Dear Kimberly... Love, Makayla

The Unraveling of My Evangelical Faith Into the Unknown

Kayla Jo McCuistion

Contents

Preface

My hope is to write this book in such a way that no matter what your religion, denomination, relationship, faith, or spirituality, you can benefit from, relate to, or learn from the content.

They say, "time heals." And it does to a point. But when you lose something that once took up your entire identity, healing may look different than you ever imagined. It doesn't mean no more pain or hardship. I remember losing my faith and God, as if it happened yesterday. I woke up one day, and my faith didn't wake up with me. I opened my eyes one morning and realized the God I had believed in all my life was gone. He left me. And when he left, he left a huge gaping hole in my heart and a vast numbness in my mind so deep and intense that I couldn't even think to try to process what was wrong with me. I just knew that my ability to have any faith at all had disappeared into thin air, without any warning that it would be performing a complete disappearing act.

To say I was devastated would be an understatement. There are not adequate words to describe the torture I underwent in my mind, trying to figure out what happened and who I was now without my belief system. My faith was my entire life. It was my entire identity. It was what defined me. It was who I was. Without my faith, I had no reason to exist. No purpose. No meaning.

I held out hope for months. I searched for God with everything I had. I looked for him high and low. I reasoned that this was a phase like depression and he would come back. I waited...and searched...and waited and searched some more.

I watched in horror, almost as an observer, as my faith continued to stay so far away that I couldn't even see a hint of it to grasp at anymore. I felt like a mentally handicapped person, lacking the ability to think a specific thought, and because of my limited ability, this God was going to punish me in hell forever, for something I was totally incapable of. This God that I had loved whole-heartedly and served with every fiber of my being for almost 38 years was going to punish me forever in hell for a thought I literally could not think. This terrified and devastated me.

Hadn't "God" promised me that "you will seek me and find me when you search for me with all your heart" (Jeremiah 29:13)? And all those verses about ask, seek, knock...and the promise to answer (Matthew 7:7-8). Where the heck was he? And if you have faith the size of a mustard seed you can move mountains

(Matthew 17:20). I'm certain I had that much faith and more, judging by the size of the search party going on in my head.

Then there's the story of Job. God allowed him to be tested and he did nothing wrong. Maybe I was like Job. Even my parents felt like Job's friends when I tried to tell them the dilemma I was facing. Labeling me a prodigal. Assuming I wouldn't go to church because I was afraid God would speak to me. (My response to them was, "I sure wish God would speak to me! Why would I be afraid of something I'm begging and craving for!?") They also told me God was going to get me good and judge me harshly if I didn't come back to him. I tried to tell them I didn't leave and I didn't want this. I didn't want or choose to NOT believe anymore. They wouldn't listen enough to believe me. They couldn't hear me because they had their own formulations in their heads from the church teachings of what an unbeliever is thinking. And those assumptions are so far from my truth, and the truth of so many others who have taken this journey. But no matter how loud or how often we speak, most fundamentalist Christians can't hear us and judge us as willfully wrong and in rebellion toward God.

I finally surrendered to the unknown (*Frozen 2* came out at the perfect time in my deconstruction). In March 2019, I walked away from the church building completely. What they offered there was taken from me. It was no longer a part of me. I still loved the people very much, but I could no longer be a part of their belief system, and I had no idea why. All I knew was it had left me against my will. Unfortunately, in leaving the building, most of the friendships disappeared as well, along with my entire community and only way of life I had ever known.

My heart was gaping wide open with the biggest wound I had ever experienced in my entire life. I didn't know how I could ever recover from this. I didn't know who I even was anymore. I lost my entire belief system, my entire identity, my sense of belonging, my community, my passion for playing in worship band, my ability to lead people to Jesus...it felt like every part of me as I knew it was gone. Dead. Lost. Never coming back. What now?

I hurt so deeply. I remember collapsing on my bed over and over for days and months, just drowning in emotions and tears for everything I had lost and couldn't find or get back no matter how high, low, deep, or wide I searched. In fact, the harder I tried to find God and my identity as a Christian again, the stronger the resistance seemed to get. Every piece of me ached. Every single part of me felt like I was not going to make it. With God mysteriously missing from my life, I had no reason to be alive any more. But as much as I wanted to not be alive, dying was not an option.

I established a new identity online. I created fake social media accounts on twitter and facebook under a fake name (Kayla Jo), and joined secret ex-Christian, exvangelical groups where I found a whole community of people like me. These communities were life savers for me. These people got me. They encouraged me like no other. None of these people knew me in real life, yet they were beside me in my deepest pain ever. They would message me and even call me when I was at my lowest. There are people before me, with me, and behind me in this journey. It's a beautiful thing how we are there for each other, each of us encouraging, grasping, embracing, and holding space for the ones behind us who are struggling. We are a community of true friends like I never knew possible. Strangely, most of us were taught people this side of religion were not capable of love and compassion, because they don't have God, and God is the source of love. Yet, here we are—and we love *big*. I've seen the most amazing, truly unconditional love on the opposite side of religion.

A year ago, when it all disappeared, the ex-christians ahead of me always told me that it will get better. That I would be okay. I desperately wanted to believe them. But my mind kept telling me, "it might get better for them, but not for you...you're gonna be tortured for the rest of your life in this hell in your own mind." I couldn't imagine how my life could ever get better without my ability to believe in God and the familiarity of my Christian community that I had lived with all my life. Especially my family. I couldn't imagine how life could get better when all of me as I knew me was missing.

I am relentless when it comes to searching. I don't give up until I find answers...one way or another I will find peace. My stubbornness and desire for wholeness come in handy in so many ways. In my exhausting search, in summer of 2019, I realized my resistance to what was happening in my life, and my constant striving to still bring back what had died in me, needed to be over. Beating a dead horse is not going to bring it back to life. I had to quit fighting and resisting my loss that I could not revive, so that I could direct my energy toward moving forward with my life. I didn't want to stay stuck.

So I hesitantly opened my hands...and I let go of trying to hold on to anything I used to be anymore. I released my desire to have all the answers, figure it out, and bring my faith back to life. I accepted where I was. Picked myself up. And determined to move forward with my life. You can't keep moving forward while constantly looking backward. And as I turned my face toward my future instead of staring at my past, I felt a glimpse of freedom in my heart. I felt a lightness and an assurance that I was going to be okay.

And this is where my healing began.

They (the people who had struggled before me) were right...life does get good again. It can get better. I am healing in powerful ways that I never imagined.

And your healing is possible too.

Reach out. Shoot me an email (kjmc0223@gmail.com) or follow me on TikTok (@makaylajo0223).

You are not alone. Those of us who have gone before you and will support you are many. I'm here for you. So many of us want to help and walk alongside you.

Part 1

A Long Introduction

I'm going to use this section to give you glimpses into my life growing up and how strong my beliefs were. I'm sure there will be many of you reading this that can relate to a lot of what I say, others will be appalled that people actually live this way, and some that are still in the movement will see nothing wrong with what I describe and defend that God's ways are higher and holier than man's ways (Isaiah 55:8-9). Part 1 sets the stage for part two of the book, when I journal my old self and my new self conversing over my deconstructing faith.

I also want to set aside whether my parents raised me "right or wrong." Because that perspective and question is not up for debate. Truth is, they raised me—they loved me—they did the best they could with what they knew. Just like I am doing for my kids. (I'm sure they will need therapy for my parenting mess-ups someday too haha). I do not blame my parents for any of this. They invested money in sending me to Christian school all my life, preschool through five years of college, and they did not necessarily realize that this "safe place" from "the world" was creating trauma and indoctrination. They were not in youth group or at church camps where the legalism was engrained into us. They were not in my classroom at school during Bible class every day where we were brainwashed with one perspective. We attended the church we did and the schools we did, because from my understanding, those places were God's perfect places and they had all the answers I needed for life. They had the absolutes I needed. We were taught that the Bible (KJV) was the *only absolute* truth...with a capital T. If anything ever didn't line up with the Bible...the Bible was right and even science was wrong. Everything I needed to know—the church or Christian school had an answer for. They spoke for God. Obeying my authority was equivalent to obeying God. Disappointing or disobeying authority, was also equivalent to disappointing or disobeying God. Which made me quite the obsessive people pleaser.

I have no anger or bitterness over my past, although I do have pain and hurt. I also have no apology for who I am now. Although, I do apologize for who I was then, when I naively attempted to force my beliefs on people who didn't believe the same as me. I was wrong to do that. And I have grown. Let me share glimpses of what my childhood through young adulthood has looked like...

First, it's important for you to know that I am both Kimberly and Makayla. Kimberly is my birth name...the name I went by until I was 38 years old. Makayla is what I legally changed my name to, the summer after my 38th birthday, when my faith shift plummeted me into an identity crisis so powerful and disorienting that I "accidentally" became Kayla Jo. (Officially Makayla on my Drivers License). This will all make more sense as you make your way through the journal pages in this book. As the journals start out, in Part 2 of this book, Makayla, (the agnostic/atheist me), is writing to Kimberly, (the *genuine*, 100% Jesus-follower, undeniably Christian me). When the journal starts out, Makayla is speaking from the future, telling Kimberly what is about to happen, assuring her that she is okay and is going to continue to be okay, despite what she experiences and feels. After it happens, Kimberly responds back to Makayla with what it was like to be present and going through that time period that Makayla has tried to describe and coach her through. So as you read my journals, keep in mind that the old me (Kimberly) and the new me (Makayla) are conversing about my faith shift...it's all me—who I am now, versus who I thought I was then.

If you would have told me that one day I would walk away from my faith, after 37 years of being fully immersed in and sold out to Evangelical Christianity, I would've fiercely and defensively opposed your ridiculous assumption. I would have thought you were crazy. That you were definitely wrong. And that you had no idea how intensely real and personal my relationship with my Father in heaven really was. My complete identity was found in Christ (Galatians 2:20). In God. I was his, and he was mine. Forever. Deal sealed. I had decided to follow Jesus, no turning back. He had chosen me—and I had chosen him. I loved him, because he first loved me (1 John 4:19). I was chosen for greatness and had a specific purpose (Ephesians 1:4-6), that he planned out for me, before time began (Psalm 139:16). He knit me together in my mother's womb (Psalm 139:13). I was fearfully and wonderfully made (Psalm 139:14). He held me in the palm of his hand (Isaiah 41:10). Nothing could take me away from him (Romans 8:35-39). I was safe. He promised to never leave me or forsake me (Hebrews 13:5). I was a child of the one true God (John 1:12). I had been taught Jesus from birth and couldn't remember a day that I did not follow him with every fiber of my being. I was loyal. Committed. Whole-hearted. 100% God's girl. I *knew* beyond the shadow of a doubt that I belonged to God forever, and that I would follow him "until death do us part."

Little did I know that death had other definitions than just me disappearing off the face of the earth. Death could also mean, my concept of God and religion dies...my ability to believe anything I had been taught and fully believed and embraced, *all my life, could & would* disappear, while I was still seeking God intensely and passionately with all my heart for 37 years. God...who was the love of my life, my best friend that sticks closer than a brother (Proverbs 18:24), my reason for living and breathing (Acts 17:28), my foundation (I Corinthians 3:11), my *entire* identity (2 Corinthians 5:17, 1 Peter 2:9), my *everything* would fall into a black hole without consent or warning. Nothing could have prepared me for this. Nothing. Nothing...unless I had been taught critical thinking, that it's okay to question, and that life & faith does not have to be one black & white way. I wish I would have been taught that nothing is for certain. I wish I had been taught that God and spirituality and how to think cannot be put in a box. Maybe THEN I could have been spared the grief of losing everything that mattered to me, and my entire identity would not have been destroyed. Maybe then the soul-crushing crisis could have been softened, even maybe avoided. Just maybe.

This is the story of (me), a girl who grew up in fundamentalism & evangelicalism, a narrow sect of Christianity that is pretty prevalent in the US, and often cultish, like any other fundamentalist religion. It was everything to me. It consumed my entire identity. If you asked me about my religion, I would tell you, "it's not a religion, it's a relationship...and let me tell you all about it and how amazing my God is!" I passionately lived out my faith with every fiber of my being. My favorite Bible verses, among so many, included Be fervent in spirit, serving the Lord (Romans 12:11). And whatever you do, do it for God and not men (Colossians 3:23-24). He must increase but I must decrease (John 3:30). Deny yourself, take up your cross, follow Jesus (Luke 9:23). Let me live so that I may praise you! (Psalm 119:175). Put others before yourself...think of them as more important (Philippians 2:3). Your good works are like filthy rags to God (Isaiah 64:6). Do what is right in the eyes of everyone...live at peace with everyone (Romans 12:18). Don't do anything that causes anybody to stumble...value others opinions above your own (1 Corinthians 8:9; Romans 14:13-23). The list could go on forever. Any verse that talked about doing things *wholeheartedly* for God, living for him, and praising him with your entire being resonated deeply in my soul. I was *all in* and I confidently knew there was no turning back. There was no other way, no other options (John 14:6). My world of faith was obviously a black and white decision to me. I was taught it was the *only* absolute truth. The *only* thing in this world that you could actually trust. There was no other option, because choosing anything but the path I was on meant eternity in hell forever, separated from God, who adored and loved me so much, and who I loved and adored in return.

I was born into a loving, Christian family. I was the first born of four kids. I was often told my smile would light up the room. I loved being around people. I was full of spunk, fun, and sassy. I was known for my goofy ways and outgoing personality. I attended church from infancy, where I loved and fully trusted my church family, and I loved learning about God and the Bible. Every time the doors were open, my family was there. There's not a time that I don't remember knowing that God loves me, and that he sent Jesus to die for me, because I was a horrible, wretched, filthy sinner that deserved hell (Romans 6:23). I don't remember a lot of my childhood, but I somehow remember my days in the nursery at church. I remember what it looked like. I remember being there every Sunday. I remember being 2-3 years old and hearing about God, Jesus, and the plan of salvation to avoid hell and spend forever in heaven, in Sunday school and children's church on Sundays (Acts 16:31). As a toddler, I knew I was a bad person, because I was told I was (Romans 3:23). I couldn't actually grasp what was so bad about me, but I knew I was required to believe I was bad, in order for Jesus to save me so that I could go to heaven. I knew God was disgusted with my sin (Habakkuk 1:13). I didn't know exactly what sin...other than I obviously didn't obey mom and dad perfectly because I would get spanked for acting out. And apparently I was a sinner just by being born because the Bible said that my mother conceived me in sin (Psalm 51:5). Because I was born a sinner, I deserved hell just for being born. This still didn't seem bad enough for a God to punish me in hell forever. But I was taught I was born bad—and needed to ask Jesus into my heart. I fully trusted what I was told. Why would they lie about something so serious? So every Sunday after church, filled with shame and embarrassment that I didn't know if God heard me the week before, I would run and *hide* under my high chair to quickly ask Jesus into my heart again in case I didn't say the right words, mean it strongly enough, or if God didn't hear me before. I was *only* a *toddler*! Each time I prayed again, I would hope that if I died, or if the rapture happened and Jesus came back in the clouds to get the Christians, I would go to heaven. I was so scared of hell. It was terrifying as a toddler, knowing that something could happen to me, and I would burn forever. Even at the age of 3, I would tell my mom, "I hope I don't be bad anymore." Somehow I was able to latch on to guilt of being bad, proving that I was bad, so that Jesus would save me. Because if I couldn't manage to admit that I was a sinner in need of a savior, I was full of pride and couldn't be saved (Proverbs 16:18). This thought terrified me. I was terrified of being tortured forever (Matthew 13:42). I was only a toddler and I felt so helpless in my ability to know for sure that God thought I was okay, and that I would be okay for eternity. Nobody knew the horror story that constantly played inside my head, and I didn't know what to do with it. I was tough. I was fierce. And I didn't want anybody to know the struggle I faced, even as a toddler. I would conquer this on my own (starting as a 3 year old y'all!!!) rather than face the shame and embarrassment that came with the questions. Thoughts and fears of "what if I said the wrong words or didn't mean what I said?" Or "what if I can't remember what I said, does it still count?" ruminated in my head constantly and spread guilt and shame throughout my entire being and soul. The anxiety, terror, and shaking that gripped my innocent heart, for fear that I wasn't enough and was displeasing to God, was unconsciously the beginning of repetitive events that would create trauma in my mind and body that would impact me through CPTSD, depression, anxiety, and in other ways well into adulthood, and perhaps last my entire lifetime.

I was taught very young, that when I die, I will stand before God and give an account of how I lived my life (Romans 14:12). I would give a report for every idle word I spoke (Matthew 12:36). And all my sins would be shown on a big screen in heaven for everybody to see. On top of that horror that awaited, I was terrified that I would be standing before God and everybody naked because I couldn't take anything with me...and we were taught our bodies were to be covered and hidden...but we would not have clothes in heaven. We were assured it was okay because we would have perfect bodies (meaning thin and physically attractive and flawless...not embarrassing), but I was not convinced. I was mortified already, thinking about my future standing naked, before God and the world, and having all the negative things about me shown to everybody. Then God would decide if I went to heaven or hell from there...because just because I called him "lord" didn't mean he would know me or accept me into heaven (Matthew 7:21-23).

In spite of the fear of hell, I loved my life. When I was not in church, being reminded that I deserved hell unless I asked Jesus into my heart, or trying to sleep at night, I was usually able to distract myself and not think about the possibility of burning in hell forever. In these times, I was a free spirit who laughed and played and embraced the happiness that being alive each day brought to me. I had loving parents, a loving church family, and 3 siblings. My family and friends cared about me a lot. We had great relationships with each other.

I developed a super close connection to God and spirituality even as a toddler. And when I was 4, I prayed for a brother and a sister at church. When my mom picked me up, the Sunday school teacher asked my mom if she was pregnant because my sister and I had prayed for a brother and a sister. My mom responded with, "no! And God would never give me twins." 10 months later, my mom gave birth to a boy and a girl, giving me the brother and the sister that I had asked God for almost a year ago. Everyone, including myself, was in awe of the amazing "answer to prayer."

I always thought I was good. I could feel it. I could sense it. And I lived it. But the people at church kept telling me I was bad—that I was a sinner. That I deserved hell. That I needed to be saved because I was born an enemy of God (Romans 5:10). That God had to sacrifice his only son to cover my horrible sin (John 3:16). "What horrible sin?" I used to think. I haven't done anything horrible. I'm a child!

I felt guilty for not being guilty enough. I felt guilty for not having a story that mattered to be saved from. I felt guilty that there was no obvious change that I was told happens to people when they receive Jesus. I needed a major life-changing story of how Jesus came into my life and changed me so that it would matter. So I tried for years to convince myself that I was bad. I would constantly push back the thoughts that I was good and replace them with the story I was taught that I was a horrible person and was like filthy rags in God's eyes, so much so that he couldn't even look at me. No one is good (Romans 3:10)

They also told me that I couldn't trust my heart (Jeremiah 17:9), but once again, I felt like an exception to that rule. I knew that I could trust my heart, that it was full of love and genuine desire to make the most of life and invest in other people. Yet, it felt wrong to trust my heart because I was told it was wrong—I felt like I was missing something.

I attended Christian school from preschool through my senior year of high school, followed by 5 years of fundamental, independent, Baptist Bible College. Between Bible stories, catechisms, and memory verses at the Christian school, church on Sunday morning for Sunday school and main service, Sunday night, AWANA & youth group on Wednesday night, attendance any time the doors were open for revival or activities, my own private quiet time (devotions) with God as often as possible, and winter and summer overnight church camps, and youth activities, I was immersed in the KJV Bible (the most accurate version according to my denomination—oddly, King James didn't even love Jesus!!!??), and I knew it forward and backward and could quote scripture from memory left and right. Attending Christian school meant I was immersed in religion most of my waking hours, most days of the week.

I started Christian preschool when I was four years old. We learned Bible stories every day and memorized Bible verses weekly, along with catechisms and scripture references, for my entire childhood including teenage and college years. I was extremely well-versed in the King James Version of the Bible, along with the

Fundamental, Independent, Baptist interpretation of what those verses meant—both stories and being able to quote scripture at the drop of a hat. People could rattle off a reference and I could quote those verses from the KJV word for word. Other translations or versions of the Bible were not allowed and were seen as inaccurate and untrustworthy. Some churches even went so far as to say you had to be saved from a King James Bible or you weren't saved.

I grew up being taught and believing that my specific denomination and church, and the way of living I was taught was the *key* to having the *right* relationship with God. All the other churches and different teachings were wrong, or "off," and God was not as pleased with them, if he was even pleased at all. Most of them were not truly acceptable to God, because the way is narrow and few there are that find it (Matthew 7:14). Some used the wrong translation or version of the Bible. Some listened to the wrong music. Some didn't wear appropriate Sunday clothing to be acceptable to God. Some held different perspectives on interpreting the Bible. But my church had the one right way. Because they said so. Other people *might* make it to heaven, but they won't have as many rewards, and God wouldn't be as happy with them, because they weren't as pleasing to him in how they were living their lives, and they were not following the right interpretation of the Bible. Their churches weren't as sanctified.

The KJV of the Bible was really hard to understand. But they said it was *the most accurate* version of the Bible—God's chosen version. The church leaders told me that if I am saved, I have the holy spirit, and the holy spirit will do the interpreting. This really created a confusing struggle in my head as to whether or not I could hear the holy spirit, but I always felt guilty and convicted, and I knew that was the holy spirit too. But maybe the holy spirit was convicting me to be saved because I wasn't really saved last time...or the time before...or the time before? Maybe that's why I struggled to understand the exact meaning of the Bible on my own? I was also taught that I shouldn't need outside sources to understand the Bible, unless they were approved by the church. Many sources could lead you astray from knowing the one true interpretation of the Bible. It was the church's job to guide you. Nevermind that the Bible wasn't written in my cultural style of English or my time period.

The Bible is the only source of absolute truth. So everything, every rule, everything I was told, everything I internalized as a child through young adulthood from my parents, churches, and Christian schools was gospel to me and must be obeyed. Those outside the church I was in that didn't follow those rules were on shaky ground. There were times that my thought patterns shifted over the years...such as listening to Christian worship music as a teen that consisted of contemporary Christian music (aka CCM), but these thoughts didn't shift without a lot of PTSD and shakiness in my entire body as I experimented back and forth in what should be allowed. I wanted to be holy like God wanted me to be (1 Peter 1:15-17). I wanted him to be so proud of me. It always threw me for a loop that one thing could be allowed at home but not at church, because God doesn't change (Malachi 3:6), so why would the rules. That seemed inconsistent to me. I often found myself literally shaking when I would play a song for my parents that I liked, hoping they would approve, and let me keep listening to it.

I remember being in my early childhood, maybe 6-8 years old, and still wondering how I could be so bad that God would want to punish me forever in hell. I loved people. I was a good person. I wanted to do the right thing. I was aware that I wasn't perfect, but struggled to believe I was so bad that I needed a Savior. I believed Jesus died for me so I could go to heaven, but I struggled to believe I was disturbing and disgusting to him. I began wishing that I had something "bigger" for God to save me from so I could feel like I was saved. We were taught that when Jesus saves you, he radically changes your life and you don't want to live the same anymore. If you smoke, he takes away your desire to smoke. If you cuss, he cleans up your language. If you dress inappropriately, he changes the way you dress. If you listen to bad music, well, that desire leaves too. Well, if I started to ask Jesus into my heart when I was 3, and I was sheltered from the evils of the world...how was I ever supposed to know for sure that I was saved, since there was nothing major to change in my life? My young naivety and innocence made the salvation process extremely complicated for me to grasp. I needed a life-changing story to share with others so they would be convinced to ask Jesus into their hearts too! Because it was my job to tell the entire world about Jesus so their blood wouldn't be on my hands (Ezekiel 3:18)

The Bible was the rulebook for life (2 Peter 1:3-4). But if the Bible wasn't clear in some cases, we were to always take the highest/holiest road. We were not to be a stumbling block to people whether it's dress, music, an activity, language, a movie...always put others before yourself. This confused me too—because if I was always putting others before myself, how could I ever even live. What could I even do, because you can't please everybody?? This was very frustrating to me as I wanted to live above reproach and not be a stumbling block or a disappointment to anybody because that would be disappointing God. This is one thing that spiritual authority is for. We were taught to obey your spiritual authority, those God has placed over you, because they watch your souls and give an account to God for you (Hebrews 13:17). These are pastors, teachers, parents, spouses, etc...They were considered superior and above you and could speak for God to you and it was truth. They had more wisdom and authority than those of us under them.

Where the Bible seems to contradict itself, we were always told it's not contradicting itself—no matter how obvious it was. It's just that we are mis-understanding something. The church is adamant that the Bible has no mistakes or contradictions. Yet, today, scholars still disagree on which books should/shouldn't be included in the canon.

In spite of trying so hard to be who God, the church, and my parents wanted me to be, I always had a heavy, guilty, anxious feeling in my heart and body when I would sit and listen to preaching at church or to Bible stories at school. I often felt heavy and guilty for no known reason at all. I was always on-edge and anxious about what I was doing right/wrong. I thought these feelings were normal. That my heart was just sensitive to God's leading. That this was God's way of saying "hey, pay attention to what I'm telling you...you can do better...you're not good enough...but I love you...but figure this out and try harder. Be perfect as your father in heaven is perfect (Matthew 5:48)." My sensitivity to pleasing God made me ultra-sensitive to pleasing authority and being on the best terms with everyone in my life, because I was taught *all* authority is from God (1 Peter 2:13-14), and you're supposed to obey them unless they're asking you to sin against God (Romans 13:1-6; Acts 5:29), and do your part to live at peace with everybody. I was always so paranoid and on edge/anxious, which was also a sin (Philippians 4:6-7). I was taught that if I have problems with relationships on earth, then I am not okay with God.

It was hard for me to hear that I was a bad, wicked sinner, and that I needed to believe this for Jesus to forgive me for my sins, so that I could go to heaven, because I always tried so hard to be good. But it was never enough. They taught that NO good thing dwells in you (Romans 7:18). I had asked Jesus to save me ever since I was a toddler. I had no horrible sins to prove that Jesus saved me from anything. When Jesus saves you, he takes away all those bad sins and bad things you do, showing his power to save you. But I was so little, I had none of that. Mostly because I was young, but on top of that, I had walked on egg-shells so-to-speak since I was mobile, trying not to be bad. So over-all, I felt like I was a good girl. I hadn't done anything "bad enough" for Jesus to have to die for. I didn't understand why God thought I was a horrible, wretched, person worthy of death and hell, but I knew I needed to somehow believe I was if I wanted to make it to heaven. This created more guilt, and another problem—pride (Isaiah 2:12; Proverbs 16:5). Thinking I was good was a pride problem. And the preachers always said that in the middle of pride is a great big "I." This horrible sin stuff just didn't make sense to me how it applied to me as a compliant, Jesus-loving kid. But week after week, I would hear how horrible I was that Jesus had to die and I must believe I am horrible and disgusting to God in my sin (Isaiah 64:6). I tried to feel the guilt and shame so I could feel saved from something.

I decided that my disobedience to my parents made me a horrible person that deserved hell, since I didn't obey them perfectly (Ephesians 6:1,2). Even though I desperately tried because I was a people pleaser to the core to help God be happy with me (Romans 12:10; Philippians 2:3-4). That became my "thing" that always guilted me and made me feel like a horrible person that didn't deserve eternity in heaven. I also decided that I was a horrible, mean sibling to my younger sisters and brother. I used these things and attached them to the unknown intense guilt I would feel, and I would constantly repent of them. Because I decided those things were true, it was also necessary for me to rededicate my life to Jesus every summer camp, because Jesus was disappointed in me because I had not been following him good enough. Never good enough. This was always reinforced and spoken over us. Nothing you do is ever good enough.

I had a passionate love for my family and everything in my life. I had an excitement that I had the best life ever and wouldn't want anybody else's family or life. I was lucky and privileged to be born into a Christian family who knew the one true God and the one right way to heaven. I was fortunate to have all the answers and it was my job to make sure the whole world had all the right answers too.

(Otherwise, their blood was on my hands and it was my fault they were going to hell). However, loving this life was also a problem, because I learned the Bible says that if we love this life so much that we do not want to go to heaven to be with Jesus MORE than being here on earth, we are sinning and we do not love God enough (1 John 2:15-17). This would keep me chained to guilt, disabling true happiness over the simple things in life well into adulthood. Over time, after hearing this over and over, eight-year-old Kimberly started feeling guilty for loving life and being happy. I worked hard at not enjoying life too much...so that I could long for heaven and eternity with God *more* than this life...even though I didn't want to die—I wanted to fully live and embrace life. That was unholy. This life doesn't matter, except for winning souls for Jesus (Colossians 3:11; Philippians 1:24). The next life is what matters. This life is only preparation for eternity, otherwise God would take you to heaven as soon as you were saved (1 Corinthians 3:13-15). This was drilled over and over and over through church and Christian school. It pained me so much that I realized I loved my life too much and needed to suppress it to want heaven and the after-life more (John 12:25). Pile on more guilt.

Knowing the blood of others would be on my hands, guilted me into feeling like I needed to obey the guilt, which was actually supposedly conviction, (which was the holy spirit) and tell *everybody* I saw about Jesus and how they can go to heaven. Even as a small child and through my teen and young adult years, every time I was out in public, I would feel the pressure build and build inside my body and I would get shaky, because I knew I had the great responsibility to tell every soul about Jesus. There were so many people I was responsible for! Sometimes I would share Jesus with that person and get relief. Other times, I disappointed God and had to find a way to overcome the hellish, horrible guilty feelings of letting God down, by not speaking up and testifying of him. I was taught to always carry "tracts," which were mini-pamphlets, telling people how they had sinned and could be saved instead of burning in hell. I was taught that the only reason we were left here on earth, after we are saved, is because God wants us to spread the gospel so that others will be saved. Otherwise, life is pointless (Psalm 57:2). And Jesus was coming back at any moment (in the clouds for the rapture)(Revelation 22:12-13). So don't love this life. Be ready! Too much fun is wrong! You would rather have Jesus find you telling others about him than enjoying life at his return to earth. You would be ashamed for Jesus to find you not "working" for him when he came back (Matthew 24:46).

I lived my childhood with a lot of secret, hidden anxiety that Jesus would return before I had enough fun and got to experience all the unknown exciting things of growing up into adulthood, etc. So it was hard to enjoy the present because I worried that I was going to miss out via the rapture. But then mom and others would say they wanted Jesus to come *now*, and we should want that more than life now because life would be better in heaven. I thought life was amazing here...but apparently that was sinful to think that, and then I felt bad. I couldn't win. The Bible says that Jesus will come like a thief in the night (Matthew 24:43). We must watch and be ready. And work for the night is coming. It was a sin that I loved this life more than my desire for Jesus to come in the rapture.

Believing in the rapture made life hard in other ways too. Because while I was enjoying the life I was not supposed to enjoy, and trying not to enjoy it, another train of thought also took over at times. This thought was... "the rapture is coming soon, so why should I _____. There's no time to _____. My life is almost over so why lose weight now? Why get in shape now? Why pursue this hobby? Why pursue that job or line of work..." These have been my thoughts I've battled since I was a pre-teen all because of the rapture and Jesus coming back soon! Even though I know he's not coming back now, I struggle to be goal oriented and view my life as "having enough time left for anything to matter." I have always lived with a sense that my life is almost over and there's not enough time left to pursue anything big, goal-oriented, or meaningful with my life. Thank you brain-washing religion that told me "JESUS MAY COME BACK TODAY!"

I was taught from my toddler years that the Bible was from God—exactly how it is. God told holy men what to write, and they wrote down what God wanted us to know (2 Peter 1:21). They were told exactly what to write. Therefore, there are no errors and everything is true and we are to take it literally...meaning the stories are not myths. They really happened exactly the way they are saying they happened...unless it's a parable Jesus is telling, that's just for an example. I was even taught to take the book of Revelation literally, believing that somehow these beasts were gonna terrorize the earth, and if I wasn't saved I would be terrorized by them too. Way down the road post-college, I started questioning revelation...and somebody taught me it's not the wrath of God toward sinners, but the freedom of Satan to release fury on Christians, so Christians would have to suffer too. So I had to be okay with that. I did my best to shove fear down and trust that God allows suffering for my good to prove my faith (Romans 8:28-29). Now I don't believe in Revelation literally for end times. I think it's apocalyptic literature that likely also includes mythology and may be partially based on some events that have already happened, so to speak, in the first century. I really don't know. I don't have to have answers. Whatever it is—it's not real. And I don't have to be afraid.

I was always told, "be sure your sins will find you out (Numbers 32:23)." This was a promise from the Bible. It felt like a threat. A threat or warning to make sure you do the right thing no matter what, because you're gonna be caught and punished if you are bad. You're not going to get away with disobeying God (disobeying authority or rules).

Eventually, sometime during elementary school, I started feeling guilty and heavy just waking up every morning. The feelings sucked the life out of me. My heart, head, emotions, and entire body felt like they were being pulled through the floor. I didn't know what I had done wrong to feel this way, but I could usually manage to push the feelings away within a couple hours, once I started engaging with my friends at school. But sometimes the paralyzing feelings wouldn't go away. Sometimes they stayed for days. Sometimes months. Certain places and events would cause them to be more heavy and prevalent. I just pressed through quietly, keeping the pain inside that kept me from fully living out my individuality and personality without intense effort. It zapped my energy, and as I grew I would take long naps behind closed doors in order to not "feel." The emotions were exhausting.

As I grew up and my body began to develop, I learned that my body is evil and needed to be hidden/covered up. If I did not cover my body modestly and appropriately, I would be what the book of Proverbs calls a "strange woman," or a slut/ho/horrible person. My clothing had to be loose. Baggy—but not so baggy that you could see anything through your sleeves hanging down too low. Long, but not so long it drags the floor. Hide the fact you're a woman—your body is shameful. As I realized my body was forming curves, I became embarrassed and self-conscious and knew I needed to hide my evil body and its development. I started layering my shirts to look less curvy. I started wearing baggier, looser fitting clothes to hide that I was becoming a woman with an evil, stumbling block body.

My school and church both required skirts or dresses. Skirts had to touch the knee in elementary, and cover the knee in high school. There was no room for dress code violations. God was holy—and demanded you to be holy too. Especially women. Women were responsible for men's sexual thoughts and actions by how we dressed. Thank you, purity culture. We were not to dress "inappropriately." Don't appear beautiful, womanly, or tempting in ways that would turn a man on sexually. Hide your body to keep them from stumbling. You are responsible for *their* thoughts and actions.

Since God is holy, he demands holiness, not just in clothing, but in every aspect of life. So many rules related to: music, movies, playing cards, dancing, tv shows, friendships, smoking, drinking, restaurants with bars, therapy, psychology, language, masturbating, sex, relationships, thoughts, church attendance, tithing, books, how you spend your time, Bible reading more than tv, yoga, new age things, mixed swimming... We were to be "in the world but not of it (John 15:19; Romans 12:2)." We were to be different. We were told that the "world," or unbelievers, should be able to look at us and know we are Christians, and that we are different and not like them. This sweet aroma of Jesus, and how we were different in appearance, words, and actions, would cause them to want what we have. We were to set an example and live above reproach, so that when the world looks at me, they see Jesus. We were to "love not the things of the world because if anyone loves the world, the love of the father is not in him/her (I John 2:15-17)." We were to "set no wicked thing before our eyes (Psalm 101:3)." And heaven forbid, as a female, don't BE that wicked thing.

Secular music was of the devil (unless it was classical music for some reason). They used 1 Corinthians 14:8 to back this. Music could not have a heavy beat, as they put it. It couldn't have drums or a loud sound. The melody must be clear and louder than the rest of the song. There must not be a syncopated rhythm (again, classical music was an exception). So pretty much piano/organ music was most of what was acceptable. An orchestra was acceptable. The lyrics must be clean and God-honoring, and theologically accurate...according to the church's interpretation of the Bible. However, a rock beat would totally destroy a good message and make a song unacceptable. We had to turn down the jingles on the tv commercials and the theme songs on some cartoons because it was a sin to allow the sound into our minds. Even Christian rock and Christian praise and worship was forbidden. Although some of the tamer stuff anxiously leaked in and out of my collection over the years. Repetitive lyrics were vain repetitions and not allowed. As a teenager, I remember wanting to listen to christian contemporary music, and literally physically shaking as my parents listened, wondering if it would pass the test or if it was going to be shut down as evil. I wanted so badly to be able to listen to songs I loved and that some of my friends listened to. I loved the energy the music gave, when it wasn't creating trauma from my belief system. My parents would get super irritated when the neighbors blasted their oldies music. My sister and I took out our "godly Christian music" into the backyard one day to "fight bad music with good music." How embarrassing to look back on. We really thought we were in a spiritual war over music. We were so deceived.

Speaking of my neighbors, I thought they were bad, horrible people because they smoked and listened to oldies music. They were hell-bound. I felt really bad for them. Christianity taught me to see them as inferior to me. As objects. As projects. And to fear becoming close to them and becoming like them. We were taught that when somebody gives their life to Jesus, they want to quit smoking, and God makes them lose the cravings to smoke immediately. Because smoking defiles his temple, which is your body, and you are not your own—you are God's...so take care of your body and don't smoke (1 Corinthians 6:19-20). People could not be Christian if they were smokers. Good Christians also do not drink. And they don't put tattoos on God's temple either.

We weren't supposed to be friends with people that didn't share our beliefs. Sermon after sermon told us to be careful about the company we keep. And bad friends corrupt good morals (1 Corinthians 15:33). And a good name is more important than lots of riches (Proverbs 22:1). One of my best friends in junior high was told she couldn't hang out with me as much because I had exposed her to some unacceptable contemporary christian music that would influence her the wrong way.

In junior high we were constantly told to deny yourself, take up your cross, and follow Jesus (Matthew 16:24-26). Life was not about having fun as a Christian, and doing the work of God was my burden to bear. But this burden wasn't to be considered a burden. It was an honor, and we did it happily for the eternal rewards we were earning. I was called to suffer for Christ (Philippians 1:29). I really believed all this.

There is an unpardonable sin that the Bible mentions—but it's a secret—it's not completely clear about what that unpardonable sin is. Nobody knows what it is. This worried us as kids that we would accidentally commit the unpardonable sin and never make it to heaven (Matthew 12:31-32).

I was terrified God would send me to the mission field someday. Going to the mission field was the ultimate sacrifice for God. I had talked to some missionaries at our church one time that told us they have to eat bugs sometimes, in order to not offend the people, so they have the opportunity to tell them about Jesus. I was told that that's what I must do if God "calls" me to do that. I thought maybe if I could just become "okay" with eating bugs, that maybe God wouldn't send me there out of spite. I was so afraid he would send me to do something I didn't want to do because people were always talking about how God breaks our will to do his will.

There were specifics I knew to stay away from because God didn't approve. We would be in trouble at school for not following several of these rules. God hated:

secular music, Christian rock, movie theaters, playing cards, dancing, holding hands/touching the opposite sex, short shorts, tight clothing, bikinis, saying gosh, crap, or other bad words, being friends with unbelievers, most tv shows and movies, cruises because they were one big sin party, inside out sweatshirts (it was the style), colored nail polish, glitter, showing your knees with shorts or dresses, dice, poker, gambling, mixed swimming, sitting in mixed groups in chapel ....the list could go on. We were taught to be in this world, but not of it. Be different. Don't look or behave like the world. Stand out. It was a sin to be carnal or worldly through participating in any of the forbidden activities.

This life is for eternal rewards. Nothing else matters. The more you do for God in this life, the more rewards you get. But those rewards aren't to keep for yourself. They are to lay at Jesus' feet. We were taught to feel shame at the thought of not having enough to give back to Jesus after all he had done for our wicked selves, saving us from God's wrath that would punish us in hell for not choosing to follow him correctly. Our works would be judged by fire and the worthless things we did (such as having fun, etc.) would be burned up and not count for eternity (1 Corinthians 3:13).

We were to show our faith by our works (James 2:18). I used to always feel guilty for how I would spend my day, as if it's not enough for Jesus. I thought when I got older and could drive and do more, it would get better. It never did.

Music was a really big deal. Music that made your body want to move was of the devil, even if it's labeled Christian. We were taught the purpose of rock music was sex and that makes it really bad and immoral for us to listen to. God hates it. They said rock beats will make you want to have sex, as the rhythm makes your body move in ways that God doesn't want it to move. They also said that the rock beat kills house plants so what do you think it does to your heart. It's definitely not

God's design for his children. Another argument they had against Christian rock/worship music was they told us that their lifestyles weren't glorifying to God. When I asked about classical music, because their lifestyles didn't glorify God either.....they claimed their music was acceptable but their lifestyles weren't. It was the music and the beat that mattered most in that case. They also said that the classical music artists weren't believers so they weren't held to the same standard as a Christian writing or singing music. Since they wrote "good" music it's okay to listen to it. How the heck do you reconcile those questions and answers?

I went to church camp from age seven through the end of high school...winter and summer. I had mixed emotions about this. I loved the freedom of being on my own in a sense and hanging out with friends. But chapel services three times a day, plus devotions and other spiritual activities, were so traumatic to my nervous system. The goal of the preaching at church camp was to get kids saved and right with God. It was a numbers game as well. They kept a tally to announce in excitement at the end of the week. We were told if we didn't have a day and a time for when we were saved, we might not be saved. If we didn't remember what we said, we might not be saved. This was so traumatizing to me because my memory was horrible, and the first time I asked Jesus to save me was when I was three, and I didn't know days, times, or calendars back then! I definitely didn't remember exactly what I said! So I always wondered which time was "official" because I *needed* to know to be saved, and I could never figure it out. Also, after you were saved you needed to be baptized....in that order...or it doesn't count. I'm still not sure if I got it right even though I was saved and baptized multiple times. In services, we were constantly challenged to live a holy life, make sure we were obeying our parents, not gossiping, being respectful, having good friends, and the list goes on. I hated chapel because conviction and guilt were extremely terrifying and intense and I never knew exactly why I was feeling the way I was feeling, but I would cry and knew I had to do something to make the pain go away. I don't know if I was crying more from PTSD or from conviction. Looking back, it was most likely extreme CPTSD—over and over and over. I would literally shake, wondering what God wanted from me...he seemed to want so much more from me than from anybody else. What wasn't good enough? What needed to be better? What will he tell me to do this time? I was terrified of not getting it right or not obeying perfectly. Then I would listen for that uncomfortable voice prompted by the preacher's emotional manipulation (wish I knew that at the time), and I would obey to make the shaking go away. I don't know how many times I committed to obey my parents better, be a nicer sibling, re-dedicate my life to God, surrender to full-time-Christian service. I never felt like it was settled. I was always shaking and on edge about my life. For a guy, full time christian service looked like being a pastor or missionary as God's highest calling. For a girl, it looked like marrying a pastor or a missionary, or even teaching in a Christian school.

Our lives were often compared to the missionaries who had suffered the most in third world countries, some who had lost their lives for the sake of the gospel. They had given *all*. Would *we* give *all*??? Would we be willing to die to take this American, westernized, white-Jesus gospel and force it on the world? We were challenged to make sure we were as focused and working as hard as the glorious Christians, who were put on those pedestals, because God was definitely happy with them. The rest of us were second class...but we could sure strive to compete for first. We were taught to say "I'm going to go to the mission field (other countries to teach about Jesus), but I'm willing to stay." I always thought, when I become an adult and can drive myself around, I can serve so much more, etc. The torture in my mind to be and do more was endless. And all I wanted was for God to be happy with me.

I cannot tell you how many times I threw away my "bad" Christian music because of camp. They would preach against specific Christian music artists that I had. They weren't even the rock-y ones. But because my music had bad songs and beats, I would throw it away because "God" told me to at camp. I also can't tell you how many times I surrendered and rededicated my life to God. While camp was fun, camp was spiritually traumatizing and stressful.

I cannot put into words the horrible dread I felt in my body during every invitation/altar call. Nobody should have to feel those feelings (called conviction in Christian circles) constantly their entire life. Especially not a kid/teenager! Living in fear over whether or not you're doing the right thing, or living well enough to please this invisible God, no matter how hard you try, is exhausting.

Sometimes at camp I would get saved all over again. It was just easier to be saved again, than to try to figure out the complex guilt and emotions that seemed forever present. Being saved again was like a "blanket pass" to start over. But that brought shame and embarrassment too.

At the time, I saw this all as just how the Christian life was supposed to be and I was doing the best I could. Now I see it as horrible, spiritual abuse by the church and Christian school that I was put through as a child, and no child should ever have to live on-edge like I did. I started dealing with anxiety over my relationship with God as a toddler! I feared hell my entire childhood starting at age 2-3! I felt the nervousness and traumatic feelings constantly, of hoping my life was acceptable to God, when I could barely even speak sentences and communicate! This is not normal! It is not okay! It is religious, emotional abuse!

We were constantly preached at about being lukewarm. God hates us to be lukewarm, and when we are lukewarm it makes him want to vomit us out of his mouth (Revelation 3:15-16). We were always told we were lukewarm, as if they knew. It didn't matter how much I was doing...I was never good enough. I could always do more. So much emotional manipulation.

There's a heavy, dark side of my childhood that I always pushed away, because I was taught by the church not to question—just trust God and obey. And I thought this was normal. So I dismissed the feelings and questions. I dismissed them by trying to think of other things, by engaging with friends, by comforting with food, and sometimes by sleeping. I tried my hardest to be happy and joyful and push through the thickness that I didn't realize was clinical depression and CPTSD from constant religious indoctrination that I needed help for. Nobody else saw it either I guess. At least nobody addressed it or did anything about it. I felt heavy and laid around since I was little. It's not a sleep issue. I don't like the lack of energy that swallows me. The weighted blanket that wraps around my body and squeezes my head. It's depression and other developmental/personality issues from religion. But I didn't know that when I was young. Depression was said to be a result of not clinging tightly enough to Jesus, and I knew I was embracing him as much and as closely as I possibly could. Therapy and medications were not options. Talking about it got you nowhere either so my depression and inner emotional struggles remained a secret. I didn't know what was wrong with me to even express it. Just read your Bible and give your anxiety and sadness to God...to solve the problem. The more I read the Bible and the deeper I got into it, the more guilt would consume me, and the more hopeless I realized I was. It was a no-win situation. And Jesus wasn't the answer to take away my depression, because I spent 25+ years begging him to take it away, and all I lost was my relationship with God and religion.

We were taught psychology and therapy are evil...they teach you to find answers outside of God. They give you too much knowledge. They weren't an option for treating depression. We were not to look inward for answers—remember, your heart is deceitful. I feel like I've said that a couple times already ;)...but once again, you need more Jesus, not medications or a chat with a therapist...or yoga...or looking inward and trusting yourself.

What other people think of you matters...a good name is better to be chosen than great riches (Proverbs 22:1). Other people's opinions matter and you better change, so you're not offending them. I remember constantly tweaking myself from who I really was, so that I wouldn't offend *anybody*, because we were always to put others before ourselves. We didn't matter. It was JOY—Jesus, Others, & You. In that order. Live your life to please other people. And do *not* be a stumbling block by doing things they don't approve of.

We were taught to embrace suffering (Romans 8:18). I'm supposed to suffer for Jesus...completing what was lacking in his suffering (whatever that means) (Colossians 1:24). If you're not suffering and you're not being persecuted, you're not living boldly enough. That was a tough one because Christians in America are *not* persecuted and do not suffer at the hands of others, other than the suffering they place on themselves.

As a youth group we would go "door-to-door soul-winning," which means we would pair up and go knock on doors and ask people if they knew if they would go to heaven if they died today, and we would give them a gospel tract that showed them how they could know beyond the shadow of a doubt that they were going to heaven. Sometimes people prayed the "sinner's prayer" (which doesn't actually exist, but we thought it did) and got saved. Now I look back and wonder if they were just entertaining us kids, because decisions don't really work that way. Paradigms don't shift like that. Not the way I saw it happen on one rare occasion, when a man opened his door and emotionlessly prayed the "sinner's prayer" with us.

We memorized the "Romans Road" and the "ABCs of salvation" so that we would be always ready to help somebody be saved. We were taught that God loved the whole world and Jesus died for everybody. The holy spirit worked in the hearts of people, to make them want to be saved, and as people responded wanting to know God, God would put a Christian in their path so they were without excuse for becoming a Christian. This is how God worked in other countries too. Nobody is without excuse. They know from nature that God exists and if they seek him they will find him, according to what we were taught the Bible says.

There are sins of omission and sins of commission (Psalm 19:12-13). Sins of commission...you know you're doing them. Sins of omission...you sin just because you're human and alive and breathing and aren't even aware you're sinning. Since there are sins you don't know about, it was impossible to ever have a sinless day. It was drilled into us that we are bad all the time, whether we think we are or not.

Yoga, new age music, and other new age stuff was bad, and all part of the new world order that will happen in the end times which is also bad. We were to stay far away from those things. One reason it was bad was because it taught you to look within yourself for answers, which we were told we can't trust ourselves, because our heart is deceitful and desperately wicked (Jeremiah 17:9). We were told the stretches were bad movements that could invite demons in. I was literally afraid of anything to do with any of that sort of stuff. We were told Satan could gain entrance or a foothold in our life. Yes I know it's silly...but I was brainwashed and deceived all my life.

When I was in high school, a grown man in my church—a good friend of my parents—kissed me on the lips very slowly...introducing me to a surge of hormones and emotions that I had never felt in my life. I felt so dirty—and I knew (thought) it was all my fault—even though I was a child and was in a long skirt, baggy shirt, and a vest. I didn't see it coming. It happened, and it destroyed me. Sexual feelings woke up and surged through my body for hours—and I could tell nobody—not a single soul—because I was afraid I would be in trouble for what happened to me, since the woman is responsible for the man stumbling. After that, I had to struggle through teaching Sunday School to 3rd and 4th grade girls. The feelings were overwhelming. The guilt was overwhelming. I couldn't focus. I could only intensely feel what had just happened to me. He awakened something that was not his to awaken that has affected me into my adult life. The weight of what was done to me was unbearable. And I had to keep stuffing it deeper and deeper into my soul and re-sealing the door. If it became known what happened I would have been brought before the church and that would have been mortifying at that age, not knowing that it was NOT my fault. This incident stole my innocence and forever changed me. I was a bad person. I had tried so hard to hide my body and be pure and it wasn't enough to protect me. I told nobody until I was in counseling at the age of 36. You may be tempted to write it off as only a kiss and no big deal. But my body screams differently. And that's what makes it trauma and abuse. He freakin knew better. And I knew the church was not a safe place to share what happened to me...I had seen what happened to others. The female was always blamed and brought before the church to confess and apologize.

Talking about sex and "things people do in secret" is wrong (Ephesians 5:12), yet I had to listen to radio talk shows about Clinton and Monica and the sex scandal for a whole family vacation trip out west one summer. I remember sitting there with my Bible in my lap trying to hear God speak to me while my heart and mind were tortured with hearing about sex over and over and over from every angle for hours upon hours. The cognitive dissonance was extreme. But fundamentalist Christianity and far right political beliefs have somehow made their bed together. Good Christians are and vote Republican ;). Didn't you know Jesus voted Republican? Oh, wait...he wasn't white OR American ☺ ☺ ☺ (insert sarcasm).

Sex was a dirty thing that only married people are allowed to do. Somehow it was special and okay in marriage, but talking about it or especially doing it outside of marriage is forbidden and disgusting. It made you trash. Chewed up bubble gum. A shredded heart with nothing left to give. Unusable to God. Worthless to any future mate. The lowest of the low. The outcast. Sex was known as what a wife owes her husband for his satisfaction once they are married. It was very one-sided in who it was for and very narrow-minded in the purpose of it.

Mom and Dad didn't trust me with boys in high school. So I wasn't allowed to hang out with them. I never even held hands with a boy. This bothered me that they didn't trust me to go out with a guy. They claimed they trusted me, they just didn't trust my "flesh" to do the right thing. Well I am my flesh, I would argue. By saying that, you're not trusting *me*! I had a couple crushes, but everybody knew I couldn't date anyway. So nobody really showed interest in me. I think this was psychologically defeating and harmful. They didn't even want me to move to Texas when I was 24, after I was engaged, for fear I wouldn't be a virgin when I got married! (I believed they could tell me what to do until I was married—I didn't know I was an adult and could make my own decisions regardless of what my parents said).

I felt safe and comforted and loved by my parents (and other authority), as long as I performed the way I knew I needed to by following the rules. I wanted to please them. I wanted them to accept me. I wanted them to take care of me and hold me and tell me that I am ok, accepted, and wanted—but for me—not based on performance. I couldn't stand the feeling of being a disappointment.

My Christian high school would not let girls wear pants. They were of the devil, and it was dressing like a man (Deuteronomy 22:5). It was snowing outside during our spring soccer practices. There was literally snow all over the ground. It was freezing cold. They decided we could wear pants that day...*but*...we had to wear long baggy shorts to the middle of our knee *over* those pants. For Modesty??? Because...God??? The irony is we all had to shop in the mens department for those modest shorts so they would be long enough, rather than wearing pants made for *girls*??? (Facepalm).

It used to frustrate me that when mom was a kid, she had no dress code or dating rules and could dance, date, and do what she wanted. She had the freedom to create her own identity. She stopped me from so many of the freedoms that she had because I guess she had regrets. Well, I have regrets that I didn't have the opportunity to create my own regrets. Okay, I'm being somewhat sarcastic here— but...not really. To this day I feel awkward in a friend group and even in my own family when people are dancing and having fun and quoting and singing things that I completely missed out on. It's socially awkward and traumatizing. To me, it's all part of the human experience and it was my culture, and it was all given to me as taboo and bad...and so I was kept from any possibility at all of messing up. Which honestly stunted my development in many ways that are still uncomfortable to this day.

We couldn't watch movies with sexual innuendos, yet our Christian school required us to read books that contained sexual relationships for lit class. They said it was culture. I called the BS as a student being required to read the literature...and of course it didn't change. So I was taught the Bible says to set no wicked thing before my eyes....well, unless it comes to studying literature and culture—then sex and porn and anything goes as long as it isn't current. How do they not see the cognitive dissonance they are creating?

We were taught to avoid the appearance of evil (1 Thessalonians 5:22)...so everything you do *must* be above reproach. Do not be in a room alone or in a vehicle alone with the opposite sex, because nobody knows for sure if you're being "good." Do not look like you are even coming close to doing something that would be offensive to somebody else, because it may cause them to wrongly assume or stumble. Life is not lived for yourself. Life is lived to please God and others (Romans 14:7-9).

Do not do anything to cause your brother or friend to stumble. In everything you do, you're to put other people before yourself (Romans 14). If somebody around you doesn't agree with what you're doing or about to do, do not do it. Do not be a stumbling block. This related to every area of life: music, language, dress, activities...*everything*. *Everybody* and everybody's *opinion* about you is more important than *you*. In the grand scheme of things...YOU DO NOT MATTER.

When I was in HS, I asked my parents if they would let me go to public school, because I could tell people about Jesus there and I always felt like I wasn't doing enough. I felt strong enough to be a witness and that was the point of life right? My dad said that he would never send me to public school because that would be like throwing me to the wolves. All my kids are in public school now—we had no other choice...guess how that "throwing them to the wolves" trauma has played into my head their first couple years there. Even now, there are days that it feels wrong and I know it's not. That's just my conditioning. It's not fair that my indoctrination does not allow me to feel okay now with things that my life and the law requires (such as education) that are not really wrong at all.

We have multiple religions and denominations in our extended family: Catholic, Pentecostal, Lutheran...different churches fascinated me and when I was 18, I really wanted to visit my Aunt's Pentecostal church. My parents said absolutely not. There's no reason to. And I thought I had to honor that. My Aunt was then told to quit proselytizing us. She wasn't. I was seeking. I was asking questions. My questions were forbidden. So once again, thinking I had to, I shut down my questions.

I graduated from high school from Faith Baptist School in 1999. My next plan was to go on to college. I had a choice of 3 fundamentalist colleges that were acceptable to attend. I chose Maranatha Baptist Bible College in Watertown, Wisconsin...because I could play soccer there. Real deep, I know. My plan was to study elementary education and become a Christian school teacher. Not because that's what I was really passionate about, but because that's all I knew. I had been sheltered from the variety of jobs that were really available. Church camp taught me that I needed to be in full-time-Christian service somehow, which meant marrying a pastor and/or being a Christian school teacher or working in a church office. Since kids are fun, I chose the Christian school teacher avenue. However, had my college offered it, and had I known I could have such a job, I would have chosen to major in photography or maybe even psychology...or maybe massage. But those majors weren't even heard of to me. I had absolutely no idea what I could be and do with my life.

My college controlled how I dressed, who I left campus with, who I dated and how I dated, what music I listened to, and where I went for activities. At the time, I saw nothing abnormal or cultish about it. Now I see everything wrong with telling a young adult how to live their life. We could not ride in cars in a mixed group without an approved chaperone. Even then we had to have a pass signed saying it's okay and exactly where we were going. There was to be absolutely no physical contact between men and women. Not even holding hands or hugging, whether or not you were dating. Women had to wear skirts on and off campus. Skirts had to cover the knee. All music had to be filtered through the music faculty at the school, which only allowed classical and piano/organ type music. Some disney was allowed. There was absolutely no drinking or smoking. No dancing. No playing cards. No TVs allowed in the dorm rooms. The campus had a TV for sports located in the student center. We had to attend chapel every day and church every Sunday (3 times) and Wednesday. We had to report our chapel and church attendance. Oh, the church had to be at an approved Baptist church too. And not all Baptist churches qualified. We were also expected to be active in the church we chose to attend and to report our service to the school.

I am not tall...at 5'3," I am the top of the shorts...so buying a jean skirt to fit me for college made them a bit long sometimes. One jean skirt I had dragged on the floor a little bit. I remember being home for Christmas one year and I stopped by my former Christian school/church office. The pastor came out of his office and commented on my skirt being long. I thought he was joking. I laughed and said, "ya, it's because I'm so short." Seconds later he got angry and said "would you roll your skirt up young lady!?" His problem was that it was worldly for my skirt to be dragging the floor. That's the kind of insanity I grew up in...that my mind still struggled to process at times. For the record, I never liked the facade I saw in that pastor and didn't do what he said, especially since I knew my motives were not what he was projecting onto me. He did not care about, or even know me on a personal level, at all. His opinion was not my problem.

I started questioning a few things that my church/schools called standards in college...such as music and speaking in tongues and calvinism, etc. I wanted to know what the Bible really said. So my preferences and interpretations started tweaking here. But I still mainly stuck to the guidance of whoever I was under at the time. I believed that if I attended college and the college said I cannot listen to a certain music I should obey them because they're my spiritual authority. Looking at that now, that is not their place to make rules like that unless they are a cult. And if they're a cult, I should not be there. But my belief system guilted me into obedience.

I worked at Christian camps every summer as a counselor between college years. I loved it. It was my favorite thing in the whole world to experience life and lead in this environment. Little did I know I was indoctrinating kids and playing a role in emotionally manipulating them into relationships with Jesus just like I had been.

I graduated from college with a degree in Elementary Education, which I used to go on and teach in Christian schools for several years. I could have taught in public school...but God's best and perfect way was Christian school so I could teach openly about him and disciple those kids to have a relationship with him.

Even when I didn't attend camp anymore, I would still shake at church all the time during invitations and altar calls. Always. Even when I didn't think I had done anything bad. The trauma continued. The invitation continued. Somebody needs to repent, etc. It was evidently always me...

The God of the Bible expects his followers to be perfect, even though he claims they're covered in the blood of Jesus. We are still disappointments. We were told that we cause Jesus pain and make him sad every time we fail. The new testament tells us to be perfect, as your father in heaven is perfect. Also, be holy because God is holy.

Our job in life is to find God's will and follow it (Romans 12:2). If you are out of God's will, you are not in a good place. However, in God's will—he has a perfect will and a permissive will. Your job is to find his perfect will, because his permissive will, he allows to happen, but it's far from his best for you. This was always a stressful task to figure out, especially when you really couldn't know for sure which will you were walking in, if either one.

In 2005, I married because we had common goals to serve God. It was not love at first sight, it was all about God and I found a man whose goals in life matched mine where we could raise children for God and retire to the mission field some day where we would die telling people about Jesus. Because of this, we knew within a week we were going to get married that year and live our lives for God together for the rest of our lives. We could learn to love each other.

I had been taught all my life that the man is supposed to lead in the marriage. I was told several times that I wasn't letting my spouse lead. Well that's not our personality. My husband is relaxed and playful. I am a go-getter, a fierce, strong, warrior type of leader. I would try to be submissive and let him lead, but then he wouldn't step up and lead. This is not an insult on him—this is an insult on the patriarchy and gender roles that need to die. Their time is over. People need to live by their unique individual strengths whether or not they fit the gender role puzzle. You know, you do you. Be yourself.

We were taught to look to external sources and never within ourselves for decisions, for validation, for compliments. Let another man praise you and not your own lips (Proverbs 27:2). But then we were also told that the validation and compliments don't belong to us...they belong to God, and we are to give them glory for those compliments we receive by being humble and admitting it wasn't you, but God that shined so brightly or did so well. God does NOT share his glory with us (Isaiah 42:8).

Spiritual authority is a really big deal. God has placed people over you that you are to submit to and obey. Starting with church leadership. Under them is your husband if you are a woman who is married (Ephesians 5). Then the wife. Then the children. There's an order of command. You must listen to and obey them because they give account to God for you. They tell you what is okay to believe and keep you from straying from God's perfect path. You don't make decisions on your own. The Bible tells us to seek counsel from our spiritual leaders/counselors and not trust ourselves. I was told I was to submit to my husband like my children submit to me. No matter what he asks me to do. That's some bullshit.

The leadership in a recent church told me I can't know for sure that I am hearing from God so I must seek counsel from older, wiser people in the church (Proverbs 11:14). They said hearing from God feels like indigestion and you can't know one from the other. I thought that seemed ridiculous and didn't agree.

We were taught we had to believe *everything* in the Bible 100% to be saved. And you had to have the perspective the church had and do things Biblically right. For example, my church believed in baptism by immersion. So if you were sprinkled, you were not obeying God, and this was a big problem.

You could call me the apostle Paul of the western world. He was the guy on the pedestal that we were taught to pattern our life after, as an example for the seriousness and commitment to serving God. Don't be a Peter...He's too impulsive and angry. Don't be a Thomas...he doubts. Don't be an Andrew or John. They were selfish and wanted to sit by Jesus in heaven. Apostle Paul was *The Man*. Anything less than him was not taking Christianity seriously enough. And yes, just like the apostle Paul with the rigidity of his belief system that he brought over from his previous lifestyle...I too, was an asshole. Just ask some of my friends!

I've spent approximately 97% of my life trying to make sure I live out my purpose and my days intentionally, according to what God had planned for my life...plans that I was told he decided before I was born. I was taught that God had ordained all my days (Psalm 139:16). He had a plan, a perfect will for me, for how I should live out those days. They were to be spent serving God by serving others, and not my own selfish self. My life was not my own (1 Corinthians 6:19). I was bought with a price—the blood of Jesus—and was created to glorify him. I was responsible to find out what God's perfect will was for my life and to live by it. I did not exist to bring myself joy and happiness, but to suffer for Christ—and in that—it was said, I could find happiness, knowing I was bringing God glory. That's different from happiness from pleasure. We were taught not to seek happiness from pleasure and things satisfying to ourselves. That is worldly and God is not pleased with it.

The burden to live the perfect will of God was so heavy. I was constantly racking my brain trying to figure out what I was supposed to be doing at every specific moment to make God happy. I was never able to just relax and just be, because fear of God wouldn't let me. I could never do enough—there always had to be *more*. Because—*what if*—Jesus came back in one of those moments I chose to relax? *What if* he wouldn't tell me, "well done, good and faithful servant (Matthew 25:23)"? *What if* I wasn't enough?

I lived with a lot of fear. Fear of...not going to heaven, not praying the right words, not listening to the right music, not wearing the right clothes, not following God close enough, offending somebody. Supposedly if you were really saved, you wouldn't struggle repeatedly...you would be holy and perfect like Jesus.

Well, I entered adulthood, got my own car, went off to college, served even more, got married, had kids, even adopted, taught Christian school, homeschooled, served in church, hosted and led Christian book and Bible studies, hosted and led small groups, served at women's retreats, spoke at a couple events...and it *still* wasn't enough. All I kept hearing from the pulpit was "we're not doing enough!" my whole last couple years of Christianity. I heard it *every. Single. Sunday.* However, now I was starting to hear a voice inside of me that said, "um, you are doing enough—you can't do anymore. You don't have any more time to commit..." And so now hearing, "you're not doing enough" from the pulpit made me start to grow a whole new frustration. God wasn't telling me this. Man was telling me this. And how dare man tell me that I am not doing enough for God!

I was constantly stuck on making sure I was doing enough to make God happy, to fulfill his purpose for me. It was so stressful. I was so stressed, anxious, and burned out. I was still always searching my mind for "what would God want me to be doing with these moments each and every day...what's his perfect plan...." I was so afraid of getting it wrong and being disappointed when I would stand before God someday and give an account for the good and bad ways I lived my life.

My purpose all my life was to make sure I was pleasing God and making him happy and leading others to him (2 Corinthians 5:9-10). I had no purpose outside of his purpose. I was taught that all my life. Life outside of God was meaningless.

I was whole-heartedly and intentionally raising my children to follow Jesus. I immersed their souls in the ways of God to protect them from the attacks of the enemy and hope they latch onto the one and only truth that would save their souls and give them peace and eternal life. We were active at church and Christian school. We even went on a family mission trip to Haiti. We constantly had Christian worship music playing around the house. We were your model Christian family. I did not take my parenting job from God lightly.

I was told by a former pastor that I was to submit to my husband like my children submit to me. He was to be in control of me. I was to obey him and do whatever he told me to do. When I asked about boundaries and what about ME, and who am I, the pastor told me that when I got married and two became one flesh, that I didn't exist anymore (Mark 10:8-10). What toxic, ridiculous theology! I didn't buy it.

The whole deconstruction process is lonely. I transitioned to different therapists several times in therapy over several years. All the transitions taught me more each time that I am ok. I can heal. And while I do need community, I do not *need* any one specific person. There will always be somebody there for me somewhere. People in our life have seasons. Whether it's therapy, family, friends in real life or online...I am not alone.

So I tried so hard for so long to live whole-heartedly for God. He was my life and my everything. My reason for existing. But things didn't always stay the same. I had always searched the scriptures. I had always been a deep thinker and went as deep as I found possible in my relationship with God. Even though it never felt deep enough, as I always craved more. This craving constantly drove me to study God's Word under the paradigms and perspectives I had been given. These paradigms *slightly* shifted over time, but never to the extreme as in stepping outside what I was taught about how to interpret the Bible and my relationship with God. However, things were about to drastically change. As I witnessed other faiths and belief systems having similar experiences, I struggled to be content with surface answers that didn't seem to adequately answer my probing questions on spirituality and faith. In fall of 2018, I began diving deeper than I had been allowed in the past with questions such as, "How can people who do not believe in 'the one true God' have spiritual experiences similar to mine?" This time I was told, what if there is more than one path to God...what if it is the same God? Freaked out about the answer I received, I hesitated to move forward in this endeavor, because it challenged the only faith I had ever known and trusted as ABSOLUTE TRUTH. This question was only the beginning of a life & identity transformation beyond what I had ever experienced before.

2018 concluded, and in 2019, as old beliefs continued to be challenged and not hold up, I sunk deeper and deeper into significant loss. Loss of childhood faith, which encompasses your entire identity, is so much bigger than the loss of an idea in your head. Loss of faith involved loss of: partial or entire identity, community, stability, comfort, and so much more. In fact, I would face such a strong identity crisis over the total loss of my child-hood faith that I would literally, legally change my name to Makayla, taken from my "fake" twitter account @kayla_jo_19, which I created as a safe place to find and explore this new world alongside of other #exchristians and #exvangelicals. Once feeling all alone and terrified of not knowing who I was or what was going on anymore, I, now known as Kayla Jo, find the strength inside of myself, through and along with other former believers, to forge this path forward and keep moving forward from where my former faith had quite literally dropped me into a deep, dark, black hole of nothingness.

Once I overcome the intense emotions of losing everything I had ever known as it was, I eventually learn that a crisis in faith does not mean it's over—it's merely a new beginning. It's not the end. It's just another chapter. I learn that I can embrace a new way of living. I learn that it's not wrong to question and change. I learn that life is just a process of: Evolve—deconstruct, change, grow.

This book is not to tell you what to believe. That's not my right or place to tell you what your belief system should be. This book is to normalize that it's okay to question, doubt, change, and shift your belief system...over and over and over. This book is to tell my story of what happened in my life to radically shift my paradigm of what I thought *everybody*'s life should look like. Truth is you are free—I am free—we are free to research, change, shift, evolve, in whatever direction our lives take us.

Part 2 of this book is written from the perspective of where I am now (as Makayla, my new name) writing to Kimberly (my birth name)...Makayla is encouraging Kimberly that it's gonna be okay and giving her a heads up on what's going to happen. Kimberly is freaking out at Makayla grasping for hope as her life-long faith and identity disappears...and never returns...

Part 2

Dear Kimberly...
Love, Makayla

July 2018

Dear Kimberly,

Hey there! I'm Makayla. Some people call me Kayla Jo. Believe it or not, I'm the future you. I've been through a lot and I want to give you a heads-up on what's ahead, because it's mind-blowing and life-changing. I want you to know ahead of time that you're safe. And in spite of how terrified and confused you will feel at times, you're going to be okay. You are resilient. You are so much stronger than you feel. And you will come through on the other side of this mess, a fierce, brave warrior full of love, dedication, understanding, and passion to help other people like you. The hard times and stretching times are when we grow. And your growth is going to be remarkable. The impact of this journey on others will challenge the status quo and what people have always "known." Especially coming from a life as genuine as your own.

You are about to embark on a journey like nothing you've ever been through before. That confidence that you have held all your life about knowing absolute truth and everything being black and white is about to be radically challenged, and you will never be the same. Don't hold things too tightly—holding the unknown too tightly will break you. Loosen your grip, even just slightly. Open your mind to the possibility that life is not what you've always assumed it was, and realize nobody's reality is exactly the same as we all have different perspectives on our lives based on the stories in our heads.

That belief that you can't trust yourself to know what's right for you and that you always need to seek 'wise counsel' within the church or from older, wiser adults, to know for sure if God is speaking, or what to do with big decisions, is also about to be challenged to the core, along with the ability to think for yourself and view situations from different angles and perspectives. You're about to start a learning process that will reveal that you have all the answers within you already. Contrary to what you've been taught, you can trust yourself. You have a natural wisdom inside of you and a spark of light that is from the beginning of time. Learn to recognize this wisdom. Your inner self is amazing and is meant to guide you into being fully you—whatever you decide that will be. There is no right or wrong. There are only experiences—and consequences. So choose wisely—and enjoy the journey.

The religious box that you thought you broke out of over the last 10-15 years only opened up into another religious box. Bigger, yes...but still a box. But it's all been part of the process. Relaxing your view on dress, music, activities, and other externals has felt freeing, but you're still tied down to thinking your spirituality is defined by your holiness in these things. That's another box.

Life is not meant to be lived in ANY box. You get to choose your journey, and you can choose to break out of any box once you realize that you are in it. But that's the key—most people don't realize they're still in a box of some sort, making them intolerant of other people's perspectives that don't match their own. You can choose to break the mold that's held you captive...the mold that has suppressed and silenced who you really are all these years.

Up until this point, you had always believed that your belief in God was a choice...yet you had no other information to compare or question. You thought that you always CHOSE to believe exactly what you were taught about the Bible and how to interpret it, as well as Christianity. You didn't understand why other people didn't just see things the same way you see them. You thought they had a choice and were purposely choosing not to believe in absolute truth, because that's what the church taught you, and you couldn't understand why they wouldn't choose the path you were on. You thought that anybody could and should choose the same path you were following. You thought that you held the one right reality for everybody. You weren't taught that all people have different perspectives and views of life and reality. You were taught there was one reality and any view of life that didn't line up with the world-view you had been taught was absolutely wrong, and it was not okay. However, you are about to find out that not even you intentionally chose the path that you were on—and it's not going to be easy. But the compassion and fresh understanding of life and people that you will develop in the process will be priceless.

Don't be afraid,

$\mathcal{D}$ear Makayla,

Life is NOT what I expected it to be AT ALL...but you've got to be kidding me. My belief in God is my choice, I do not live in a box, and I am not going anywhere. True, if you would have asked little Kimberly where she would be at the age of 38, she would have told you that she would probably be telling people about Jesus on the mission field somewhere, and eating bugs. If I was lucky, the bugs would be covered in chocolate...but still gross, and I hated and feared the thought that following God would require me to do that, but I knew I had to embrace it and be willing to sacrifice anything. Not kidding on the bugs. I learned early in life that God wants you to sacrifice your life on the mission field and you have to do whatever the locals do so you don't offend them, so that they will ask Jesus to save them. Sometimes this meant eating bugs. I knew even as a toddler that I had to and wanted to give my entire life to God, because he sent his only son Jesus as a sacrifice for my sins, because my sins were a filthy abomination to my loving heavenly father. Meaning I was a filthy abomination to him too, when I would sin, because he couldn't look at sin. I was born a wicked, disgusting, wretched worm, and I owed him my entire life. Every single aspect of it. It was the least I could do for the sacrifice he made for me by sending his one and only son to die on the cross so he could love and forgive me for being such a horrible person and rebelling against God's will. Otherwise, I would have to die for my own sin. His son Jesus was my substitute. Jesus loved me so much he died for my wickedness and rebellion toward God so that I could have eternal life in heaven one day (Isaiah 53:6). He gave his life for me, I owe my life to him—every breath.

I have always taken living for God and my relationship with him VERY seriously. Nobody could take God and the crucial need to give my life to him on a daily basis MORE seriously than me. I am an example of what it means to follow Christ. I am a leader. And I wanted you to walk with Jesus as intensely as I do too. "Follow me as I follow Christ" (1 Corinthians 11:1), is a Bible verse that I passionately pattern my life after. I lead by example. After all, it is a sin to not be an example. Because if I am not being an example of how to live for Christ, I am failing and souls are being lost and their blood is on my hands for not leading well enough. And if I am not being an example of giving 100% for God, I am wasting my life.

I lead worship playing in our church's band. I just finished leading a Christian book study on Boundaries. I am enrolled in a Christian college for grad school. I am a key speaker at a women's retreat in September and my topic is all about walking with God in daily life. I am active in church and in my life group! I just adopted 3 kids to add to my biological 3 and I'm raising them all for God's glory! I have no intention of ever leaving my relationship with God or Christianity. God is my entire life, my entire identity! I am absolutely NOTHING without him. Everything I have done up until now is for him, and will continue to be that way. It's impossible to separate us. Makayla, you've got the wrong person. You are not me, you don't know me, and I am not ever leaving Christianity!

Wrong Number Girl,

Kimberly

August 2018

*D*ear Kimberly,

You have had a hell of an emotional year and a half in therapy, and this month is going to throw you for a loop. You've been in therapy for depression, along with working through the intensity of foster care and adoption, and your time with your current therapist is going to abruptly end. This therapist has walked you through so much darkness and the attachment that you feel to this person is going to exponentially increase your pain as you leave her and move on to somebody else to try to help you through all your emotional pain. It's going to sting...A LOT. You're going to feel like you can't make it. But you can. You are strong. The pain won't last forever.

You will reluctantly switch therapists, to another Christian in town who seems to get you, giving you hope that maybe this was the answer. You chose him, knowing his faith was like yours, so you felt safe that you wouldn't be led astray, and you believed he would not allow anything contrary to your faith, which was extremely important. You will continue to question why God would allow you to struggle with depression so deep that you wish you didn't exist anymore, when you've begged for healing ALL YOUR LIFE. But that's not what will cause your faith to waiver. Your faith in God and his purposes was strong. You trusted that God's ways were perfect, and we can't know his purposes, but we can trust that the outcome is for his glory and our good...no matter how much it hurts. You were taught that our suffering here on earth completes where the suffering of Jesus was lacking.

You've got this!

♥Makayla♥

$\mathcal{D}$ear Makayla,

Life has gotten so hard. I've been battling severe depression and suicidal thoughts daily for over a year. Sometimes I wish I never started therapy. Less thinking sometimes means less pain. Life is so hard. I don't know how to do this. I'm devastated. And adding to all the emotional pain, I'm officially switching therapists. It needs to happen, but I hate the idea of starting over. My current therapist and I have done as much as we can do I guess. I don't want to start over. I thought she was a great Christian woman and I could trust her to not lead me wrong. But at the same time I'm not so sure she is a healthy relationship for me to be in as it seems to be "her way or no way." Something about my relationship with her made me suicidal. Until her, I never had those intense thoughts...life became unbearable. She did recognize I have symptoms of PTSD for some reason. She's not sure what it comes from, but she thinks my previous churches are cultish.

Therapy was scary to get into because I have always been taught that psychology is evil and studying it or learning about it can do things that lead you away from God. Thinking is dangerous. Exploring how the mind works is not the Christian way of healing because Jesus is supposed to be the answer to all that, and my relationship with him was supposed to be enough to make me whole, no questions asked. Simple answers. No deep, critical thinking. Just Jesus is the answer. Don't try to understand life or the ways of "God." Accept what is and realize God's way is perfect. Surrender any questioning or anxiety about anything to him, and let him carry the load. You quit thinking about and worrying about what could go/be wrong and leave it all in the hands of God and just let go.

Getting help from "worldly sources" outside of the church is not what a Christian is supposed to be doing, because it can let the devil sneak into your life. Fortunately, I will be seeing another Christian, but I don't like the idea of transitioning or starting over. I've worked through soooo much dirt over the last year and a half and the idea of starting over is overwhelming.

I don't know what to do. I feel lost. I feel like nobody can help me. I believe it's God's will for me to suffer, but I don't know how much more I can take. My husband and I have even discussed that this depression and suicidal ideation could be my "thorn in the flesh" and it's God's will for me to suffer with depression in this life. But I'm not able to be a good mom, wife, or friend because this emotional pain is consuming me and pushing me through the ground. I don't want to keep going. But in regard to all this, I am taught that God says, "his grace is sufficient for me—for in my weakness he is made strong (2 Corinthians 12:9)." But this feels unbearable and hopeless. I can't keep going at this intensity.

I feel emotionally spent.

Kimberly

September 2018

Dear Kimberly,

You have already been in counseling for depression and struggling to have a desire to exist since May, 2017. Yes, you've struggled with depression over not being good enough and falling short of life's expectations since you were 11 or 12. But these last couple years have been the hardest mental and emotional years of your life. You are still really struggling to find answers, and while you still completely trust and love God with all your heart, you are starting to think critically about what is life, what is God, and what is actually the point. You still believe the actual point of life is to glorify God and love him with every fiber of your being, but questions relating to spirituality are growing. You've always gone above and beyond in your part in your relationship with God. It was not a religion to you. It was a relationship. An intense love relationship. Even though, in my "future you" opinion, looking back, it often felt like you were making up the other part of the relationship in your head. You didn't realize that the relationship you had was just with the inner you, which will never go away. You didn't realize your inner voice was "God's" still small voice. Role-playing or filling in the gaps for how you believed God was Biblically speaking to you, according to the spiritual teachings you were given on how to interpret the Bible and the God of the Bible. Going to "his word" like you were taught to find his reply to you on any given topic. Orchestrating this relationship to be as genuine as humanly possible, all while believing that ultimately it was God orchestrating it by moving in you to do as he desired you to do. However, eventually, one question in particular is going to be the key that unlocks the turn to the greatest life-change you ever imagined.

Your faith will be rocked when you ask the question, "How can people in other religions have spiritual experiences just like me? They think they hear from

God. But not my God—their god. Not the One True God—false, sinful gods. Idols. But that doesn't get rid of the fact that they have things happen spiritually like I do—but if their god is not my God, the one true God, how do they have these experiences?" The church had taught you the answer to this was "demons" or satan. Satan is an angel of light and makes darkness look like God is at work when he is not.

You will expect black and white answers from your new, current Christian therapist for how these other people experience spirituality apart from the (your) one true God—but you won't be given the Christianese or cliche answers you're expecting and looking for. You will actually expect him to blame the similarities on satan being an angel of light (2 Corinthians 11:14). You will be shocked that your Christian therapist does not present a concrete answer to you, like you thought he should...like every other "authority" has, all your life. When you've always been told what to believe, and that it is the one and only truth, and everything else is evil, you don't develop the ability to think critically for yourself. You literally become dependent on outside spiritual sources to tell you what to and what not to believe and follow, and you are taught that you cannot trust yourself. This becomes extremely overwhelming when you don't have the critical thinking skills to realize you can have your own beliefs and make your own decisions and be okay even when they don't line up with what your authority has taught you all your life. It doesn't feel okay. It doesn't feel safe at all. It actually feels quite terrifying. Traumatizing. The responses you will be given will rock your world. For the first time in your life, you will be given permission to question. Questioning outside the box will scare the crap out of you. You'll try to shut it down, but this time, your brain won't let it happen. It will be up to YOU ALONE to figure out the answer to that question, rather than have it be fed to you. Panic will set in as your mind begins to whirl with "what if" possibilities that contradict everything you've always been told to believe and built your entire life upon.

The response you receive, "what if it is the same God?" will blow your mind. Your heart will race, and you will majorly freak out inside at the dilemma you are now facing, with a therapist you trusted to stay "Christian focused," according to your own definition, that you had constructed from your upbringing and belief system. Later, you will realize that these therapy sessions where you were free to question and grow in uncomfortable ways were a huge stepping stone in you growing into the adult and individual you were meant to be...even if it was 18 years later than "normal."

In the process of all the questioning and ambiguity, you will get scared and angry, and you will shut down. How could a person be a Christian and allow this much freedom for the God you were raised with? Is that even possible? You will stay far away from that topic in therapy for months...occasionally dabbling with a brief question or comment, but the fear of letting your mind go into the unknown will tailspin your emotions and thought patterns into a world they have never been.

The realization that things may not be as they seemed to be, in their absoluteness, has just begun. Peering over the edge of that abyss was terrifying. Too terrifying. You were not ready to go there. As far as you knew, you are not ALLOWED to go there. The enemy lives there. You were wanted there, but you were a child of God and not supposed to be there—not even entertaining the thought, questions, or doubts.

You will start to read a book your T recommends to open your mind to different perspectives of Christianity. You have no intention of leaving Christianity. And he has no intention of convincing you to leave. That's not his job. His job is to help you realize you can figure this out on your own. You have the answers for YOU. This book will look nothing like your fundamental, independent, Baptist upbringing to you. It will not even slightly appeal to you, as you will see it as lies, and you will decide, in your still black and white mentality, that this dude you're reading a book about is screwed up because how can he view

Christianity so freely and allow "sin," while claiming to be Christian and thinking God is okay with that. Progressive Christianity will look like a joke to you. You will quickly head back to where you came from and revert back to your old black and white thinking, as it will seem so obvious that this is not the right path to take. You were taught that the Bible was a rule-book for life. To be followed exactly. You were taught things that applied to today, and things that did not, and which commands applied to today that you were responsible to follow. You know the Bible inside and out from 37 years of church, 14 years of Christian school, and 5 years of Bible college, not to mention the hours and hours of personal study, teaching Christian school and Sunday school, leading small groups, etc...you "knew" your literal interpretation of everything was RIGHT and spoken from the mouth of God to be put on the pages of the Bible. You knew God didn't want his children to be ANYTHING like the pagans and how angry he was with people in the old testament to the point of death. And the new testament may state that God is love, but it also states God does not change. He demanded holiness and living above reproach. And you knew that the Bible warned you not to depart from the ways you were taught as a child. To hold tightly to the truth, and not let go. Funny thing is...how does the Bible know what ways you were taught as a child that you are not supposed to depart from? Ironic, isn't it. Which interpretation? Translation? Which were you and others taught was right? And how do you know which is right other than insisting that it's the one you were taught?

You will be a major speaker at a three-day women's retreat this month. You had been chosen to give the 40 minute piety talk...the talk on what it meant and looked like to daily walk with God. You were so excited when you were asked to give this talk at the beginning of the summer. You were honored, pumped, confident, and ready for it. Living a life of service to God, in spite of your feelings that lie to you, was your passion and you had so much to say! You even had to cut probably 10 pages out of the talk to make it short enough!

Now the time is here and while you will be excited, the torture in your spirit will make it hard to even speak. You will still 100% believe in what you are saying, and it's fitting, because you will be talking about doing the hard, serving God, even when you don't feel it. That will be exactly what you are doing, pushing past your feelings that you were taught you cannot trust, to teach these women how to do the same. You will believe this is the devil fighting you because God is using you for amazing things, and the devil wants to stop you. But really, it's the cognitive dissonance, and not being able to make sense of what's involuntarily happening in your head. The acrobatics your brain is trying to do to stay afloat and hold onto your beliefs is actually quite impressive and saddening at the same time.

The cognitive dissonance you will be experiencing more and more will both make it difficult, and tie in to the key that you kept going back to, "I can follow Christ regardless of my feelings. My feelings lie. I can't trust myself or my feelings. But I can keep doing what I KNOW I need to be doing, that being, serving God with all my heart, moment by moment, every day, and encouraging others to be the same. Lead by example."

You will be numb the entire talk. You will not even feel like you are in your body. Then when you go back to the prayer room, as you are supposed to, when you are finished, you will have an intense, emotional breakdown. You will not even know what's going on. You will not know how to explain both the numbness and ironically the pain you feel inside or where it's coming from, but you will not be able to stop the waves of emotions surging like rapids and the tears streaming down your face. Nobody in your circle understands the depths of pain that's going on deep inside your soul. Nobody. Nobody gets it, as much as some seem to think they do. Others looked very confused.

You can handle this—I believe in you!

*D*ear Makayla,

I have struggled with depression and suicidal ideation for 2 full years and I am so tired of struggling. I don't understand why God won't take it away. I mean, the feelings are so intense and I battle them every day. It feels like I walk around with a weighted blanket covering my entire body. It feels like my mind is being tortured and squeezed. I can't find a way out. Not even God answers.

I've spent the last two years seeking God with all my heart. Actually, I've spent my entire life seeking him, but we're talking about this specific situation. I have a genuine relationship with him, it's not about religion. I talk to him, sing to him, listen to him, worship him...with my entire being! He has my heart, mind, soul, and body! Everything I do, I do for his glory. Every day I live, every breath I take is dedicated to my God and Savior, Jesus Christ. I've been vulnerable about my struggle with depression and suicidal ideation. I've asked for prayer at church. I've listened to countless sermons on renewing my mind. I've researched how to heal. I've been active in therapy with Christian counselors. NOTHING is working. NOTHING. Sometimes I even feel worse. I feel stuck. I feel like I will never get better. I want to give up, but I can't. I don't know where to go from here. I wish I wasn't alive anymore, because I hate the emotional and mental pain I am in. I can hardly move or function.

I'm definitely still a Christian. I don't know why God would allow me to struggle like this...but I will be faithful to him, because according to the Bible, which is also known as HIS HOLY WORD, he has called me to suffer. Suffering is completing what was lacking in the suffering of Jesus somehow.

I do not understand why I would beg God to heal me of my depression and thoughts telling me I would rather not exist, and he won't. I have an amazing, close relationship with him! I pour every fiber of my being into serving and worshiping him! Living for God consumes me! My life in Christ controls everything I do and think.

Why does he tell me that all I need is the faith of a mustard seed (Matthew 17:20), and to ask in faith and I will be healed...and yet he doesn't answer me? I have enough faith! I know he can heal me—IF HE WANTS TO! I also know sometimes he wants us to suffer for his greater purpose and for his glory and that's very possibly why I am so intensely suffering. So it's my job to let him shine through me and persevere through this hell of a trial.

Yes, I am still a Christian, but I do have questions. How can other people in other religions or faiths have spiritual experiences like I do? They seem so legit. So real. Their spiritual experiences are very real to them—as real as mine are to me. How can that be? I expected my therapist to give me the black and white answer for that...like demonic activity mimics God activity...which is what I had always been taught...because Satan is an angel of light and appears good...but that didn't happen. Instead he let me question, so I could find the answers for myself instead of being fed pat answers like I had all my life. He was allowing me to explore and come to my own conclusion. He wasn't spoon feeding me what I was supposed to believe, as I had been spoon-fed all my life.

Questioning outside my religious box was frowned upon in Christianity...because if you listen to the "wrong" people, they will lead you astray (Matthew 7:15). The right and wrong people to listen to were determined by my church and other spiritual authority in my life. I wasn't even supposed to listen to other Christians who didn't agree with my church because they were wrong, and straying from God's truth.

My therapist encouraged me to read Brian McLaren, to get a broader perspective on my black and white perspective of Christianity. So I did—and it was very unsettling. I couldn't reconcile his beliefs to my "true brand" of Christianity. I was totally black and white—and Brian didn't fit the mold. But let me say, I think it's awesome that Brian can have so much peace and have his relaxed form of Christianity without any guilt. I'm not allowed to do that. The way I was taught to interpret the Bible does not allow for freedom like this.

I was a main speaker at a three-day women's retreat this month. My job was to give the talk on Piety. The Piety talk was meant to be the key, turning-point talk for the weekend, as I spoke for 40 minutes on what it means to follow God in every-day life. I talked about how we can follow God, regardless of our feelings. I taught the women that our feelings lie to us and we can't trust them. I fully believed this 100% at the time of the talk. I believed that my feelings and inner self could not be trusted because according to Jeremiah 17:9, the heart is deceitful, who can know it!? And we are only to trust GOD with all our heart (Proverbs 3:5,6). Trusting yourself was dangerous, prideful, and sinful.

Something just wasn't right inside of me. I was still really battling how other religions could have spiritual experiences like me. In my black and white thinking, I was pretty confident that it could NOT be the same God that I was serving. And if it was not the one true God, what/who was it? This was really bothering me. And it messed with my head the whole time I was giving the talk.

I finished the talk, walked back to the prayer room, and had a complete melt-down. I didn't know why. I just could not stop shaking and crying. I felt horrible. We all chalked it up to spiritual war-fare. The enemy (Satan) was at war for our souls that weekend...and we just kept praying for strength and that the enemy would be bound and taken away.

I felt so numb inside the entire weekend, yet I felt so much pain at the same time. I didn't know what was going on inside of me. But I took my own advice and went against my feelings and continued to serve and love on these women at this three-day event. I had a group of women that I sat with all weekend, that I was responsible to minister to with all my energy. I definitely had to dig deep. In my head, it was because Satan was working over time because he didn't want me doing all the good that I was doing.

I really hate how I feel inside. I hate living in ambiguity. It's hard to live with the unknown when the unknown is fighting against my belief system and creating questions that I can't answer. I don't know how to live with this cognitive dissonance. I don't want to live with it. I hope I find my answers soon.

What the heck is happening to me!?

Kimberly

October 2018

Dear Kimberly,

You will hope for peace and try to back away from the intensity of all the confusion, questioning, and research this month. But when you want answers, the questions always drive you to do more research to find whatever it is you feel you're supposed to know to have peace. You will keep looking for definite answers to questions that are not black and white. This makes sense, because you were taught that God has a perfect path that you are supposed to find, and if you're not in the perfect will of God, you're not living your best life...which is a disappointment—to God and to you. You were taught that the Bible is the absolute truth and rulebook for life and godliness. Everything you need to know to live your life is written in the Bible, and you should always refer back to it for answers. You knew the verse and the song that said something like, he has given everything for life and godliness to the knowledge of him who called us by his own glory and goodness in Christ Jesus (2 Peter 1:3-4)

You are going to struggle through realizing that there are different perspectives and interpretations of the Bible. It is going to radically challenge your black and white thinking. It is going to feel like it's destroying you. But it's not. It's going to be beyond scary having your paradigm challenged. But you're going to be okay. It's growing you. It's creating you. It's teaching you to think outside this religious box we just mentioned.

You will intensely struggle with uncertainty and will not want to allow yourself to entertain doubt, at least not for long. You want answers fast. You will still hold on to black and white thinking and wonder if doubting is a sin against God like you were taught. Your therapist will keep telling you that doubting is a part of having faith—but you don't want to buy that. You've always been taught that God is disappointed with doubt, and you should put away your doubts because they are sinning against God by not trusting him to have your best interest in mind. You were taught to not be a "doubting Thomas" because God was disappointed with his lack of belief. You were always taught not to follow his example and just believe and have faith, without question. You were taught in James that we were to have faith without doubting because he who doubts is like a wave of the sea, driven by the wind and tossed...and that person shouldn't think he will receive anything from the Lord (James 1:6). Your need to not doubt continues to drive your need for concrete answers. You do your best to try to let go of black and white thinking. You will try super hard to embrace ambiguity. But it feels impossible to buy into ambiguity when you've been taught absolutes all your life. You were taught YOU had all the RIGHT answers and it's YOUR job to spread that to the world. The Bible said to ALWAYS be ready to give an answer.

You will beg God to help you through this depression manifesting as a mental and physical storm you are facing on a daily basis..for over 2.5 years now. Not to mention most of your childhood and young adulthood off and on. It will feel like you are not getting answers. It will feel like you keep slipping because you expect God to answer you by taking away all your doubts so that you can be on the same page as your church and family again with your entire belief system. But in spite of your begging and searching with all your heart, that God is not found and you are left to yourself to find answers. You will feel forgotten by God and alone. You will struggle to find friends that can identify with your radically challenged beliefs...but there will be a couple who get it. You won't really be completely alone, even though it feels like it.

Later in the month, you become more content in your walk with God. But what you see in the church doesn't seem to line up with how you perceive we should view ourselves and this life. This will create another roadblock in your black and white belief system as you are desperate to be in agreement with the church on your beliefs, while also not having the ability to maintain a full grasp on your old belief system anymore. Things feel out of control in your mind.

You will also change your harsh views that you've always held on the gay community. You will realize how judgmental you've been and you will apologize to one of your best friends from college for how you treated her when she decided to have a girlfriend. You will realize how wrong and how hurtful you were to her. You will make things right and heal the friendship this month. Her forgiveness and acceptance will blow your mind. You will even eventually fly out to attend her wedding, and you will see the most amazing genuine love and teamwork between her and her new wife, as they create more family stability for the foster kids already living in their home. Your paradigm will be challenged beyond anything you've ever experienced before, as this is not how you assumed things are supposed to work, but you see it working beautifully.

You will also continue to be so hard on yourself—needing to have all the answers and have the perfect life. I wish you could just let go of the need to have concrete answers and be okay with not knowing everything anymore. This is bringing you a lot of mental, emotional, and physical pain. The struggle is real. I hate this for you.

Hang on girl! You got this!

Makayla

*D*ear Makayla,

I want answers so bad! I want certainty! I've been told all my life to believe beyond the shadow of a doubt! That's extreme certainty! Although reading Peter Enn's book, "The Sin of Certainty" really helped bring peace to my spirit about all this questioning I'm doing. Maybe it is okay to doubt and question. Maybe. ...MAYBE. I'm encouraged when I read books like his. They make sense. They make me feel better because I can identify with them so much! But then I get back into my reality where my family and friends do not see eye to eye with me and I feel the floor fall through again because I don't want to be different from them. I want them to see what I see. I want them to at least say, "ya, it's possible, we don't know for sure..." and accept me where I'm at, without seeing me as a heretic or falling away from the TRUE gospel or only true way of life. It's all or nothing with them, and I'm trying to break free from that, but it's so hard and scary and lonely.

I've been very skeptical and freaked out about the idea of exploring Christianity through any lens other than the lens that I grew up with. It's one thing to switch music preferences, denominations, and other surface things. It's a whole different ball game in my head to view the Bible from somebody's perspective that doesn't line up with the way I was taught to interpret the Bible. Even though I have made denominational switches through the years, the core of my belief system remained the same as far as doctrines of salvation and baptism and things that supposedly "really mattered." We were taught that the way our church interpreted the Bible was the way closest to how God wanted us to interpret the Bible. There was no better way. My spiritual leaders and authority had the best connection to God and I could 100% trust them to lead me right. That's what they had been to college for. The "right" colleges that taught the "right truth" and correct perspective about the Bible. Their degree qualified them to know the Bible and will of God more than me, and their job from God was to teach me how to interpret and follow it. If I was not following the path that they were following, then I was disobeying God, because God put them in charge of me to watch over my soul. Bill Gothard's umbrella theory was alive and well even in my current church. If you don't know what that is, just google it. Pretty much—Jesus is over the church/spiritual leaders, who are over the husband, who is over the wife, who is over the children. It's a hierarchy of command so to speak. My children obey me. I obey my husband. My husband obeys the church leadership. You answer to and obey the one above you. And in doing so you are obeying Jesus/God. If you get out from whoever is over you, they say satan can "get you." Which didn't make sense because Satan can get you anyway, if you let him.

I'm talking to a friend from high school who deconstructed. She's still spiritual...but views things quite differently. She introduced me to the liturgists. I then found Michael Gungor and Science Mike. I started reading Rob Bell, and then I found Peter Enns. I started listening to Paul Young, on YouTube, and his amazing story about how he wrote "The Shack" and his view of God. When I heard his story behind how/why he wrote the book it made so much sense and was so amazing. It was really cool to hear where it all came from. Things are clicking and make sense to me in a whole new way. It's exciting, but it feels risky. It feels like I'm an outsider...because none of my people believe any of this in this way. So I don't feel like I'm allowed to either. While seeing the Bible with a fresh perspective and "new eyes" is invigorating and refreshing, I also don't like not fitting in. As much as I love pushing the envelope and being different, this difference is so big it risks not fitting in with my community and being told I'm wrong. It isn't like a preference in favorite colors or which jeans to wear. It is a matter of heresy vs non-heresy, wrong vs right, to the group of people I am a part of. It separates me from my entire community.

Somehow, in the middle of all this thought transition, I realized how much I had hurt and been judgmental of one of my friends who had chosen a path different than my own as far as relationships go. She had taken the hard road and announced her love for her girlfriend, while I was the judgmental pharisee condemning her for her sin against God and humanity. I was horrible, unforgiving, mean, but from my paradigm at the time, I saw it all as love and bringing her back to God. I messaged her (she was one of my best friends from college) to apologize for condemning her for being with a girl. I feel like I just woke up and realized what love is, and I can't believe how judgmental, condemning, and unaccepting I had been. The more disturbing part was, I fully believed I was doing all of that in the name and love of Jesus. I was so wrong and she even invited me to her wedding because she could tell I was genuine and trusted me.

I'm changing a little.

Kimberly

November 2018

Dear Kimberly,

Your human development class at Liberty University will reveal to you how your belief system actually formed. Things will begin to make so much sense to you in a scary, even more life-changing sort of way. Your mind is about to enter shock as you realize that even though you had always thought your belief system was yours and you owned it, it was not as clear-cut as you thought. You will realize that, while yes, you chose it, and you were genuine and fully committed to loving and serving the God of the Bible, you didn't realize there were other perspectives of how to interpret the Bible. This will blow your mind and actually excite you as the Bible and the history of God begins to make more sense to you through an alternative lens. You will fall in love with a more historical lens of viewing the Bible, a lens that will allow you to make more sense of the angry God you see in the Old Testament vs Jesus being love in the New Testament.

The historical view of the Bible, from what you understood, viewed the Bible as written by man, and their own unique view of who they thought God was and what they thought God said to them. They often got it wrong—just like we get it wrong. It wasn't made to be taken literally or without mistakes necessarily. But more like a journal where different people in history recorded their stories, myths, perspectives on what they interpreted God and life as at that time. And some of this had foundations in earlier religions. This perspective really made the Bible come to life to you, and it didn't discredit a thing. In fact, it made the Bible even more special to you—and the story of redemption even more cool. It gives you a greater appreciation for what's written in the Bible and makes you hungry to read it again to see it all from this new, fascinating perspective.

These new perspectives will make it possible to see a God of love in the OT, by viewing the stories as written by man, from man's perspective of God intertwined their culture and their previous religions and views of war-like gods, rather than saying the Holy Spirit told men exactly what to write so we could read it later. But by having significant people in your life label these men heretics, you also will take on the label heretic, and you will despair... "Why believe anything at all then? If I am a heretic either way, and I lose my people & my community, why even try?" But you won't be able to stop searching, because you are so hungry for truth and for answers. You still want the concrete answers that you can't have. You want to prove that you're ok and be accepted as you are. Your brain will struggle to realize that you can have ideas about history, but you can't and don't need to know every detail for certain. It's just not necessary or possible. Not for the Bible, not for anything really. You can choose to trust what you see written. But you weren't there. You don't know the full culture. You don't have all the details. You don't have all the answers. And it's okay.

You will get hooked on listening to podcasts, sermons and YouTube videos by more progressive Christians and individuals with a historical view/interpretation of the Bible. This new-to-you view of the Bible will be so refreshing and invigorating to you! However, it won't be easy to embrace because of your intense need for approval from those in your community and the fact that your husband and friends at church label these individuals and their views as heretical. Those beliefs weren't just different, They were viewed as inaccurate to them. Heresy. Blasphemy. They weren't an option to believe in and remain "right." And since your husband and the leaders of the church are supposed to lead you and be in charge of you (so you were taught to believe), you are really going to struggle with wanting to believe what seemed to be so accurate and true for you, but feeling the pull to submit to your spiritual authority and ignore the evidence of another way to believe. The struggle will be intense and feel impossible and unbearable as you will see plainly that these beliefs that these "heretics" held seem to be more historically possible than the literal interpretation of the Bible you had been taught all your life. You don't want to be known as a heretic. You desperately want to believe and find the truth. You will be exploding with excitement and also feel like you have to keep everything a secret to be accepted, as you see glimpses of truth in what your friends and family consider "lies" and you struggle with what to do with these answers that don't match up with what you were taught to believe. You want to fit in, but you also desperately want to explore this exciting new possibility of belief that seems to make life make so much more sense in your thought process.

You will keep trying to find black and white answers and reconcile everything, and you will start consuming books like never before. Your thirst to know more and find a way to interpret the Bible that fits your paradigm will send you digging deeper and deeper. You will become consumed with Rachel Held Evans, Rob Bell, Peter Enns, Paul Young, and many others.

You will leave Sunday morning Bible study this month. Not because you do not want to identify as Christian, but because you will decide you have had enough of the political crap and meaningless talk going on in class. The class will have felt too "churchy" for you for a long time by now. It also felt superficial and shallow. Not that the people were that way...you love and appreciate the people. While you love each one of the ladies in that class, you will have known that you did not fit in that box for some time. So as you step out, it will be a breath of fresh air, where you feel free to be you. While you don't see it in the moment, this step of independence is the first of many baby steps to learning to trust yourself, think on your own, make your own decisions, and follow what you believe is best for you, regardless of what others think.

Leaving Sunday school will mean that for once in your life you will be choosing to not do something that everybody else is doing, simply because it's not a fit for you and you do not want to. This will be an extra big deal though, because the activity you are stepping out of is a religious one. But you will realize that's okay. You will grasp that you do not have to attend "every religious class that's available whenever the doors are open" in order to be a good person, a good Christian, or okay with God. Which is contrary to what you were taught by the church growing up. However, while you sit in the lobby at the church between band practice and the main service, you will overhear your children being told that God views them as filthy rags (Isaiah 64:6). This will unsettle your heart and not sit well with you. But you will not know what to do about that at this point in your life...other than make sure your children know that that is simply not true. You will not let them go down the road of thinking they are disgusting creatures to God. A God of love would not view your kids as disgusting bloody menstrual cloths. Ew. Gross!

Keep moving forward!

Dear Makayla,

I am in a Human Development class at Liberty University's grad school this month. I love this class because I love learning how we develop, and what is normal/abnormal, and all kinds of stuff like that. I love seeing how I compare to the averages. One thing triggered me though. As I was reading about developing critical thinking in adolescence and about how teenagers create their identity from their early years into young adulthood, I realized I had been robbed in this area. Not intentionally...I mean, I can't blame my parents...they did the best they could with what they knew. But I realized I had experienced identity foreclosure. Identity foreclosure is when a child/young adult takes on the personality and identity that an authority assigns them. My church, Christian school, and family had assigned and manipulated my identity all my life. I ultimately didn't have a choice, because I didn't know there was a choice. There was a right choice and a wrong choice. I had been exposed to the "only right choice" since birth. And what child, desperate to stay out of hell, is going to choose the wrong choice. My "choice" was conditioned into me so that it looked like it was my choice, but I had no mental ability to make any other choice because I was not given the information necessary to make any other decision. I was only given the information needed for the decision my authority wanted me to make. So while I thought I was making a choice, I was not aware of other choices to make. People that experience identity foreclosure may or may not realize this is what's going on at the time. I didn't realize this—because I grew up in religion. I didn't know I had other options. I genuinely thought I was choosing this identity—and I was with as much as I understood. But the fact that my authorities at Christian school, church, and home kept me from being exposed to other perspectives of the Bible and other worldviews for fear that I would take on the wrong belief system really hurt me developmentally. Choosing differently than what I was told was rejecting my ultimate purpose in life—and why would I want to do that? I wanted to live out my life's purpose whole-heartedly every day of my freakin life—with zeal and passion—for the God who loved and created me and wanted me to spend eternity with him in heaven! I fully embraced the story I was given to live out from the day I was born.

When I realized I had experienced identity foreclosure, I kinda freaked out inside. My first thought was denial. I remember thinking. No, my life was perfect. My parents were perfect. My church was perfect. This kind of stuff doesn't happen to me. I'm being dramatic. I am the one that's wrong here—not them. (Not that they intentionally did me wrong—they did what they thought best— they genuinely loved me). It's me—always me. I can't trust myself. But I couldn't let go of the thought that I had no comparison of anything to choose from. I wasn't even allowed to visit other denominations of family members for Pete's sake. Not even when I was 18! My parents had told my Aunt to quit proselytizing me—I AM THE ONE who had approached her with questions, and she got reprimanded for trying to answer my questions. Honestly, this angers me, because this was intolerance to other perspectives of Christianity. They weren't the enemy. This was definitely controlling me and hurting my critical thinking development into my young adulthood, and I had no idea.

Thoughts raced through my head...would I have chosen the same? Who would I be if I had a choice? Who would I be had I been given all the information from every perspective I had been learning about? Of course I assumed I would still believe in God, but what branch of Christianity would I be? And would I have lived life feeling free and unashamed, not guilty? I had been learning so many different perspectives. At this time, the issue wasn't "does God even exist?" But rather, what is this God that exists really like, and what does he want from me and how do I interpret or know him.

What if I had been raised in a different family? Who would I be then? And would I think that it was the only right way? I began to realize that I am who I am because of where I was born and who I was born to. My belief system was not an accident but a natural conditioning from my environment. So of course I'm going to believe what I believe—but born elsewhere and to a different family, I would not be the same person with the same belief system—and I very likely would fully believe that I had all the right answers then too…at least in a fundamentalist group. I was shocked when I learned that the other religions in the world all think they have the one right way too. What this tells me now—is that there is no one right path. We're all in some sort of story or illusion…we believe what we are taught as children because our brains are wired to do so. Our paradigms, or ways of thinking and believing, are formed in early childhood. So you're kinda destined to believe what your family believes and hold as tightly to it as they do, risking identity foreclosure for children growing up in stricter, more sheltering families. Sometimes, later in life, something rocks our belief system enough to shift the paradigm…and any direction is possible. But this only happens to a small percentage of people. The exact reason is not necessarily known.

I got tired of Sunday School a long time ago. The political talk and the church lady stuff…I just didn't jive with. I always felt out of place, judged, different, like I didn't fit in with a couple ladies in there that I knew to be busy-bodies, and those ladies dominated the conversations. The class was small anyway, so I sucked it up and left, because I had better things to do with my time than sit there annoyed and uncomfortable. It was unfortunate because there were also some of the sweetest ladies in there too, but the environment I was subjecting myself to was not healthy for me. And it wasn't fun or beneficial. So I thought I'd practice some self-care by exiting quietly.

Leaving the Sunday morning Bible study was definitely a huge step in becoming an independent thinker for me. Before this moment, I really didn't realize I had a "choice" to not attend Sunday morning Bible study. I felt like a rebel in choosing what was best for me. But it felt really good. It felt good to have the courage to make choices based on what my gut told me I needed, because I knew what was best for me in that situation, and I took action. I knew the traumatic feelings that my body was experiencing, and I knew I had to get out, even if I didn't understand the exact reason. Looking back, this marks the beginning of listening to my inner voice, my gut, and learning that I CAN trust it. Contrary to what I was taught. I can trust myself to take care of myself and do what's best for myself. I am not broken. I am whole deep down inside.

When I quit Bible Study, I was still very Christian in my beliefs, although my perspective of the Bible was changing. So I would bring my kids to their Sunday morning class, and I would wait in the lobby and read or chat with other people as they arrived until the morning service. Most of the members of my (former) class didn't say a thing about it when they would see me. A couple sweet people would comment that they missed me. I was mostly okay with that, since I didn't know how to reply to any questioning anyway...at least not with an answer that would be satisfactory to some.

One Sunday, as I was sitting in the lobby, I heard my kids Sunday School class being taught. The teacher was telling them that they were like filthy rags to God. This struck a nerve, but I was not confrontational. Not at this point in my life. My kids are good! God created them GOOD (Genesis 1:31)! How dare you tell them they're filthy rags! I was frozen and angry. I addressed the issue after church with my kids. I assured them that they were NOT disgusting to God.

I smell freedom, but I still feel chained.

Kimberly

December 2018

Dear Kimberly,

You will continue to read, study, and learn at rapid speeds. You'll finish your college classes and consume books in 2 days...one right after another. Your hunger to know more and figure things out will consume you with intensity deeper than ever before. You will experience extreme excitement as you see new, refreshing perspectives on the Bible. You will have hope that even though people don't share your perspective, you can still hold on and grasp this radical view of Christianity because it made so much sense to you. You were rejuvenated and in love with the historical perspective of the Bible.

But in the middle of it all, the idea that people you love view these authors, who also claim to love God with all their hearts, as heretics because they have a different perspective on how to interpret the Bible will be almost too painful to bear. It will feel like your heart is being torn out of your chest as you try to find ground where you can allow your beliefs to shift as you learn new information, but your rapid growth will not agree with those you love most. Oh, and you won't see this as growth. You will feel like you're losing because it creates conflict in relationships that you care about. You will feel like you are on a giant emotional rollercoaster of beliefs. Why can't it be okay to disagree with people and be okay? Why can't it be okay to not see eye-to-eye and still remain "okay?" Why does it need to be a definite one way or the other? Why does somebody have to have the absolute right answer? Why does one way have to be viewed as absolutely wrong? Why can't we just all admit we really don't know?

Life is hard. It's frustrating. It's discouraging and you can't make peace in your mind about what's going on in your head. You'll feel so divided. You'll hate life and what you're going through. You'll be so tired of existing in the mental turmoil. So you'll do the "safer" thing and you'll perform a virtual suicide. You'll randomly disappear off the social media grid for several weeks without telling anybody. You figure maybe you can get some relief from utilizing this option, and it's not as complete as real suicide. Little do you know, when you come back, you won't be "Kimberly" much longer.

I promise you're going to be okay,

Dear Makayla,

UGH, it's Christmas season. I have not been a fan of Christmas for soooo long, but especially not this year. In the past I had fear of displeasing God in the way that we celebrated and commercialized Christmas, even though it was not originally a Christian holiday. But this year, my heart was so confused and in so much pain, I wanted nothing to do with the Christian form of Christmas.

I spent December reading as much as I could, trying to keep my faith and make it work for me. So much of scripture was becoming confusing and unbelievable, the way I was taught to interpret it. The more I studied, the more I researched, the more questions I had. It didn't help that my husband and his friends didn't hold back that the people I was reading books by were heretics. One man in my church even reported to my husband to warn him and make sure he was aware that I was reading a "heretical book" (in his biased, narrow-minded opinion of course). They weren't heretics. They just held different perspectives of Bible interpretation. But it didn't agree with the church I was in, so these men who loved God were labeled heretics, making me a heretic too. There's the Gothard umbrella theory at work again with spiritual friends making sure you are in check and your wife is in check (Ephesians 5). It's seriously all portrayed to be done in love and concern over how a person lives their life. But it's so cultish because it binds me to things that aren't necessarily true! Well it attempts to bind me. It attempts to keep me in the box and not ask questions.

I am so distraught. Why should I even try, if when my beliefs are different from yours, you call me a heretic...why even put forth the effort that was stressing me out!? I'll tell you why. I wanted to KNOW! I wanted to know TRUTH! But some things, you just cannot know. EVER. And some things you know through study, research, and experience, you can't UNKNOW.

Midway through December, I was so perplexed, I commited "virtual suicide." I told nobody. I just did it. It felt freeing. It felt amazing. I virtually killed off me because it was as close as I could get to not existing without really not existing. It was something that was not permanent, but felt like I had ended a part of myself. I disappeared from all social media without a goodbye. They didn't deserve a goodbye. Would they care? Would they miss me?? I was hurting so freakin bad.

Life in this limbo is hard. It sucks. I hate being stuck in this abyss of uncertainty in between beliefs. I hate my life. I hate that I can't believe what they want me to believe and they won't accept what I believe where I'm at. It's not even a question. It's an absolutely not. Absolute heresy. No entertaining of different perspectives at all. I feel like I am lost forever. I feel like I'm sliding into nowhere. I can't ever go back to where I was. Maybe someday I will be okay with where I'm at even though I'm different from everybody else.

One can hope...

Kimberly

January 2019

*D*ear Kimberly,

Then, just when you think "hey, I can handle interpreting the Bible like this..." Everything, EVERYTHING you believe spiritually is going to fall away. You are going to wake up one day and feel like ALL THINGS SPIRITUAL are COMPLETELY gone. You will not sense your former god--who claimed to be a friend who sticks closer than a brother--anywhere. The God you had an intense relationship with all your life (even though it often felt one-sided, but also often had what you thought were real experiences and conversations), will be gone. The God that you had always testified was about a personal relationship and not religion will be nowhere to be found. You will not be able to pray. You will not be able to sing. You will feel empty, lost, scared, no—make that terrified. You will feel like there's a huge wall or block between you and anything spiritual. Your brain will be fuzzy like the static on an old TV. You will have nobody in real life who understands your situation. Nobody you know personally has lived so freakin whole-heartedly for Jesus and left the faith...on purpose or on accident. People will even tell you it's not about religion, it's about a personal relationship with God...which is a slap in the face because you of all people know that, but they don't trust YOUR idea of a right relationship with God, because they claim God wouldn't leave you (Hebrews 13:5) . They will doubt your experience. They will think and talk lies about you, according to what the church has taught them or even from their own personal experience. But it's okay. Trust your experience. These people don't know how to think any differently. And you know that, because you were just there months ago. That won't make it easy, but it will make their accusations make sense, when they choose to believe the brainwashing they've been taught over your actual story about what's happened to you. You will realize they don't have a choice from their paradigm to think any differently.

You'll keep holding on to hope that this is just a temporary experience, that God will return to you...he has to. He said he would never leave you. This is a test. Right? Because if it's not, and he doesn't come back, but he's real...you're screwed and apparently chosen for hell. Believing was not a choice. That choice was taken from you. Thoughts of what if the doctrine of calvinism is real will periodically play through your head. In Calvinism, God creates some for heaven, and some for hell (Romans 9:22). Even the Bible says faith itself is a gift from God, and God enables one to believe (Ephesians 2:8-9). You realize, if that's true, you don't have that "gift" anymore.

You will create a fake twitter account to try to explore what this radical shift is. You will start out with the initials KJ, since you had gone by that in college, but then in order to hide yourself more and feel a little bit safer, you will quickly turn "KJ" into "Kayla Jo." You choose Kayla Jo because you just really like that name. It's cute, fun, and feels good. You will immerse yourself in the twitterverse and quickly become an active part of the #Exvangelical community. These people resonate with you, get, you, believe you, and have had similar traumatizing, mind-blowing experiences. You will find your people through hashtags such as: #exvangelical, #emptythepews, #exchristian, #agnostic, #atheist, #exfundy, and eventually #RTS, #religioustrauma and #religioustraumasyndrome. You will start living your "real" life online, where you can hide from the world you know in your immediate community, and you are safe to question and be real. Offline was full of too much pain and you couldn't be real without being triggered and misunderstood.

You'll open facebook back up and join some secret groups on fb where you can secretly explore and question like on twitter. Social media becomes your lifesaver. You will be amazed at the community you find and the people that care about you, have experienced what you're going through, and are there for you, non-judgmentally. It's like the church outside the church, except better. It's like the Christian community like it's supposed to be. The love and acceptance that you will find outside of religion will blow your mind and encourage your heart.

I'm here for you.

Makayla

*D*ear Makayla

Oh My GOD MAKAYLA!!!!! HELP!!!! I have no idea what has happened in my head or how. I can't even begin to process this deep black hole that I woke up with! I am terrified! I'm scared! What if I go to hell because I can't get my belief back!? There are no words to describe the void I feel!! God has left me, and I can't even try to imagine him back! What am I going to do?!? Who can I even talk to about this!? What if I'm chosen for hell? For ETERNITY!!?? I didn't freakin leave him! I love him! Where is he!? He is my entire identity and my entire life! What is going to happen to ME?!? To my family!? To my community!? Surely in a week or two or three everything will resurface...God will return, my ability to sing and read my Bible and pray will return, and it will all be okay. Everything will surely come back. Right!? I hope!? This is just a test. Just gotta wait it out. But something's not right. Something's wrong with me. I've never felt this way before. My brain is spinning. I have so many questions. I'm so confused! If Calvinism is real...I'm not chosen. You know, there's verses that say God creates some for heaven and some for hell, some he loves and some he hates...so maybe I'm one that's created for hell. Because I literally am NOT CAPABLE of believing anymore. I can't even find the words to explain the impossibility! But then there's a version of Christianity that says "once saved always saved"...so then I'm safe (John 10:27-28). But then there's the verse in Hebrews that says some will fall away and it's impossible for them to be brought back (Hebrews 6:4-6). What if that's me? OMG HELP ME!!!! I'll wait a bit—it'll be back. Faith will come back. It has to. It's who I am.

A couple weeks have gone by, and my faith is not coming back AT ALL. As hard as I want to believe in God, I literally cannot. My faith just won't return. Faith is a gift from God. I don't have that gift anymore! The consequence of Hell is scary! Because even though I literally do not have the ability to believe in God anymore, even though I miss him and crave him, what if he IS real and I DO go to hell because I can't believe!? I'm literally not capable of grasping what I used to believe. But hell—fear of hell is so real...I've got to find a way to purge my mind of hell. Through search engines and making connections, and previous research that I have done, I came across Brad Jersak's book: "Her Gates will Never be Shut." I bought it on Kindle and immediately started reading. See, Brad Jersak is still a Christian. And if Brad Jersak can be convinced that hell is a man-made structure and not religion has made it out to be, and he can use scripture to prove it, then whether I'm a Christian, agnostic, or atheist, I can be safe. Amazingly, the book did the job. Half way through Brad's book, my fear of hell disappeared. I was convinced, through Brad's interpretation of scripture, that even if I did end up in a "hell" for unbelief, it would only be purifying and temporary, and the gates of heaven would never be shut, and I would make it there someday. And if there is a God—he is love...and does not want to hurt and torture me forever, especially over something I cannot choose. I need my belief back. But at least I'm not afraid of being tortured in hell for eternity anymore. A loving God could never do that. I mean, I would never throw my kids into a fire! And the argument that God lets US CHOOSE hell!? Well no, I wouldn't let my kids jump into a fire even if they wanted to if I had the ability to stop them! Even if the pain is over temporarily. It's unfathomable to imagine torturing my kids in a fire forever. I wouldn't even do that to my worst enemy, because I don't have that much hate in my heart. Therefore since I cannot be more loving than God, if love really came from God, then I am safe.

With nowhere in real life to turn, I opened up a fake twitter account. I found my people on twitter and eventually on secret Facebook groups too. I took my initials, KJ, and created a new account under the name Kayla Jo, using a new email, so that I could not be found. Kayla Jo was real. Through the name, Kayla Jo, I spoke my frustrations. I vented my hurts. I screamed that I didn't want to exist anymore. I questioned EVERYTHING. I poured my heart out under the hashtags #exvangelical, #exchristian, #emptythepews, and a few other random hashtags at times. Through searching those same hashtags, I found a new community of once-Christians, who had left or fallen away from or lost the faith just like me. I private messaged some, talking to them for hours. I found podcasts, like exvangelicalpodcast, mindshift2018, the secret life after.... and started hearing other deconversion stories like my own. While they were heartbreaking, they were also encouraging because I got them. I understood. They got and understood me. We had community. We had something very deep and important to us in common. I feel hope in the middle of my pain and emptiness when I am interacting with these people. I know I'm not alone. I wish I lived closer to them so I could be with them in real life. Most people like me are scattered across the globe...we only have online community. We are alone in our real-every-day-life communities.

I learned about "deconstruction." Deconstruction is what happens when an individual's pieces of faith start falling apart and not fitting the way they used to. The individual can sometimes choose what to hold on to and what to let go. Other times, you realize a belief disappeared before you even had time to think about it. Holding things too tightly is extremely painful. But so is deconstructing. Some deconstruction is done on purpose. And sometimes deconstruction happens against one's will and even the foundation crumbles, which is what happened to me. I learned that people believe whatever they're born into. I learned that most religions teach that they are the one right religion/way of viewing life...not just mine. Muslims, Jews, Mormons, JW's, you name it...they're all taught what I was taught in view of their religion...this is the RIGHT way...the ONE RIGHT WAY...walk in it.

That's thought provoking.

Kimberly

February 2019

Dear Kimberly,

You will leave life group this month. You will have grown weary of your leader always saying things like "we need to do more" & "we're not doing enough," followed by weekly homework assignments to choose who you need to evangelize for the week and go out and do that (seeing people as projects). You will not understand why you can't manage to sing anymore. Singing worship songs used to be your absolute favorite. You will struggle to connect when you are called on to pray. You will feel depressed and so, so heavy every time you meet for life group, which used to be your favorite time of the week. As the disconnect keeps growing more and more intense with the group that you once loved to hang out with, you will decide that it's time to stop forcing something that you can't have and you will stop going. In stopping what doesn't work for you, you will experience freedom in your body and spirit. You will feel lighter. You will be able to breathe. You will have peace that you did the right thing for you. Kind of similar to leaving Sunday school.

Just Breathe,

 Makayla

$\mathcal{D}$ear Makayla,

I cannot stop crying. I randomly sob mega tears. I walk into my bedroom, fall down on my bed, and just melt into a mess of tears over my loss of faith, community, purpose, and ultimately my ENTIRE identity. What the hell was I even alive for if I had nothing specific, no known purpose, that I was born to live for. What's the point now!? Why do I even exist?? I always thought I existed to glorify God and do his work while I was here on earth, and now he's gone and he's not coming back! My beliefs have vanished into thin air, and nothing is resolving them the way I hoped they would resolve. To compound that, the reason Drew and I got married was INTENTIONALLY and SOLELY to love and serve God together for the rest of our lives. We were going to raise our kids passionately Christian and even go to the mission field to share the sweet story of Jesus and salvation when we retired. NOW WHAT!? I have failed our marriage. I have changed. I did not WANT to change. And there is absolutely nothing I can do about it. I tried so freakin hard to hold on and adjust my perspective with my shifting beliefs as I was growing and learning. It got too heavy to hold onto anymore and slipped right through my grasp and disappeared out of sight. I'm so distraught and heart broken, and I don't even know how to cope or where to go from here. I'm so disappointed...in life. In myself. In my community. In my lack of beliefs. In what I thought was God. I'm a disappointment to my former community too. And to my family. Nobody gets me. I don't even get me. I'm so alone and I hate my life. I don't want to be alive anymore. I want this unbearable pain to be over.

I'm leaving life group. I can't play the part anymore. I've tried so hard for the last couple months to join in the singing. Singing worship songs used to be my absolute favorite! But the last couple months, when it comes to go from enjoying dinner conversation to our time for singing and Bible study, my emotions just plummet. I choose the song, or take a request, and play it on my phone and bluetooth speaker like I always have. But I can't sing the words. I can't fake it. I'm not a fake person. I'm genuine. I'm real. I don't do things just to go through the motions when I can help it. I took my spirituality seriously. VERY SERIOUSLY. SO SERIOUSLY, that apparently I studied so hard, I studied belief in God and the Bible right out the window. I talked over my dilemma with my husband and we agreed that I would not go to lifegroup anymore. I have caused so much pain in our marriage from my faith crisis, and I wanted his "ok" to not attend lifegroup. I knew it would hurt him even more on the inside, but I was trying to include him. I feel horrible that I am not who he married. I'm not who he married at all. How does one deal with that? Not just me, but especially him!!?? I can only imagine how I would feel if roles were reversed and I would NOT be okay. I would be devastated and not sure what to do from there. I just could not take the cognitive dissonance any longer. I have a war inside me. I am trying so hard to break free in my mind, and I don't even really know what I am trying to break free from.

Trying to reconcile what had happened to me, as well as trying to assure myself that I was okay, I checked out statistics on Christianity. I learned that roughly 30% of the world is Christian. Really!? Would a God send 70% of the world to hell for ETERNITY!? But wait, I was taught that Catholics weren't really Christian, so there goes 20% of the "Christians" according to my legalistic belief system. That leaves us with 10% of the world going to heaven someday according to what I was taught (not reality obviously). OH, but WAIT AGAIN...I was taught that most of those "Christians" weren't really following Christ but were putting on a show...these are the ones God would say "depart from me into everlasting punishment because I never knew you." So, what does that mean...God will save 5% of the world and condemn the rest to hell? REALLY!? A good, loving God would create humans just to save 5% and to torture the rest FOREVER!? The way is narrow and few there be that find it (Matthew 7:14)?? No, not buying it...not buying it at all. Not okay with that. That is not unconditional love. The statistics were key in my turning point for finally feeling the freedom that it was okay to let go of the fight and completely leave evangelical Christianity. That, and I would never throw my children in a fire for not choosing me or for any reason. Love is deeper and stronger than that.

What about the people that had never heard (Romans 10:14-15)? (Christianity says if they want to know God will send somebody to them). What about the people who are born muslim, hindu, or any other religion or philosphy of life? There are over 40,000 religions in the world! There can't be only ONE right way! Not to mention, you're going to become whatever you're born into. Those paradigms, or ways of thinking, are created beginning at birth and solidify early in life. Which is how I faced identity foreclosure until I was 37 years old! So knowing how the brain works, I could no longer buy into the belief that you HAVE to believe a certain way or face eternity in hell. That is a horrible set-up against humanity if it's true.

This is such a mind-game!

Kimberly

March 2019

*D*ear Kimberly,

You have not quite given up on church yet. You will attend a women's retreat this month, and you are still playing in band at church. You are still desperately trying to hold on to God, your spirituality, and your entire identity. You love playing in band and you do not want to let that go, but you will realize there's no point in holding on anymore...You will eventually have to leave the church, because you will realize your former beliefs are probably never coming back. You will work hard to accept where you're at. You will stop fighting the desire to believe again. You will stop resisting this new life that you didn't ask for, and you will do your best to accept it. It's one of those things you can't change or make happen. You're still the same person (but at the same time you're not the same person)—you're still full of love for people and what's good. You're not evil. You're not running from God. And you're not rebelling against anything. After accepting it for some time, you will learn to start embracing it. You will open up to different belief systems. You will see that there is nothing to be afraid of. But that's still farther down the road. You will see that you are ok—even though by now, you have very concerned Christian friends that are convinced you are not ok. That will bother you for a while, but eventually, as you accept that, the pain of that will go mostly away too. You will still ache for them to know you're ok, but it won't bother you anymore like it used to. Remember, their opinion of you is not your problem.

You are strangely going to have more peace and love in your heart than ever before. That "peace that passes understanding (Philippians 4:7)" that the Bible talks about for Christians is going to be yours as you step away from the church and accept where you're at. This peace is going to continue to grow in you more and more every month in ways you never imagined. And of course, people won't understand it.

You THOUGHT you were accepting of people before, not judging them, but now you are going to realize how judgmental you still were, without realizing it. Blinders are going to fall off your eyes as you see humanity with an even deeper love than you've ever experienced, even without God in your life. Which is crazy because you were taught you can't love apart from God. Part of this love is because people are no longer projects to be rescued. They are just simply people to be loved and accepted right where they're at, regardless of your difference of beliefs. There is no longer any agenda or motive in how you treat people, just to purely love them, where they're at, without an agenda or desire to change them or their beliefs.

In spite of the intense peace, love, and joy that you feel inside like never before, you will be accused repeatedly by a person you love deeply of being angry and hostile. He will bring that accusation over and over. No matter how many times you try to tell him that you do NOT feel what he is saying, no matter how many times you try to convince him how much joy and peace you have and how amazing you feel inside, he will still keep telling you how angry and hostile you are. He sees you standing against what hurt you and speaking what is true for you as angry and hostile. But also let me interject here. Being angry is not a sin like you were taught...it's not wrong. Anger is a secondary emotion that protects you and moves you to action. And there's absolutely nothing wrong with that. Embrace anger whenever you feel it—and use it for good and for change.

The fear, isolation, loneliness, confusion, inner turmoil, intense emotions, loss of identity, and more that you are about to experience are going to be deeper and darker and more scary than anything you've ever experienced before. BUT YOU ARE GOING TO BE OK! I am here for you on the other side of it all. And

I am stronger, happier, less judgmental, and more peaceful than you could ever imagine. I've got you—you've got this.

You're going to slowly learn that you can trust yourself. You can trust your inner voice. You can trust your heart. You are going to think that God left you—and you are slowly going to learn that the inner voice that you thought was God all along, is still there, and it's YOU! It will CONTINUE to guide you into all truth. You will know the truth—and the truth will set you free. But it's not the truth in a box that you imagined. It's sooo much bigger.

Love,

Makayla

$\mathcal{D}$ear Makayla,

I opted to go to Pine Cove on the women's retreat to hang out with the ladies from church, in an effort to maintain friendships. And because I was really trying to hold on and give God every last chance to come back. I could skip the sessions if they were too uncomfortable. I went to the first session, because I'm a good sport. And I'm not angry, not bitter, just not fitting in in this religious social box anymore. That should be okay, but instead others view me as something is wrong with me. I decided to give it a try rather than saying absolutely not. It ended up more awkward than I expected. I felt dark. I felt depressed. I felt like everybody was wondering "what's wrong with her?" Maybe they were, maybe they weren't. But sitting down, trying to look like you're okay, in the middle of a bunch of ladies standing, singing, and raising their hands to Jesus is a little obvious that you're not a part of that particular party. After that session, I opted to stay back in the room at our cabin and read for the other sessions. I was still trying to read through Brad Jersak's book about heaven and hell, even though I no longer held on to the fear of hell...it was still a book with great content that I wanted to try to finish.

I struggled through the weekend. I talked a little bit about censored parts of my story to a friend or two, but knowing that they wouldn't understand, because they had never been where I am at, I saved my breath, and spared myself of the anxiety that increased with talking about my loss. It was so hard to handle the depth of despair and loss of identity that I was going through. It's strange to be surrounded by a great community of women, yet feel so alone. However, at breakfast one morning, an older friend leaned over and said "I know what you're going through, and I want you to know that I love you no matter what." This was a woman about 12 or more years older than me that I highly respected and loved. She was one of my favorite people. Thinking she understood me and knew and cared and loved me anyway, I broke out sobbing and melted into her arms. "How did you know!?" I asked her. She said that she had known for a while. Wanting to know exactly what she knew, I asked her...how and what do you know!? Most people, especially from church, didn't know the depth of my loss of God and my faith. She assured me that she just knew. Then she leaned over and whispered words in my ear that hit me like a ton of bricks all over my already wounded soul. "I know that you struggle with same-sex attraction." WHAT THE FUCKING HELL!?!?!?!?? "What!!?" I freaked out. "I DO NOT! WHY WOULD YOU SAY THAT!?" (Let me interject here that some of my best friends are gay/lesbian, and I'm all for them, but that's just not me). We got up from the table and went outside to talk. Where I sobbed some more and told her my story. I don't know why I felt obligated. I don't know why I felt the need to defend myself and prove I wasn't a lesbian. Oh wait, yes I do...I felt the need to defend and prove I was who I said I was because my fundamentalist upbringing taught me to be above reproach and that I had to answer to those older than me. BULLSHIT.

My grandma's health went downhill. The kids and I took a quick trip home to Michigan where we hung out with my parents for a couple days and visited my grandma too. At this point, my parents were unaware that my faith was gone. While home, I visited my parents church, where I was reminded that yes, fundamentalism really is as sick as I was remembering it was. The guest speaker in the pulpit that day, spoke against liking anybody's picture on facebook that had been divorced and remarried because if you do, you are condoning their sin. OMG people!!! This was the last straw in the church for me. I knew I would be leaving soon. Not because I was angry at the people. Not because I was bitter. But because this was an institution that I really didn't care to invest my energy in anymore. I needed to invest in people outside of church and religious rules. I needed to be free to genuinely love humanity not based on a list or rules of do and do not in order to be accepted and loved.

I still play keyboard in the band at church back at home. I absolutely LOVE playing in band, even though the words in the songs do not resonate with me anymore at all. Band is what keeps me at church right now. But as much as I love playing, I don't know how I can handle continuing to attend services. I talked to my husband about taking a short break. He told me to go for it. I figured I would take a couple months off and then come back, because surely God would come back for me by then. But he told me not to give them a coming back time frame, to just take it easy. Thankful for the freedom and "permission" to do what I needed to do, I texted the family pastor, who headed up the band, and told him I was taking a break. And then it was over—church membership and attendance became history. A past me. A past life. Who was I really now? Who is this person that doesn't go to church and has no clue about God? I am a stranger to myself. What do I even do with my life from here? Would my identity ever come back? EVER? I'm scared. I'm lonely. And I have no idea who I really am or where I belong. I feel so lost.

Who am I now?

Kimberly

April 2019

Dear Kimberly,

You will work up the courage to tell your parents that your faith is different. This will actually be more discouraging than expected. You record the conversation so that you will remember accurately what was said. What they say will not fully surprise you because it matches what the church teaches about people who "leave the faith." Your dad thinks you don't go to church anymore because you're afraid God will speak to you. He clearly doesn't hear what you're saying. Your mom tells you God's gonna "get you good" if you don't repent. They will also try to blame your psychology classes...until you say this all happened at Liberty University. They will end the conversation with "the conversation didn't go where it needed to go" because you didn't conform, and they say they'll try again some other time. They're so disappointed in your "decision," even though you repetitively told them that you didn't choose this. They don't understand.

Your dad will text your husband asking if you are leaning toward being a lesbian because your fb leans that direction. He thinks that since you are an advocate for your gay/lesbian friends on fb that you may be gay too. You will be so angry that he would ask your husband and not you. You confront him and his defense is, "he wants to know how to pray for you." This is not acceptable. This is not your fault or your problem.

You will also tell your siblings. They don't speak to you much anyway so not much changes here. One of them says they'll pray for you. The others don't have much to say.

You can do hard things!

Makayla

*D*ear Makayla,

So I've been using a fake twitter profile, under the name Kayla Jo, for four months now. It's on twitter that I have built a community of people like me where I can find support, encouragement, and understanding for what I'm going through. The crazy thing is, all these atheists and agnostics are more accepting of where I'm at in life than the Christian community I grew up in. By this, I mean they gave me freedom to believe whatever I wanted to believe and to question anything and they told me I was going to be okay. They walked with me through it all. Nobody told me I had to follow a certain path. They were giving me constant encouragement to keep going, and that I was going to be okay...all under the name Kayla Jo.

There were strangers, former Christians, who had also deconstructed their faith after serving God for countless years, who would talk to me for hours in private message and even on the phone. They were there for me closer than family. They were my rock. They heard me. They saw me. They didn't question me. They genuinely care about what I'm going through. They didn't threaten me or doubt my story or experience. They loved me, listened to me, encouraged me, and held me through the pain.

As I sat thinking one day, I realized that in the conversations I would have with myself in my head, I was identifying as Kayla Jo. I remember the strangeness I felt as I realized that "Kimberly" had actually accidentally disappeared now too. Everybody who knew who I really was inside now, knew me as Kayla Jo. They had absolutely no idea who Kimberly was. I had accidentally created a double life, being that I had to hide who I was becoming in order to avoid criticism and disapproval. There was no room to question and change your mind where I came from.

I can't explain how split I felt at that moment, like I was dealing with two different people...and I had accidentally done this part to myself, not realizing how even more powerful this identity crisis would be when included with a name change. It's like being one person the first half of my life, and somebody else the second half of my life.

I am such a genuine, authentic person. It's so hard to not be absolutely real with everybody in my life. What you see is what you get is the motto I have lived all my life. This is me—nothing to hide—is how I lived. It was killing me, hiding my unbelief from my family. I needed them to help me bear the excruciating pain if they could. But I also knew the pain that it was going to cause them when they found out that I no longer followed their belief system. They wouldn't understand. They wouldn't understand that I literally and legit didn't choose to walk away and not believe. They would be so hurt and disappointed. I knew the things the church taught us to think about people that stray from the faith...the lies...the brainwashing...it's all simply not true...but we were trained to believe the church's view over what the person who deconstructs actually says. Believe the church and Bible over actual experience. When one contradicts—only the Bible can be accurate. Which goes back to telling me I can't trust myself or my experience—simply not true. I know what I have experienced and I know what I do and do not have control over. And I see things clearer than ever before and will continue to do so as I keep growing. Obviously my confidence in trusting myself is growing. Still have a long way to go though, but I see progress.

In my desire and need to be real and genuine, regardless of the lack of understanding I knew I would face, I built up the strength this month and told my siblings and my parents that my faith is gone. I did it all by text message, because I legit didn't know how to talk about it out loud. I didn't want to have to answer questions in the moment. I knew I couldn't. My brain was often in freeze mode (a trauma response) and articulating a loss of faith that I couldn't understand for myself was not even an option at this point.

I hate this.

Kimberly

May 2019

*D*ear Kimberly,

Your Christian therapist will continually tell you that you're still Christian, that he thinks you're just in a phase. You will feel invalidated and misunderstood, as you realize he thinks you will come back around to Christianity. All this will seem to confirm that he does not seem to see what you see or hear what you are saying.

You'll realize that you've accidentally taken on a new name with your identity crisis over the last few months. That fake name you used to create a twitter account with, has become the real you. In your mind, the real you is Kayla Jo—she's not faking anything...she just is who she is. She's real...with those who accept her and allow her to be that way. She's very cautious with who she shares her questions and struggles with, but she has found many safe places online to open up, be encouraged, and also encourage others in their every-day life outside of religion.

 Makayla

Dear Makayla,

I wish my therapist would realize that I'm not coming back to christianity. I feel like I can't adequately explain what's going on in my head. He keeps saying that I'm in a phase, or I'll come back around. But I know I won't! And I can't get him to understand that. This is so painful. I hate where I'm at.

I'm struggling with this identity crisis. I don't know who I am any more. My life was so wrapped up in my relationship with God that it was my ONLY identity. I believed them when they told me that my identity was in Christ (Galatians 2:20). When they said, "he must increase and I must decrease," (John 3:30)... I lived it. I believed that apart from God, I was nothing, and I could do nothing (John 15:5). But with him, ALL things are possible (as long as it is God's will) (Luke 1:37). I lived and breathed all things God, Christianity, church, and the Bible. I fully trusted all my spiritual authorities without question...I was taught from the Bible that they were placed there by God and they will give an account for me to God some day, and it's my responsibility to obey them so their report to God about me will not be done with grief (Hebrews 13:17-21). Do not question. Just obey.

I have felt horrible and confused for months that my faith is gone and I can't get it back. I am dying inside because I have hurt so many people by simply losing my ability to believe. They don't understand me. They don't understand that I didn't walk away. I didn't choose this. I didn't want this. I would never wish this on anybody! I can't choose to "come back." I would be living a lie. I would be faking it. God would see right through it. It would be lip-service. I wouldn't be genuine. Those fakers still go to hell (Matthew 7:21-24). And I can't live a lie. I am a genuine person—I am who I am.

I don't want to go on living like this. But I don't have a choice. I no longer have the ability to think on that level. I can't be Christian any more. I can't even try. I can't even fake it. The pain inside me for what I have unwillingly lost is so intense. It's like I have been kicked out of the game. It's like my brain has been completely erased of any ability to have any connection to my relationship with God that I valued and grew and held on to all my life. There's been an intensely strong disconnect. And I am not the one who cut the connection. This connection was cut while I was doing everything I could to trust in God's promises and keep living for him. This was the ultimate abandonment that I had absolutely no control over. I have never been so judged or misunderstood or attacked by Christians who once called me friend.

I can't take the pain!

Kimberly

June 2019

*D*ear Kimberly,

You will address an issue with your former church leadership in a private meeting. A couple of your children will bring up an issue that was inappropriately and purposely done to them that needs to be addressed. The person guilty is one of your favorite people ever, and a leader in the church, and your heart and stomach will be in knots over the entire situation. You will go into this meeting with no intentions to harm or hurt anybody, but with intentions to validate and protect your children. Your motive will be to address the issue, for the guilty party to be warned that what they did was not appropriate, and to quietly remove your children from the situation and let time play out. The person guilty will deny having any idea what you are talking about. The person's spouse will insist you can't believe your children because they are just children. The Pastor will ask what you told your children when your kids shared the story with you, rather than addressing the offense of the offender. They will want to make sure you taught them to forgive the offender for his inappropriate act (which he claims he didn't commit), rather than addressing the offender's action as a very inappropriate action against children. Instead of this going through peacefully, like you really expected, the meeting will turn on you and you will be accused of being angry at the church. You will be told that you've already left the church anyway, and that you are trying to destroy a good person's reputation. You will be told that you are bringing the law and not grace. Your husband will be told "sorry you have to deal with this." You will be shocked at the turn out of the meeting, and when the leadership tries to lie about what you said, you will hold up your phone denying the lie, saying you recorded every word, and the leadership will dismiss the meeting on that note. At the end of this meeting, they will try to tell you how much they love you. You see straight through the bullshit and will push through as they attempt to hug you. You will not be treated this way. You will not be gaslighted. You are growing stronger and stronger and see so much more than ever before. You were not angry at the church—but you were very angry at the turn out of two grown men (the teaching and family pastors of the church) in this situation, where they refused to protect the innocence of your 8 year old girl and 10 year old boy. You were very angry that you were made to be a liar and a reputation destroyer. That man's actions were destroying his OWN reputation. Except the church pastor protected him and threw you and your kids under the bus instead. NOT OKAY. You had always heard stories like this from other people about church throughout your life. But you never imagined, especially now that you were not a part of the church, that anything like this would ever happen in a church you belonged to. Especially to you, because you had a clean reputation and were well-respected.

You are fierce!

*D*ear Makayla,

Some unfortunate, inappropriate events happened with some people from my old church. It directly involved my younger kids seeing things they shouldn't see. They were still attending the church, and so I gently brought the truth to the attention of the leadership in a private, quiet meeting. Was it a joke? Maybe, but it was very inappropriate and needed to be addressed. I expected this to be an easy meeting with a simple admitting to a wrong-doing and an apology. I would have been okay with that. Instead, the offender acted like he had no idea what I was talking about, and his wife tried to accuse my kids of lying because they're kids. This meeting turned against me, and I was accused of being out to destroy a good man's reputation and running from the church. I was told I was bringing the law against this godly man, and not giving him grace. I was told that I needed to teach my daughter to forgive this (pornographic) offense that was done against her. I even had proof of the offense on security camera, proving that the man was blatantly lying about not being aware of what he did. There's no way you purposely moon my kids and forget about it.

I had not left the church because I was angry with the church. These men that I met with in this meeting were some of my best friends. I was honestly shocked when they lied, made me out to be angry with the church, and said I was out to destroy this guy's reputation. He destroyed his OWN reputation. He performed the stupid act himself. He got called out by my 8 year old daughter and 10 year old son. He got caught. And he got protected because to the church leadership, I was a wolf. I didn't matter. Saving his reputation and the reputation of the church is all that mattered. I am so misunderstood. I am so pissed off at the injustice. They know me better than that! They know THEY are in the wrong here!

NOW I'm angry!

Kimberly

July 2019

*D*ear Kimberly,

You will really struggle with your identity and who you actually are. You will not feel like Kimberly any more at all. Your loss of identity will have been torturing you for months, and you will start tossing around the idea of actually changing your legal name to Kayla Jo. Early in the summer, you will decide that if it gets to be the end of the month, and you still want to legally change your name, you will. You keep it in the back of your mind. That's not hard to do because it's who you feel like you are. You will do the intense research like you always do, to figure out what you're doing and what effects it can have on you, and you will have very little doubt that you want to go for it. Your only hesitations will be that it has the potential to hurt your parents and people will not understand and may think you're crazy. However, since your motive is pure, and you know you need this to move on, you will decide to go for it. This is self-care. This is solely for and about what's best for you. And I'm proud of you!

You will find that the cost to change your name is $279 for the court fees and $21 for the fingerprints. You will need $300 to proceed. You will list several items on Facebook in an effort to sell them and make money for your name change. To your amazement, in just 24 hours, you will have exactly $300!!!! This will remind you of one of those "God-things" where you knew it was meant to be and God made it happen. Except this will confirm to you that this was not a "God-thing." This was a universe thing, and somehow, you are connected to something, somewhere, that isn't limited to biblical definitions. You have and will continue to experience these coincidences over and over and over.

You will hear through the grapevine that there is gossip going around your previous church that you have "gone off the deep end." A former member will ask a current member if they have heard about you and that will be the conversation. Don't let this bother you too much. She's a busy body and has nothing better to do. Her opinions don't matter.

Keep moving forward!

Makayla

*D*ear Makayla

I can't take it—this identity crisis is still going strong. I think I'm going to change my name to Kayla Jo. That's the real me. I never expected to start identifying with that name the way I have, when I created my fake twitter account. Everybody in real life knows me as Kimberly. But Kimberly, the old, Christian me is gone. She's not coming back. She can't. I can't make her come back. And it grieves me so much! It tortures my heart! I miss my community. I miss my people. But I'm coming to terms with the grief of the loss. I feel like maybe I'm just around the corner from being able to move on.

I decided early this summer that if I still feel this strongly about needing to change my name at the end of the month, I'm going to go for it. I am going to legally change my name. Crazy, I know. But I've lost so much already. I feel like I've lost everything about me EXCEPT my name. I really don't know how to move on from here. I don't know how to accept this new way of life that I never asked for and never saw coming. Maybe changing my name will help me accept what has happened to me and move forward. I know it won't be a magical answer. But it's how I truly identify now, and I don't know how else to do this. Everything that was "Kimberly" is gone.

Well, it got to the end of the month and I still desperately wanted to make Kayla Jo my legal name. Actually, I tweaked it a little because I am a person who likes options as far as names/nick-names go. So I decided that my legal name will actually be Makayla Jo. I like the power I feel with the name Makayla. It's a strong name.

I found out that it was going to cost me exactly $300 to change my name. $279 for the court fees and $21 for the finger prints. So I rounded up some random things from around the house and listed them for sale on FB. Weird stuff happened. My first sale was to a girl who's name was actually Makayla. Funny how if I was still a Christian that would have been a "God-thing." Then, I made

EXACTLY enough money to change my name in 24 hours...another "God-thing." Except not. We are all just somehow connected. It's pretty cool and mind-blowing.

I found it really intriguing that these circumstances, similar to what I experienced as a Christian...were still happening to me as an atheist...and were supporting my transition away from faith and my former identity and way of life. Could this be the answer to my question that started the disappearance of my faith in the first place? This journey all began with "What's the difference between my spiritual experiences and spiritual experiences of other religions and belief systems. They all seem to be the same, but how can they be if there's only one true God?" There seems to be some sort of connection here. And it's not in a concrete, absolute religious-type answer.

My name change is in the process. I can't believe I'm doing this! I am so excited! Next month I will officially be Makayla Jo McCuistion! Or Kayla Jo :). This feels so refreshing and empowering. I can't wait to be able to write my new name on everything legally.

One of the ladies from my former church, that I knew to be a busy body, told a mutual friend that I had gone off the deep end. She doesn't even know me. But she was key in why I had left the Sunday school class. Thank you for the confirmation that she was toxic. Words like hers from "Christians" are hurtful when you're fresh into all this confusing deconstruction. Truth is—I didn't go off the deep end. Truth is—she doesn't know me and never asked. Truth is—her opinion doesn't matter...and she needs to shut the fuck up. She has no idea what she's talking about.

So excited for my name change!

Kimberly

August 2019

Dear Kimberly,

Your name change will become official this month! You are actually going through with what you want because you want it, and you are changing your name to Kayla Jo! I'm so proud of you for doing what is best for you! This is a huge step in self-care and doing what benefits you, so that you can be whole, to do the work that you desire to do to help others.

You will switch from therapy to coaching. You will start working with a coach who specializes in trauma. This will be an interesting transition. You're going to learn a lot from this and the vast range of experiences you're going to have. You're going to become more and more free to stand up for yourself in the process and you're going to explore paths you would not have explored otherwise.

You will jump into methods of processing your emotions that would have been taboo to you before, but you will find that they have potential to bring relief! You will learn that they are not 'bad.' There are many paths. You can't really go wrong. You choose what's best at the moment...and you keep shifting, as needed, as you go. Mistakes aren't bad, they're signals to redirect.

You've got this!

Makayla

*D*ear Makayla,

I can't believe it! I am legally Kayla Jo. Actually, I am legally Makayla Jo, but I go by both. Changing my name is one of the most empowering things I've ever done. I have no regrets. I don't want to go back to Kimberly. I absolutely LOVE being Makayla!

I feel like a new person. I feel like this is exactly what I needed to be able to let go of the past and move forward with my life. I feel like it frees me for such a drastic "start over" in the middle of my life.

I started working with a coach who specializes in trauma. We meet several hours a week. I'm learning so much from him! A lot of the stuff he asks me to do or ways he asks me to think are hard. Hard because I am not used to thinking this way. It makes sense—I kinda get it. But I'm struggling to apply it. But the important thing is I am growing on this journey. I am feeling more normal again. I feel like there's a light at the end of the tunnel. I still have waves where I struggle intensely, but I'm not as hopeless as I once was.

Moving Forward!

Kayla Jo (aka Kimberly)

Part 3

Moving Forward

September 2019

My name change was exactly what I needed to continue to grow into my new life and move forward. It was not a fix-all, but I would be lying if I said it didn't feel empowering and magical. The name Makayla is such a strong, powerful name to me. I love the sound of it. I love the confidence that it carries.

I got tired of hiding my loss of faith from the world. I got tired of feeling fake and living a double life. So, this month I announced the reason for my name change on facebook. That reason, being, my faith-shift. I faced extreme feedback and results from being so bold and vulnerable. I lost some people I thought I would never lose. But I gained some friendships beyond what I could have ever imagined. It's so good to not feel like I'm suffocating anymore. It's not easy, it's still shaky, but I can finally breathe again. I feel so free! Everybody knows now and there is nothing more empowering and freeing than being vulnerable. Was it hard? HELL YES! Was it worth it?? ABSOLUTELY!! Since everybody knows now, I don't have to hide, and my job is to continue to boldly and powerfully live my truth. To continue down this path I'm on. To be vulnerable. To not hide. To reach out to others to help them heal too.

I realize that Christians don't understand and they're terrified for my soul, but some of them are down-right mean. A group of women that I thought were close, loyal friends decided I was an enemy of the cross of Christ and had a huge public gossip session about me on social media. I know they thought it was tough love, because I have been in their shoes. But it was downright cruel, and ugly and the most un-Christlike thing I've ever seen. I mean, would Jesus have gossiped about how horrible I was because of my unbelief? No! But he certainly would have condemned the self-righteous pharisees who were bringing me down.

I was bold and interviewed on an Atheist podcast. This was both insanely weird and freeing. To hear myself say these things out loud for the public to hear was shocking to me. But it was the truth. It was who I am now. It was speaking up for what had happened to me. You cannot deny experience. Something's different. Something seems off. But something seems right. So, so right.

October 2019

I started a facebook group to encourage people. (Don't go looking for it because the rollercoaster of emotions reconstructing isn't always easy, and part of self care for me several months into the group was to cancel the group—Yes, I felt bad. But it was best for me, and I was learning to take care of myself). The page did really well with activity. We used it to encourage each other to move forward and keep growing, and we tried to keep the negativity and venting at bay. There's a place for venting and anger. But I saw a need for a safe place for calm emotions where we could just rest and be refreshed.

I started to feel my confidence and excitement for life coming back. I loved the idea that I get to create my own reality. I'm the creator and owner of my life. I don't have to remain a victim. I refuse to be a victim of my past. I choose to reframe my past and not stay stuck there. I may stumble, but I won't stay down. I have a warrior mentality. I'm a fighter. I am a world changer and I have a purpose—I exist to help others heal from their pain. I have been through intense mental, emotional, and physical pain that has empowered me and continues to empower me to hold space for other people who are also in pain, and to help them heal.

One thing that's been a big adjustment for me is realizing that I create my own reality now. I am in charge of my world. It's easy to get stuck in a victim state of mind, thinking that the world and things happen to me and I am a victim of my circumstances. But that's not true. I am a creator of my reality. I am creating what I WANT my reality to be, every day through my thoughts and actions. If I do not like something about my reality, I can change it...whether it's the situation itself, or my perspective of it. Don't get me wrong. I still struggle a fucking lot. But I'm learning. I'm growing.

I texted an older, Christian friend who I was very connected to pre-deconstruction. She was like a mom to me—no reply. I actually texted a couple people...no responses. I wonder what they're thinking. But really, I won't entertain that much because it doesn't matter. I won't waste my energy wishing for what's not. I will pour my energy into what is and where I'm headed, and the things I can control. I will pour my energy into people who accept me where I am and love me back.

I may sound strong here but I still struggle. Religious trauma syndrome (RTS) is very real. It manifests as CPTSD...and I fit almost every description of RTS to a T. But that does not define me. It just reveals how strong I am because of how much pain I've been through.

November 2019

This month is hard. I'm getting tired of trying. I feel like I'm getting pulled into finding one right path again. Like there's one best right way that's superior to all others. I don't want to go there. I won't!

Religious Trauma is NO FREAKIN JOKE! My body is strong, and it will not let go of the trauma it is holding. My brain will not let it process...I have a big wall that is keeping me stuck. I'm frustrated that I can't seem to get anywhere with processing. It makes me wonder if it's even possible to heal.

I feel like I'm going in circles in therapy/coaching. I feel stuck there too. I feel like I do not want the approach that we are taking, but I do not know where else to go. I wish I had clarity on what path to take and who to go to for the fastest healing. I feel like I'm lost in the woods and the only path I can see is not one I can or want to take. There's a lot of pressure in my head to take that path. But my body and my gut give me a great big NO—and I am learning to trust my gut. I can trust myself. I know what's best for me. I want to quit therapy. I keep trying. But I'm afraid to quit, but I'm running out of $ to pay for therapy anyway. I don't know where to go next...I don't know what to do. I hate decisions, because my brain always searches for the perfect path since I was always trained to find God's perfect will. Old habits die hard...especially when they're ingrained in your development. I hate feeling this way.

I am learning to stand up for myself and put my foot down. It feels powerful and good to be adamant about what I do and don't want. This is huge growth progress for me! In some ways, I feel like I'm just now experiencing the fight for independence that a teenager faces.

I used to play piano for my great grandma when she lived in the assisted living home when I was in high school and college. I miss that a lot. I love encouraging the older people there by playing the hymns they once sang in church and loved to hear again. They would make requests and I would play whatever hymn they wanted me to play and they would sing along. An hour would go by and feel like minutes. My great grandma would sit by me and be so happy as she sang "In the Garden," her most favorite song, and tons of others.

So I looked into playing for a nursing home in town. I started playing for them once a week. It made the residents so happy. They looked forward to my time with them and I looked forward to the smiles on their faces and the joy that the music would bring them. However, as the weeks went by, it got harder and harder to not feel the trauma responses of hearing the hymns repeat in my head as I played them on the piano. The words were still there echoing in my head from long ago, except now they weren't true to me. They couldn't be. Sometimes I would hold back tears as I played for the happy residents. I thought, I can love these people in spite of our different beliefs. Those don't matter. But as time went on, my method of loving them echoed religious abuse and trauma throughout my body. It was taking me back and I was reliving memories that were not healthy for me to relive, and I had to quit. Once again my emotions sank as my heart intensely grieved over the depth of the loss that I had suffered, and continued to feel.

December 2019

I have finally decided that I am taking a break from therapy/coaching. I have mixed emotions about taking the break. I think I just want a break from thinking and trying to figure things out, as I feel kind of stuck. But I also hesitate to go back to doing life "on my own" again, because I know I still have stuff to work through, but I can't quite figure out how to work through it. I guess I'll just let time play out.

Christmas is weird. I haven't "felt it" for years...but this year is strange. I'm not opposed to it, but really just want to pass by it too. I've been hesitant about Christmas for the last few years anyway, so this is nothing new...but this is my first Christmas without God. So I'm not looking forward to Christmas for different reasons this year. In the past it had been related to how am I supposed to celebrate Christmas in relation to Christianity...what would God want? What about commercialism? What's the right way? So many questions pulled at my heart that I struggled with wanting to get it right and not hurt my kids. Because, you know, God has a perfect will, and it's my job to find that path as closely as possible to ensure that my kids turn out right.

This year I felt freedom to celebrate however I want to, but the emotional draining of the entire last year made me just not want to go anywhere with it at all. I didn't want to decorate or have anything to do with it...because I didn't HAVE to. I just wanted to be still and breathe.

January, 2020

I can't believe it's been a whole year since God and my faith that I held onto for my entire life completely fell into a black hole. It blows my mind. I don't get it. I still don't fully understand what happened or why it happened but learning the psychology behind it all has helped me know I'm not crazy. Learning how the mind develops and works has also helped me kind of understand the science behind it all.

I've continued to realize and learn more about the fact that where you are born and to who you are born makes a huge difference on what your belief system will be moving forward. If I was born to a muslim family, I would follow Islam. If I was born to a Hindu family, I would subscribe to Hinduism. If I was born to a Buddhist family, I would follow Buddhism. There are thousands of religions, and whichever you're born into, your brain is going to most likely grasp onto it in the early years and not let go, unless a big event shifts something, causing your paradigm to drastically shift.

I kinda understand what happened to me, I think, but it still freaks me out. Why me? This is fucking hard.

I still struggle with the fact that Drew and I got married to serve God for the rest of our lives together. I wholeheartedly meant it at the time. I was 100% genuine. I'm the last person I would've ever imagined turning from her commitment to God and her faith. But the truth is, I didn't turn from it. It left me. People can't understand that. They think I walked away. I know that's what it looks like. But it's like holding on to a helium balloon. You get caught up on something and accidentally lose your grip on the balloon. You grasp for the balloon and it's too late, it's already gone, floating into oblivion into the unknown. That's similar to what happened to me. I grasped to hold on to any form of Christianity...yet it slipped so far out of reach, I can't even barely see it anymore. Like a run-away-balloon, my faith as I knew it is never coming back.

I followed through and quit playing piano for the nursing home this month. I love the people there, but I have to step away from any form of spirituality or religion and breathe. I realized this is okay to do. I was doing a good thing and loving on and encouraging them, but it was not healthy for me in my healing to keep putting those songs back into my head.

Drew spoke words to me this month that healed my soul. I was having an emotional breakdown, incredibly upset while trying to reconcile that I was free, but my freedom had destroyed our marriage as we had planned it. Drew's words to me were something along the lines of, "I know you didn't choose this. I believe you." Oh. My. God...SO MUCH FREEDOM...And of course I sobbed even harder at his compassion and trust he showed me.

Surprisingly, our marriage has actually grown stronger over the last year. We've both grown a lot. Our relationship is in a great spot. We have both learned to love the other where they're at while giving them space to hold their own belief system, even if it's contrary to the other. Because that's okay. It's okay to not see eye to eye. It's even okay to see opposites. You can still love and respect the other person and give them freedom to be themselves.

I've continued to blog my story of my deconstruction, or my shift in my faith. My blog has reached thousands. I get emails and private messages about how people resonate with my posts. About how I put into words how they were feeling, but couldn't find the words to speak. This is one thing that keeps me going. It keeps me vulnerable. Because I want to help people. I want to do for them what others have done for me. I want them to know that they're not alone. That I am here for them. Because of all this, and because I accept who I am, I have gotten more bold about speaking out. I am learning to embrace and not hide who I am becoming. I do not push myself on people, but I do not hide myself either. I'm learning to let go and release things that I can't control. It's so good to be free.

So considering all things, overall, I'm doing amazing...it's still hard...it's a rollercoaster...there are good days and hard days...but I'm shifting...I'm growing...I'm learning...I'm finding my path...one step at a time...it's freeing to know that none of it's wrong...and I'm okay.

February 2020

I'm struggling with depression a little more this month. I shared my story with some people, and one asked me if maybe I had religion and not a relationship. The other told me not to trust my heart. That I needed God's wisdom. I know they're speaking out of love, from what they know. I get it. So I just didn't continue the conversation. I'm not mad. And I love them back. But I know it's impossible to have a conversation about what a mountain looks like from two different sides of the mountain, and still agree it's the same mountain, if they don't realize there's another side, multiple sides... that still lead to the top.

It's kinda scary being between therapists when I am still in the middle of everything. When things pop up that I need to talk about, sometimes I wonder who to unload on. It can't just be anybody. There's always been somebody to listen though. It's always worked out. And I've grown a lot. I'm beginning to realize that I am enough. Yes, I need people. But when I can't always depend on them to be available for me, I can depend on myself.

I was privileged to be able to be on a podcast this month. Talking things out, outloud, with people who understand, is so therapeutic.

Part 4

Reconstruction

*T*his has been the hardest few years of my life. I would never choose this or wish it on anybody! Sometimes ignorance and illusion is bliss. Certainty and absolute truth and having all the answers is night and day different from the world of ambiguity that I now live in. But at the same time, being on this side of things, I will gladly walk through healing with anybody entering this experience, letting them know they're not alone and assuring them that they are okay. I now have the ability to hold space for them. To hear them. To let them hurt and heal without judgment from me. To encourage them that they are strong and they can do this.

It's super hard to lose the only identity you've ever had in the middle of your life. People that aren't born into Christianity or other branches of fundamentalism get a chance to create their identity. If somebody becomes Christian later in life, and then they deconvert, they have a self that they identified with before religion to look back on. However, if somebody is born into Christianity, and later they deconvert, they have absolutely nothing to go back to that they were beforehand. They have to start completely over with their identity, beginning with the foundation....and where the heck do you find that when you were taught the only foundation is Jesus Christ???

By the time this book is published, I will be 40. I spent the first 37 years of my life immersed completely in religion/spirituality/relationship with God/whatever you want to call it. Over my entire life, everything I enjoyed or started to enjoy has slowly died. Why? Because I was told I was not supposed to be enjoying it. I was to be about God's business of winning souls for Jesus and saving them for eternal damnation. From an early age, it was drilled into me that Jesus was coming back soon to take the Christians up to heaven. When he returns, would he find you playing games or telling somebody about him? We were to always be watching for him to come back in the clouds, and to be constantly serving so we could be found faithful. We were actually constantly shamed for being more excited about a football game, where we would yell and cheer, which exceeded the excitement that we brought into a church service. Here's the irony...in a Baptist church, if we would've brought the same level of excitement that we brought to the football game, we would've been kicked out of the church service and shamed for that too! You can't even hardly raise your hand in a Baptist church service without being looked at as pushing the envelope and being a little rebellious. Especially not where I came from. You could always feel the thick cloud of judgment and religious expectations. I felt it deeply. All the dang time.

It was several years ago that I realized that I had become numb to the ability to enjoy anything anymore. I had lost all my hobbies. I had lost the ability to fully enjoy anything at all. Yes, I could laugh in the moment, but my ability to be at peace and enjoy the present did not exist anymore. Somehow, I would dissociate from the present experience in a way where I couldn't connect to the joy I used to feel inside as a small child. Traumatic experiences have a way of taking their toll on your body and mind. Trauma is your body's response when it doesn't know what to do with the information it has been given. And my body was clearly storing a life-long experience in religious trauma.

When you spend your entire life striving to be 100% whole-heartedly sold out for Jesus, who wants to find you working when he returns at any moment, your purpose and identity are completely wrapped up in this deity that exists outside yourself. It's a lot of overwhelming work. It's stressful. It's draining. It's frustrating trying to find the right, perfect path.

Believing the feelings and fears I faced as a child were just normal, I didn't realize it was a problem until recently. Over the years, I have battled a vast majority of the symptoms of Complex PTSD, but when my first therapist enlightened me about that, I dismissed it as nothing because how could I have CPTSD when I had such an awesome childhood? Impossible. I had a great family. My parents loved me. They invested their time and money into me to give me a great Christian education all the way through college. They attended all my home games when I was a cheerleader, basketball player, and soccer player. I had a great childhood!

They sacrificed *everything* because they loved me and my siblings. They did their absolute best to raise us the way they believed was right. I admire that. I thought I turned out pretty great from their parenting techniques. Come to find out, the emotional trauma I carried all my life from religion has strongly manifested itself as complex PTSD, depression, anxiety, borderline personality traits, and dissociative identity traits. These things don't define me, but they help me get the help I need to grow and heal.

I have spent my entire life, taking life *way too seriously*...thank you fear-based-religion.

So when your entire belief system shifts, or even completely disappears, you're left not even knowing who you are or why you exist anymore. When it's drilled into you all your life that life outside of God is meaningless and purposeless, it's hard to make sense of why you even exist when God disappears. What's the point? I've tossed ideas around in my head over the last couple years and I came to the conclusion that well, I didn't choose this, but I can choose to love. If nothing else, I exist to love. And to help other people hurt less, by being with them in their pain. I can choose to be kind. I can choose to invest in people and make their lives better. I can choose to do good. But that still wasn't enough. There was still an emptiness that I've felt all my life, that I was told was a God-shaped hole that only he can fill if you're following him closely (Well, y'all...I no doubt proved that wrong for me at least—the rest of y'all have to decide that on your own ;).

All my life I have dealt with depression. Not just the blues. Not just feeling sad. Deep, dark, clinical depression. There are days that I don't want to do anything with my life. I wish it was over. I wish I didn't have to go on. I wish I didn't have to deal with what has happened to me. I wish I could be loved, understood, and accepted by everybody. I've got everything in life I've ever wanted. But depression doesn't care. Some days are really dark and difficult. Other days are not. But I really think my depression stems from the religious trauma I went through for so long. It seems to have started when I was trying to stuff my joy and happiness of loving this life more than wanting to go to heaven. Maybe I killed my ability to feel healthy happiness and peace on a regular basis. I trained it out of my body. But I keep going. And I keep searching for answers to overcome this trauma that lives in my body.

Just yesterday I was thinking...wouldn't it be great if life didn't have to be taken so seriously? If there didn't have to be an agenda? If we could all just enjoy what each day brings, as it unfolds, and just be in the moment? I feel like that's what I'm learning all the time on this side of things. I can slow down. I can enjoy the moment. I can just "be." Life can be simple if we let it. We can detach from religion and drama and people that aren't healthy for us. We can decide our meaning and purpose for each day as we go, and it doesn't have to be complicated. We can have our own opinions. Other people's opinions of us don't matter. In fact, other people's opinions of me are none of my business.

I don't hate anybody. I'm not angry at anybody. And I did not leave the church or Christianity over hurt or being angry either. I left because I simply could no longer believe.

My new role in life is to enjoy each day and be the best me I can be. I don't have to worry about measuring up to anybody or anything. I just need to live a satisfying and fulfilling life. This is done by loving and caring for myself, and then pouring that love and care into other people so they can also feel loved and fulfilled. Kind of reminds me of the words of Jesus when he said to "love your neighbor like you love yourself" (Matthew 22:39). In order to do that, you have to take care of and love yourself first.

Life does *not* have to be taken seriously. There is *no agenda* for *me* to follow to please a deity and be in right standing. I *can* enjoy what each day brings, as it unfolds, and enjoy just being in the moment. There are no requirements for life that I need to fulfill to make a god happy with me. I get to create my own purpose and reality...and that can simply start with enjoying the human experience in any wholesome way possible! I can't go wrong here. That is so freeing! It's completely okay to enjoy the day by doing nothing. It's okay to stay in bed all day if you're sad or exhausted or tired or just want a day off. It's okay to enjoy playing video games. It's okay to enjoy an exotic, amazing vacation. It's okay to spend the day coloring with your kids. It's okay to go out with friends and have a blast laughing and having drinks. It's okay to let loose, have fun, and enjoy the day playing games, chilling, swimming, hiking, and doing whatever you want with your family and friends. It's okay to float in the pool all day. It's okay to laugh and be silly. It's okay to chill and watch tv. It's okay to eat a lot or a little. It's okay to enjoy yourself at a ball game and cheer for your team. It's okay to spend money on whatever you choose to spend money on. It's okay to miss a Sunday service...or all of them...to do something else you'd rather do that excites you...it's okay to not be religious at all. It's okay to not know something or to lack answers.

IT'S ALL JUST OKAY!!!

Don't ever give up!

Follow me on TikTok: @makaylajo0223

All scripture verses are summarized from the KJV Bible.

LEADERSHIP
BEYOND MEASURE

Profound learning with horses to transform leaders and business

Jude Jennison

Published by Leaders by Nature Ltd
First printing: 2015.

ISBN-13: 978-1511971560
ISBN-10: 1511971568

British Cataloguing Publication Data
A catalogue record of this book is available from The British Library.

Illustrations by Jerry Longland
Photos by Ed Phillips Images and John Cleary Photography
Cover design by Alice Cook of Mercia Digital

Also available on Kindle from Amazon

To Kalle and Opus
In honour of your profound leadership wisdom
and with gratitude for never letting me off the hook

Contents

Author's Note

You might think that I've been around horses all my life, but nothing could be further from the truth. With little horse experience, I had three major incidents around them: two of which landed me in hospital and a third, where I narrowly escaped being seriously injured. As a result, I became terrified of horses. Working with them could not have been further from my mind.

Then, in March 2011, I decided to confront my fear because it made me feel powerless. I recognised that riding was not for me, but I wanted at least to be at peace with horses. Nothing could have prepared me for what was about to happen.

I learned how to have an incredible relationship with horses with my feet still firmly on the ground. But, more than that, I discovered the work I was born to do. Learning with horses was such a profound experience that I became accredited with HorseDream, a European Equine Guided Leadership Development qualification aimed at working with corporate leaders in business.

I left my corporate career and started a leadership and coaching business, thinking I would incorporate Leadership with Horses after my business was established. In fact, once I'd completed my training, I never signed another conventional leadership or coaching contract. Clients were only interested in the work with the horses, and I was drawn quickly into doing this work — and

9

never mind that I had little experience with horses and no idea how to care for one! My clients challenged me to my highest leadership potential, and I responded accordingly.

Despite 16 years of senior leadership experience in a large global IT corporation, and 10 years of personal development, coaching and world-class leadership training, nothing could have prepared me for the leadership skills I would need to work with horses. They challenge me mentally, physically and emotionally every day. The horses question every decision I make. Moment by moment, they are clear about whether I'm up to the job or not. They present this clarity without judgment.

For example, if you are compelling as a leader, a horse will readily come with you. If you are not, they plant their feet. It's that simple.

Horses give you an opportunity to explore what is happening *in the moment*. The second you become compelling again is the second the horse re-engages. There is no judgment from the horse: they simply respond based on whether they feel safe — right now — with you as a leader, or not.

It's not about horses; it's about leadership

We are all leaders by nature, whether you lead others or only yourself. In this book, I share with you some of the raw and honest accounts of my personal experiences around horses, while exploring what it means for leaders in business.

I'm on a mission to remove the masks and peel back the layers. I believe in order to live and work in harmony with each other, and to make our world a better place, we need leadership skills. At the very least, business requires us to work through our differences. At its best, we should do this with love and compassion in a way that allows us to speak our deepest truth from our hearts with mutual acceptance and appreciation. We're mostly not trained to do that.

Whilst the stories in this book are about horses and what they teach us, this book is about leadership, not horsemanship. I am a novice horse owner, but I believe that puts me at an advantage: I'm able to observe horses at face value, with an open mind and without preconceived notions regarding their behaviour.

Some people find this work challenging because it is honest and transparent. It's like being under a magnifying glass and examining the consequences of your actions in minute detail. The beauty of that is, as you find out how you 'show up' for others, you can practise using your strengths and experiment with how to adjust behaviour that blocks your effectiveness.

Most leadership books focus on what leaders **do** i.e. how to be strategic, create a vision, develop relationships, and so on. Of course, these things are important, but this book is different. This book focuses on the "being" qualities of a leader: *who you are* rather than *what you do*.

The seven skills described can fundamentally change the way you live and work. More than any other, these seven skills repeatedly arise when interacting with horses and are the foundation for exceptional leadership. Subtle shifts in these skills transform the way people lead and the results they get.

The skills described in this book are experiential, and can only be developed through first-hand learning and practice. A bodybuilder doesn't build muscle by reading a book. He must apply what he's learned and practise until his muscles are well developed.

If you expect to read a book and become a better leader in the process, then you've missed the main point of leadership and of this book. If you think you've got a handle on all seven skills, dig deeper. Exceptional leadership requires physical training where you keep building these skills to greater depths.

In writing this book, I became acutely aware of my own growth opportunities. When I wrote the chapter on courage, I noticed where I continue to wimp out and not be courageous. Many people tell me I am real and authentic and much of the time, that's true. Yet whilst writing about the masks we wear, I noticed where I still hide behind one. In digging deeper, I see how much more digging there is to do. There is always more trust, more compassion and more respect that I can reach for. This is the challenge we face as leaders: to be all we can be and to be gentle with ourselves when we fall short.

Leadership is a work in progress. You are a work in progress.

I want to inspire you to reflect on your leadership, fine-tune the way you lead, explore new ways to create a different result and invoke a more conscious approach. You will never be the perfect leader because the perfect leader doesn't exist. You have the potential to keep learning, growing and becoming more skilled as long as you are open to it. As a leader you are expected to do things you've never done before. You need to be able to think in a different way and say things you've never said before. You are being called on to be vibrant, compelling and courageous.

My own leadership continues to be a work in progress. This book is a part of that. I hope you enjoy the stories and embrace your own learning.

Shine bright. Release the mask and be all you can be. The world needs you.

With love
Jude

Introduction

"It's not that people don't want peace;
it's just that they don't always know how."
Jude Jennison

In today's global economy and rapidly changing business environments, new ways of working and new styles of leadership are required. Competition and hierarchy are being replaced by collaboration and shared leadership. That involves relating to others as human beings and working together. When you have the skills to work through differences, you can explore new concepts, generate new ideas and create new solutions to new problems.

Horses can demonstrate a new style of leadership: my horses and I are a herd, of sorts. We have developed a relationship based on trust and mutual respect, and everyone knows their place. Yet as in the world of business, that place is always in flux as I move in and out of the herd. The horses are always questioning and testing and redefining our relationship as the circumstances change. We don't always agree, but we find a way to work through our differences without breaking the relationship. This is the lesson of leadership. This is how to work through differences with people at deeper and deeper levels.

Instead of seeking personal power and reward, leaders

15

of the 21ˢᵗ century need to recognise the value of empowering others and find ways to inspire and influence them. It doesn't happen by following a process and logic.

Leadership requires self-awareness as well as inter-relational skills. These are typically not taught and not easy to teach because they are embodied experiences rather than intellectual ones. You can only fully accept others when you accept all of who you are. You can only embrace yourself for who you are when you acknowledge your brilliance as well as the places where you get stuck.

When we work with horses, they show you clearly where you are brilliant as well as where you get stuck. They do it honestly and without an agenda in a way that is compelling and memorable. The horses have provided the greatest learning opportunities both for me and my clients. Through fine-tuning and subtle shifts in direction, the results are sustainable and transferable to the workplace. Through this book, I share some of those skills so that more people are aware of the profound learning that is available from working with horses.

A paradigm shift

New ways to lead in a capitalist society require us to value more than money and economic growth. Financial achievements are not enough. People want to lead from the heart and soul, but they often don't know how. Employees crave community and connection. Most people want to make a difference and get frustrated when they can't.

Business has a significant impact on society. Business is succeeding in breaking down global barriers where diplomatic talks have failed for decades. When companies choose to do manufacturing in China, diplomatic negotiations play a critical role in supporting any decisions, but businesses make it happen. Leaders overcome differences for the sake of commercial success. The choices you make in your daily working life impact your immediate team as well as the wider global society. You are part of something much bigger than your local department. That's why I believe it's essential for everyone in the workplace to be highly skilled and to understand their impact.

What's the impact of the decisions you make?

Working in a global economy highlights our differences and creates a need to be more flexible in our approach. The old style paradigm of a management approach is no longer valid. When businesses drive a top-down, hierarchical command and control style approach, they lose talented employees. This is a significant switch in leadership.

Up until now, most of your role models in life will have taken this approach, including your parents who told you to sit still at the dinner table, and your teachers who praised you for getting things right and reprimanded you for getting things wrong. In work, the performance culture rewards those who stand out from the others and achieve at the highest level. Although most businesses say they want collaboration rather than competition, they encourage and reward the latter.

A paradigm shift in leadership requires a change in the skill set, a change in approach and a desire to grow and develop collectively. It requires a global awareness and a willingness to operate as a global citizen. That's where business can make a fundamental difference. As technological advances speed up the rate of change in business, it is no longer possible for one person to have all the answers, information, skills and abilities that are needed to create success.

Are you ready to lead, inspire and influence?

My driving force

I desire peace in the world. It's my driving force. Most people want peace even though it doesn't always look that way. Conflict arises out of unskilled behaviour. When we do not have the skills to be in relationship with people whose opinions differ from ours, we disagree and fight one another. As a result, we have conflict in our homes, our families, with our friends and at work. At a country level, we have conflict within society and an abuse of power. On a global scale, there is conflict between countries that all want to be the most powerful because they are scared of what might happen if they are not.

More importantly, you have inner conflict. You know the inner voice that tells you that you are not good enough, you can't do it, people will judge you, and so on? That internal conflict is painful, uses inordinate amounts of energy and prevents you from being who you can truly be. It's a flag to show you are at the edge of your capabilities as a leader.

Through working with horses, I not only overcame my fear of them, I learned to finely tune my leadership in the process. In particular, I learned how to be in relationship through our differences because horses are quite willing to be clear about what they want. They are less compliant than people and more authentic in every moment.

I want to reduce the pain and stress caused by conflict. If it starts with one individual having the skills to live and work in harmony in the world, then I believe I've made a difference. When you expand that to teams, the difference becomes ever greater. We are all change-makers in our way – big or small. Whether you are a corporate leader or an entrepreneur or look after a family, what you do and how you do it has an impact on society.

There are times when fighting for your rights is essential and times when it's easier to walk away. I want people all over the world to collaborate more successfully, and reduce the fight. Shared leadership and relationship provide an alternative way and we can learn so much from horses about both.

I have a vision of the future where we have the skills to treat each other as human beings. When we look each other in the eye with open hearts, we work together more collaboratively.

We are tribal by nature. We gravitate towards people like us and gather together in work or society based on shared interests and beliefs. Nobody teaches you how to stay when the going gets tough. How do you work things through when opinions are at the opposite ends of the spectrum?

How do you collaborate when you disagree with someone fundamentally?

I'm raising a lot of questions here. They are important for everyone to consider if we are to change the way we engage in differences of opinion. I wish for peace in Syria, Egypt, Nigeria and other places in the world. I wish for peace in your workplace and your homes. Most of all I wish for peace in your heart so you can live and work in harmony with others. Only then will we create peace in the world and put an end to conflict. I hope the skills in this book help you navigate your leadership challenges more effortlessly and peacefully. Working with horses has been instrumental in helping me and my clients to do exactly that.

Leading on purpose

This book is also about leading on purpose. It's possible to overcome enormous adversity when you know you are on the right path.

It's not enough to go to work, do a great job, come home and expect to be fulfilled. Work needs to light your fire. People who show passion for their work are compelling. The other evening I switched the television on and watched a woman present passionately about flowers and different varieties. I found myself drawn in and watching her for a full ten minutes before I realised I wasn't particularly interested. The flowers did not inspire me but the woman's passion did.

Work is full of people who are existing. You drag yourself out of bed, crawl into the office, find yourself getting stuck in the negative gossip and chit chat. You probably do great work, go to the same boring meetings that you don't want to be in, go home and repeat the following day. You do the same great things and get stuck in the same places. You find the same people challenging to work with, get frustrated by the same problems, and hold back because you concoct stories about what you can and can't do. The musts and shoulds. Along the way, you are leading, but you know there is more to you behind some of the struggles.

Leadership requires you to influence and inspire. Find your passion, find the thing that lights you up and helps you do extraordinary things. If you look at the great leaders in history, every one of them was aiming towards something that mattered to them. I believe that is what leadership is. Whether you are leading your individual life or leading a team of people, leadership is about the choices you make in every moment and the impact on you, others and society.

In one role I did, I managed a budget of a billion

dollars. It was primarily a cost reduction role and it could have been an uphill struggle. In parallel to running a cost reduction programme, the company was making redundancies. I was passionate about saving the company money because I recognised that when I saved money, fewer people were made redundant. I helped my European team understand that. When we hit resistance, we reconnected with knowing we were making a difference by saving jobs. It helped us keep going and achieve significant cost reductions in a two-year period.

Every morning, consider what will make the biggest difference in your work and then do it. Too many people go to work, sit in boring meetings and come home again. That's not leadership. That's doing what you think you should do. You won't be passionate about work if you get stuck in a rinse and repeat cycle. Business needs shaking up. You can be part of that. Leadership requires you to step up.

I believe I'm ordinary. I've been a high achiever and overcome enormous challenges in every step of my career. At my core, I'm a leader. Except when I'm not because I'm unskilled in places too. I'll share some of those experiences in this book as well as the times I got it right!

I'm driven by my passion for peace – inner peace and outer peace. I only realised that in the last few years, but it is the theme that runs through my career. Find your passion. Find what makes you come alive and make decisions that align with your values. Lead like you mean it because business and society need that. There is no room for mediocrity in leadership.

What's your purpose that inspires your leadership?

How this book is structured

If you have picked this book up expecting to be told how to be a better leader by doing things differently, then you are going to be disappointed. This book is deliberately not a how-to guide because I don't know how you lead.

*How do you find **your** courage and compassion?*

*How do **you** build trust and mutual respect?*

*What's the impact **you** have and how do you change it?*

The skills outlined in this book are experiences you feel. They go beyond language. That's why no matter how much you sit in a classroom and learn about leadership, it doesn't make a lot of difference.

Your way of leading, inspiring and influencing others is unique to you, just as learning to ride a bike and find your balance on it is unique to you. You won't have the language to describe what you are doing to find your balance on a bike, but if I produced a bike and asked you to ride it, most people would be able to.

Leadership is much the same. That's why this book is designed to inspire you to think about your leadership in a different way, to feel what is working and what is not and to notice your impact.

Part One of the book is the story of my background with horses, including how I survived three serious accidents. It sets the context of how I came to do the work with horses.

Part Two explains what Leadership with Horses is. It provides a brief background to the work, as well as an introduction to some of the exercises we do, some of the experiences my clients and I have had, and how those experiences are relevant to working in business. If you've not come across Leadership with Horses before, this section will put the work into context and help you make sense of some of the stories described later in the book.

If you have already experienced Leadership with Horses, it will help you further your learning, remind you of some of the things we cover and look at how they inform your leadership.

Part Three introduces the equine team and 7 Leadership Skills that people typically learn around the horses. I could have included 347, but I had to stop somewhere. The seven skills identified in this book are ones that are a foundation to leadership, and clients repeatedly deepen their learning around these skills.

At the end of each chapter in Part Three, I provide a case study explaining some of the benefits clients have gained from working with horses. The case studies are examples of learning that more than one client has experienced at different times. Names have been changed to protect the people who have had these or similar experiences. Chapter 16 provides further examples of learning that clients have gained.

If you think you can tick off the skills in this book as complete, you have missed the point. Every one of us can continue to go deeper and deeper with these skills.

With this book, I hope to provoke you into exploring your leadership practically in your everyday life and work. Tweak small things here and there, notice the impact and recalibrate.

Your leadership is a work in progress.

PART ONE

How it all began

*In which I childishly declare
my intent with horses
and overcome enormous challenges
as an adult to achieve it*

Chapter 1

My background with horses

"I'd like a horse, and if I can't have a horse,
I'd like a rabbit."

Jude Jennison, aged 8¾

As I lay in the hospital bed, I noticed that I wasn't in a normal ward. I was in an intensive care unit. There were only two other people in the ward, and they were both wired up to all sorts of machines that looked quite frightening. I looked around and saw I was also wired up to beeping machines.

I was frightened. What was happening? Would I live? It wouldn't be the last time I asked myself that question. Suddenly the lights on one of the other patient's machines sounded an alarm. The nurse came in, did something to make it go silent and then went again. A few minutes later, a priest arrived and read the last rites to this patient.

I felt my heart beating. Why was I here? Would I die too? Was I really in such a serious condition to be on this ward where people were dying around me? I had no intention of dying, but I knew I was badly hurt.

"I'd like a horse, and if I can't have a horse, I'd like a rabbit." I distinctly remember the conversation with my parents as I neared my ninth birthday. I had never been around horses and, living in the suburbs of the city of Nottingham, I don't think I'd even seen one before, but I had the clarity of an eight year old who knows what she wants. I was also clear that I wanted a horse, not a pony.

Early in the morning on 23rd June 1977, my parents led me blindfolded down to the bottom of my garden in my dressing gown. There was Bumper, the white rabbit. He wasn't a horse, but I loved him for the nine years he lived, and I spent hours of my childhood, training him to leap through a show-jumping course that I designed especially for his shorter legs. It was the next best thing to having a horse.

Yet I still wanted to work outdoors with horses. I wasn't

specific about what kind of work that might be, as the only reference point I had was to be a riding school instructor. My mum warned me it would be cold and wet in the winter, that I couldn't earn much money working with horses, and that I needed to get a proper job. I dropped the idea. It wasn't until thirty-four years later I remembered having that conversation.

In addition to Bumper, I was also given six riding lessons and a riding hat for my birthday. I rode for three or four months and then stopped. I liked being around the ponies, but I didn't particularly enjoy riding, and I didn't like the riding instructors.

A couple of years later, I took up lessons again with my sister and her friend Diane, who had her own pony. The ponies were mean, the instructors were still mean, and I didn't enjoy it at all. I never liked being told to kick the ponies to make them move, and pull on their mouths to make them stop. I remember asking if it hurt the ponies, and the instructor said no. I was never fully convinced, but I found myself yanking them around like everyone else did because I didn't know how else to treat them, and what else are you supposed to do when you are eleven years old? I spent a lot of time doing pointless exercises that were intended to help me find my balance, but we did them repeatedly, and it was boring.

I used to watch the girls who mucked out the stables and did jobs around the yard. I longed to get involved, but I lacked the confidence to ask because I didn't know what to do or how to do it.

When I look back now, my overwhelming memory is the smell. The scent of the ponies always touched my heart, even though my relationship with horses was lacking, and I was never particularly competent as a rider. I longed for something more, but I didn't realise that a different relationship with horses was possible. I rode for less than a year and then gave it up again, having never made a connection with any of the ponies I rode.

Learning to ride and my first accident

Twenty years later when I was 32 years old, my friend Dot persuaded me to go riding with her. This time I got to ride a horse! He was a tall thoroughbred called Troy, and he was beautiful. He was not a novice ride and was quite spirited. I explained that I'd not done much riding, and I felt a bit out of my depth, but the riding instructor seemed to think I could handle him. I got on even though I'd not ridden since I was a teenager and had never gone faster than a trot before.

It was at a time in my life when everything was going well, and I was living at breakneck speed. My career was rocketing; I was being promoted, travelling extensively and living life to the max. But I ignored all the signs that I was close to being burned out by the speed at which I was living.

Life was about to make me slow down in no uncertain terms.

My new teacher assumed that I'd done more riding

than I had, and I joined a class of mixed ability. When she told me to canter, I just put more pressure on the horse in trot, and he cantered. I went with him – just. It felt unstable, but I was having fun. The teacher didn't seem to notice that I had no idea what I was doing.

Next, she directed everyone to jump over a fallen log in the field. It was nearly two feet high. I explained that I'd never jumped before. She told me to watch everyone else, to lean forward and let the horse do the work. I was on a very tall horse, so a two-foot high log was pretty easy for him. I watched everyone else jump; I saw how they leaned forward when they took off and sat back when they landed. (To my readers who are experienced with horses, I apologise for this crude description that may be completely wrong. I'm just explaining what I saw, and I copied it.)

Troy and I took off. We landed. I bounced around a bit and pulled up behind all the other horses, who were not far away. I regained my balance once we were stationary, and so we continued for the next five weeks. It was a disaster waiting to happen. I should never have been jumping solid fences as my first attempts.

On my sixth lesson, there were only three of us booked: me and my two friends who rode there regularly. Because they were regulars, the teacher said we could go off into the field of cross-country jumps on our own, and we were encouraged to do whatever we wanted. We walked, trotted and cantered as usual. We did a few jumps too. Only things were different this time, and I felt more unstable than ever. In the previous lessons, we would go from the front of the group, jump one log and pull up at the back of the group. That meant if I was losing my balance, we would soon come to a stop, and I could regain my seat from a stationary position. Now there was no group to cause me to pull up.

We were coming to the end of our hour, and we decided to jump a final log that was on the path leading towards home. Dot went first, and I followed. As I landed, I lost my stirrup and my balance as usual. I fidgeted my foot around, trying to get it back in the stirrup and continued to be slightly off kilter while Troy carried on. I tried to slow him down, but he decided instead to head for home. Without the group to pull up behind, he had no incentive to stop, and I continued to bounce around trying to get my foot back in the stirrup. Had I been more experienced, I might have realised that it was better to find my balance than my stirrup, but I wasn't, and I didn't.

As we continued cantering faster, we were heading towards another two-foot high fallen log. I had no intention of jumping it, and neither did Troy. At the last minute, he veered sharply to the left. I fell off to the right, landing on the edge of the log. I heard a loud bang as I landed.

Tracey, who had been behind me, saw what happened and pulled up. I lay on the ground unable to breathe. I knew I was badly injured. As I struggled for each breath, Dot said: "Don't worry. You're just winded."

I gasped: "I'm not. I'm seriously hurt. I can't breathe."

Tracey knew I had hurt myself severely, and she cantered off to fetch an ambulance. (This was in July 2000, before mobile phones.)

As I lay on the ground, I could feel myself getting incredibly hot, and the world around me started to go black. I felt as though I was going to lose consciousness. I didn't want that to happen. I knew that if I allowed myself to black out, I would have no control over what might happen. I willed myself to stay awake. It took every ounce of physical and emotional strength. I could hear Dot talking to me, but I couldn't hear what she was saying. Instead, I focused on breathing as much as I could and told myself that I would stay conscious so that I knew what was happening. I was going to be in control, and nothing was going to stop me. I wasn't afraid. Just incredibly focused. It shows the power of your mind under pressure. We can achieve extraordinary things when we decide we want to.

The ambulance arrived. I was taken to hospital, and it turned out that I had broken nine ribs, fractured my shoulder blade in three places, and I had a collapsed lung. I later discovered that I was an inch away from being a paraplegic. I was alive, and I was grateful. The doctor operated to insert a chest drain to re-inflate my collapsed lung, and by the time I was transferred to a ward it was midnight.

I was given an epidural to relieve the pain and transferred to intensive care, where I was wired up to heart monitors in case I went into cardiac arrest with the shock of what my body had experienced. My husband was in Edinburgh and had missed the last flight so he would not be able to come and see me until the following day. I lay in bed wanting to get some sleep as my pain was finally under control.

Two days later I was transferred to a surgical ward where I stayed for two weeks. The pain was horrific. When you break ribs, they break like broken bottles. Every time I breathed, the two ends of each broken rib pulled apart and moved back together again, trapping muscle and soft tissue as they did so. I had broken nine ribs resulting in eighteen jagged ends trapping muscle and tissue. It was agony, despite being on an epidural. Every day, the anaesthetist came to increase the amount of drug I received through the epidural. By day 10, they had to take me off it and put me on morphine instead.

The first night they gave me morphine in the evening, and the doctor told me that he had prescribed some additional morphine that I could have overnight if needed. All I had to do was ask the nurse. Coming off the epidural was agony. I'd had the pain numbed for ten days, and now I was feeling it and the morphine was only just keeping it at bay.

In the middle of the night, I could bear it no longer. I called the nurse and asked for the morphine. She said I'd had painkillers and didn't need any more until the morning. I explained that I was in agony, and that the doctor had said I could have it. She said I didn't need it and left.

I couldn't lie down because my ribs were stabbing me. I sat on the edge of my bed, but that was hard too because I needed my back muscles to hold me upright, and they were so shredded by the ribs. I sat with tears coming down my face, feeling helpless. With no mobile phone, I considered walking to the phone box to call my husband, but I could only walk about four or five paces, and I still had a chest drain attached.

As the tears fell, I felt powerless. I had no choice but to sit on the edge of the bed. I sat there and wondered if I could die with the amount of pain I had. I wasn't sure if I would make it through the night. I surrendered because in those moments of helplessness there is not much else to do, and I didn't have the physical or emotional strength to fight. I thought: "If I can't make it through the night with this amount of pain, then I will die and so be it. It's a shame, but I can't do anything about it. And if I live, then I will have to bear it through the night until the morning when I will ask the doctor."

Of course I lived. In the morning, I asked the day staff for the doctor as I was still sitting on the edge of my bed rocking back and forth because I had found that was the most comfortable position to be in. I explained that the doctor had prescribed morphine and that I had been refused it. They called the doctor, and he gave me the morphine and apologised for what had happened. It turned out to be a lack of communication between the day and night staff.

One of the problems was that I was on a surgical ward because they considered my collapsed lung to be more life-threatening than the broken ribs. The majority of people on the ward were dying of bowel cancer. I watched three people die during the two weeks I was in hospital. The nursing staff on the surgical ward didn't understand the severity of broken ribs and how to manage me, so they left me to my own devices. They kept telling me to drink more, but I couldn't lift more than half a glass of water at a time. I needed someone to pour the jug of water into a glass regularly, but they were understaffed and couldn't help. On an orthopaedic ward, this would have been understood, but on a surgical ward they just thought I was precious! It was a painful two weeks, emotionally and physically.

I finally came home and embarked on a long road to recovery. I hadn't yet learned to let go, so I was attached to getting back to work as soon as possible. My career was on hold, and my work was such an important part of my life that I didn't know what else to do. I could barely sit and had to spend long periods of time reclined on a garden chair padded with pillows.

Six months later I returned to work for two hours a day. By the time I left work, I was in so much pain that I often had to stop on the five-minute drive home, crying uncontrollably. I would calm myself and continue the drive home. I remember the two places where I used to stop. One was just round the corner of the office, and the other was halfway home.

In hindsight, I should not have returned to work so quickly. My body needed more time to recover. It was still in shock. The muscle and soft tissue damage was so severe that my whole back would spasm with the exhaustion of just sitting upright at a desk. My work was important to me, and I desperately wanted to hang on to my career. It was a great example of how we can get things out of proportion in life.

It took me three years to return to work full time. I had to lessen my hold on my career at that time, and I struggled to do so. I was so driven, and doing work that was below my capabilities was boring. I wasn't able to travel, and I wasn't capable of managing clients, so I was performing back-office functions that were not critical and not that interesting either.

Throughout my recovery, I wanted to ride again. I wasn't put off by the severity of the fall because I realised that I'd been doing too much and far beyond my capabilities. I still hadn't realised at this point that there was a different relationship that I could have with horses. I only knew that I wanted something more, so I focused on wanting to ride.

A declaration and two more accidents

Seven years later, my career was back on track, and my back was finally strong enough for me to consider riding. In February 2007, I declared to my husband that I was going to ride again in a few months' time when I had got fitter. That afternoon, I slipped over on the kitchen floor and broke an inch and a half off my elbow. I had a three-hour operation to pin my elbow back together again and a second operation six months later to remove the majority of the pins holding it together.

Any thoughts of riding again were pushed to one side as I embarked on another road to recovery, which would take me two years before my elbow was strong enough. In January 2009, when my elbow was strong again and my back was feeling reasonable, I told my husband that I would start riding again. He groaned and rolled his eyes, but I assured him that I'd learned my lesson this time. I was now aware of the importance of pacing myself, and I would be careful and take it easy. What I didn't know was that there was still a lesson for me to learn by being around horses.

You can almost guess what was going to happen next! The following day, my husband Paul and I walked across a field of horses with our dog Gracie on the lead. Two horses thought Gracie was a threat and galloped over, bucking and rearing in front of us as they tried to stamp on Gracie's head. With their hooves flailing above our heads and less than two metres away from us, I was terrified – and rightly so, because we could have been seriously injured. We managed to escape unharmed, but the incident shook me up. I couldn't sleep for a week and would wake up in the night thinking about what had happened and what a close escape we had all had.

From that moment on, I was terrified of horses. Whenever I thought of that incident, I would feel my heart pounding, my head would feel as though it was going to explode, and I'd feel incredibly stressed. I continued to have sleepless nights about it for quite some time.

I'd now had three dangerous incidents as a result of even thinking about riding, and life was trying to tell me to slow down. I also realised that I am not meant to ride! Finally, I got the message and to this day, I have no desire to ride.

Of course, that could have been the end of my story with horses, and for most people it would have been. It wasn't the end. In fact, it was just the beginning. Any events up to that moment were to educate me about the fact that I could have a different relationship with horses and to provide me with the experience I would need to do the leadership work with them.

My new story of horses and leadership was about to begin.

PART TWO

Leadership with Horses

*In which I explore how horses
teach people to be human*

Chapter 2

What is Leadership with Horses?

"If you can lead a horse, you can lead anyone."

Jude Jennison

People often ask me what I do. If I say: "Leadership with Horses," a typical response is: "Oh, do you teach horses leadership skills?"

Er, no.

They follow up with: "Do you teach horse riders how to lead a horse better?"

Still *no*.

I work with *people* – senior leaders and executive teams

– to help them fine-tune their leadership skills. What have horses got to do with that? Quite a lot! The horses are the training partners for the day and my clients work with them to learn how to influence and inspire their own clients and teams through powerful use of non-verbal communication.

As one client commented: "The simplicity belies the depth of the experience."

Whilst leading a horse might sound simple, the skills that people learn are profound, and life-changing. These skills are repeatable in the workplace and create sustainable changes of behaviour.

There is no riding involved. In Leadership with Horses workshops, you lead the horses on the ground in a variety of different situations and discover your strengths. When you see the impact of what works in your leadership, it creates greater awareness and an opportunity to use those strengths even more.

Conversely, horses will quickly identify the places where you get stuck. This non-judgmental feedback gives you an opportunity to try new ways of leading and enables you to recalibrate your leadership style at that moment, in a variety of situations. The result is you learn what you most need to learn to have more impact and influence. Like riding a bike, once you have found your balance, you can find it again in different situations. If you can ride a bike in Manchester, you can ride it in London. It might be a bit more out of your comfort zone, but the feel for it and the skills you draw on are the same.

Leadership is similar. Once you have discovered your courage, you can invoke the same feeling again and again in different situations. Working with horses provides an embodied leadership experience. By finding what works and what doesn't, you learn how to modify your leadership behaviour and find your new way of working. One client was surprised when a horse head-butted him. He had been so focused on the task that he had completely lost sight of being in relationship. Every time the horse had resisted, he was more insistent that she did as she was told. He was treating her quite roughly without realising it, and the horse would not tolerate it any more than people would.

Why are we willing to listen to a horse when we shut down to what people tell us? A horse provides feedback without judgment or agenda. When people provide feedback, they usually have their own agenda and intend to change you. The horse is only interested in whether you are a compelling leader, can keep them safe at that moment and build a relationship based on trust and mutual respect. If the answer is yes, they come with you willingly. If not – for whatever reason – they make it clear.

A typical workshop

We start the day by observing the horses. It helps people adjust to a new environment that is very different from their normal place of work. Another reason we observe the horses is to practise observation and emotional intelligence as leadership skills. Observation is hugely underrated. In a busy working day, you may overlook what is happening in both the team and the environment. If your team is unhappy or stressed, it has an impact on how they perform. Your role as a leader is to be aware of what is happening so that you can identify issues early on.

Many clients report being much more aware of what is happening in their team as a result of learning to observe at a deeper level. Through practising observation, they learn to notice what is not said as much as what is verbalised. They start to pick up on emotions in others and gain a general feel for the environment. They learn to notice when people are confident, afraid, tentative, focused, determined, resilient and much more.

All of these things can be identified at minute levels if you hone the skill of observation. People quickly learn the importance of paying attention around horses and recognise that things can change quickly, just as they do in business. People often describe horses as unpredictable because things happen when you are not paying attention. The same is true of people in an office too. Learning to pay attention can help you navigate complex business change because you learn to notice the subtle nuances of behaviour.

During the day, we move on to building relationships with the horses. We explain to clients how to meet the horses in a way that makes both people and horses feel safe, and we explore the importance of relationships in business. The horses instantly show people how well they build relationships by engaging when the relationship is solid and disengaging when the client focuses too much on the task or their own agenda. It's another simple exercise that often has a profound impact on people and encourages them to consider how well they build relationships with others.

The first active session of the day is a straightforward leading exercise. Clients are often surprised by how much they learn from something as simple as leading a horse around the arena. It doesn't matter if people have experience leading a horse or not. They learn through discovering where they are confident as a leader and where they get stuck. Often clients who have been around horses a lot are used to telling the horse what to do in a "command and control" style of leading. It surprises them when my horses refuse to cooperate when being told what to do. My horses expect you to engage with them as a sentient being with opinions and feelings, just as people in your team do too.

People often ask me how I train my horses to do this work. I don't. All I ask is that my horses be themselves – nothing more and nothing less. Instead, I encourage them to have an opinion. I never use force or coercion with my horses. That way, they learn that if they don't want to do something, they don't have to. It makes them more demanding to lead, and I always have to be on top of my game when I ask them to do anything too! It means that clients need to lead, influence and inspire instead of cajoling and forcing. As long as clients are compelling enough as leaders and build strong relationships, the horses are willing to follow their lead.

For those who are still sceptical, I have worked with a variety of horses in different locations, from an 11.2 hands high pony in Devon to a 19 hands high Percheron in Ohio (a hand in horse measurements is four inches). In addition to working with my horses and those of my business partner, I've also worked with retired racehorses, retired police horses and retired horses from the Household Cavalry Regiment of the British Army. Horses naturally want to engage in a team and readily accept leadership when it is offered honestly, with congruence and integrity. They don't need to be trained to behave naturally!

We do a variety of leading exercises, each designed to bring out different skills, some individually and some as part of a team. Throughout the day, we balance the focus on leading self, building relationships with others and working within a cohesive team.

Why horses?

Horses show us how to be present in the now, at this moment where life and leadership are happening. They teach us to be more creative and flexible, and to respond to whatever happens. These skills are desperately needed as business continues to transform in the 21st century.

There are varying schools of thought on how much of your communication is non-verbal. I don't want to get into a scientific debate here. Most scientists agree that the majority of your communication is non-verbal. Non-verbal communication is much more than body language and facial expressions. It includes your energy, emotions and intentions.

Your non-verbal communication is the biggest portion of your impact. How many times have you done a presentation and thought about what you are going to say and how you say it? How many times have you thought about the impact you want to create? Usually, you do a presentation because you want a certain impact or outcome. Most people focus on themselves and their material rather than the outcome and impact. Your impact is primarily non-verbal.

Are you interesting?

What emotions do you invoke in others?

Do you show passion for your subject?

Consider some of the great orators of our time. Martin Luther King's "I have a dream" speech wasn't so much about the content as the delivery. His passion, emotion and desire to create a different outcome were so compelling and still are today. Even now, it's hard to watch his speech and not be moved by it. It creates a profound impact.

Horses communicate almost entirely non-verbally using body language, movement, space, intention and emotions as their communication. They mirror your leadership behaviour. It's not what you say but how you say and do it that makes a difference.

Unlike humans, horses only interact with authentic behaviour. They are sensitive to subtle changes in body language, sense what is going on and mirror it back to you. If you think one thing and say another, it causes confusion, and they show this by refusing to cooperate.

Horses will only follow an assertive leader who leads with strength and gentleness, courage and compassion, trust and mutual respect. You learn how to step out of your comfort zone and create maximum impact with minimum effort.

Horses are a prey animal and work cohesively in a team as a single herd. Their primary goals are safety, health and wellbeing of the whole herd. They are inclusive and show us how to embrace differences of opinion with ease. They model trust and mutual respect, where everyone gets a say in what they want, and you improve your ability to handle conflict and differences of opinion. All of the skills that horses demonstrate are needed in business today. They show you how to make subtle changes in your leadership that have a profoundly different impact.

Some clients are more resistant and cynical than others, especially when they don't get the outcome they want. They may not like the feedback they get. That doesn't matter. The work with the horses causes shifts at a cellular level. Once people have worked with them, they are changed forever – not always in ways they understand or can articulate, but nevertheless they are changed forever.

When I meet up with clients several months later, I see the difference. I see more power, focus, confidence and self-belief. The shifts might be minor, but the impact is major. Common responses include changes in leadership teams, greater respect, better relationships, improved teamwork, promotions and pay rises. People tell me they are doing things they never dreamed they could.

It's not unusual for there to be tears when people work with horses. It happens to me too. When you reach the limit of your verbal communication, your heart and soul are moved at a deeper level, often resulting in tears. A coach once said to me: "Tears are the language of the soul." I do know the horses are trying to reach us at that level, and when they do, tears are the result.

It's also common for people to open up and tell each other things they wouldn't normally say. They often stop and say they are not sure why they are telling me things. It's the impact the horses have on us. Around them, you become more congruent in behaviour and more likely to share your experiences, thoughts and feelings.

There are enormous benefits for teams who open up in this way. When people show up more transparent and vulnerable, others in the workshop find them more compelling. They put aside prior judgments and support each other because they see and understand each other at a deeper level. Often team conflict is resolved as people open up and have deeper conversations.

Horses operate primarily from their limbic system. The limbic system governs your emotions, feelings, relationships, nurturing, images and dreams, play and creativity. Scientific research has shown that when you are in the presence of horses, you have greater access to your limbic system and greater awareness of your emotions.

People become more authentic and more honest and have an emotional experience that they own honestly. It's not unusual for people around horses to start telling stories about themselves and say: "I've never told anybody this before." People share things they wouldn't normally share because they have access to their emotions and are aligned with their authentic selves.

In the following chapters, we'll explore some of the different exercises in more detail, including client experiences, the learning they get and how it helps them lead in business.

Chapter 3

Watching and assessing

"Observe and listen to everything around you,
and the leadership action is usually obvious.
The problem is that we are so self-focused
and task-focused that we forget
to pay attention at a deep level."

Jude Jennison

Angela stood quietly, wiping tears from her eyes. Part of a group of eight senior leaders, she stood outside the arena, watching the horses. The whole team was scared, but many of them were trying to suppress it. Picking up on the fear, the horses mirrored it by bucking and rearing round the arena. The fear only increased further.

Angela said she was terrified and overwhelmed. She was not the first to feel this and won't be the last. When I asked how that informed her, she said: "I'm not going in the arena on my own with the horses." As soon as she said it, her fear reduced. Owning what she was feeling reduced the hold it had on her. She turned and said to me: "I realise I won't have to, will I?"

I said: "Not unless you want to."

Her fear dropped some more, and her tears dried up. She became more focussed and said with confidence: "OK great, then I'm ready to begin." In that moment of owning her fear, it no longer had a hold on her, and she was resourceful again as a leader, making powerful choices about what she would and would not do.

In our Leadership with Horses workshops, we often start the day by observing the horses interacting in the arena. Depending on how they feel and what emotions are running in the clients, the horses will mirror the clients' energy. They may wander about, roll in the sand or charge around if they are picking up a lot of anxiety.

I ask everyone in the team to name one thing they're feeling. Most people struggle to find the words. They've spent so long shutting down their emotions and no longer know how to feel. They don't have the language for their emotions. Often people focus on the horses and say they are wondering what the horses are doing and why. I explain that's not a feeling. It's their information brain wanting to know the facts and figures. That can be a default for people who are uncomfortable with their emotions.

I also name how I am feeling because all of us are having an impact on the horses, including me. I model transparency when working with clients and the horses. By doing this, I'm leading by example, and it encourages others to be transparent. The horses mirror what you feel so there is nowhere to hide with this work. On the day Angela and the team came, I said I was feeling trepidation. Everyone turned and looked at me, shocked. I explained that I felt responsible for their experience and safety, and I didn't want to go into the arena when the horses were bucking and rearing the way they were. This often surprises people. As the workshop leader, they expect me to have everything under control.

We talk about how the person leading is vulnerable too, how they don't always have to have all the answers, how being transparent builds a bond with a team because it's real and honest. Clients often have expectations about what a leader should and shouldn't be. We start to unpick the beliefs that a leader has to be confident, strong and know everything. Clients recognise that all leaders are vulnerable, get scared and need help at times too. They learn that all those feelings of insecurity they have ever had are normal, and they don't need to suppress them for fear of being found out. Transparency in leadership builds bonds instead of alienating people.

Most people find a way to express what they feel eventually. Some clients are terrified to the point of overwhelm. Some people get bored watching the horses, especially if they are not doing much. Others are excited and impatient to get on with interacting with them, or they may feel calm and relaxed.

Each client has an emotional response, and each one is different, even though they are watching the same horses doing the same thing. Usually, clients think everyone has the same emotion as them, or they think they are the only one who is scared. It's often the first time they've been asked to name their emotions – not to do anything with it but simply to notice.

What emotional responses do you have in different situations?

How do your emotions inform you?

I ask clients to notice if their emotion changes when the horses do something different. It's interesting to see how your emotions change with external circumstances. They then consider how they want to use it as a source of information and what it tells them.

With Angela, a number of things were happening in the discussion with her. Her emotions were no longer having a hold over her. She was using them as a source of information, making decisions about what she was and wasn't willing to do and then clearly communicating them to me.

In the process, we were building relationship. I

respected her fear and her transparency in owning it. She respected me for asking her to do something that felt so terrifying and out of her comfort zone. At that moment, mutual respect was at play. Immediately, trust was built. I trusted she would be honest about her emotions, would name them when she did get to a place of overwhelm and fear, and we could work through it together. She trusted I was not going to throw her into an arena with horses charging around. As a result, her fear reduced.

We had built the foundation for a solid relationship in such a short interaction. She felt safe. I knew what her boundaries were at that moment (they are always changing), and we were able to work powerfully together throughout the day based on clear, honest communication. By the end of the day, she was in the arena on her own with a loose horse, and she loved it!

The role of emotions

You are an emotional being. You have emotions. They are real. What do you do with them?

Do you shut your emotions down in business and make them wrong?

Or do you use your emotions as a valid source of information?

Emotions are part of your makeup. They are a valid source of information. Whether you are happy, angry or sad, there is a reason. If you bring your emotions powerfully into your leadership, it shows people that you are open, flexible and human. It helps you build trust and mutual respect. It shows you have compassion for others and in return, helps them to have the courage to have more open conversations and dialogue with you and the team.

Consider the different meetings you go to and different aspects of your job. What do you find frustrating? Are you moaning about it or taking action? As a leader, your role is to notice what is happening in you and others and decide what to do. Notice where you pay attention. Next time you catch yourself being negative and complaining about what you don't want, consider what you do want instead and how you might achieve it.

Do you have emotions, or do your emotions have you?

By that I mean when you have an emotion, do you recognise it and use it powerfully as a source of information? Or do your emotions take you over, and you do things unconsciously because you are stuffing the emotion down?

Take anger, for example. Anger is often deemed not to be appropriate for the workplace. You judge it as wrong. When you feel yourself getting angry, you make yourself wrong, and you may try to push it down. Except you are angry, and it doesn't go away until you address it. Before you know it, you've lost your temper, either directly at the person or situation or indirectly by going to someone else, letting off steam and complaining vehemently. Then you feel better for a while until the same person or situation frustrates you again, and the frustration builds until you feel angry again.

This is an example of your emotions having you. It is unskilled use of emotions. There is another way. You can use your emotions as a powerful tool in your leadership tool kit, as Angela did. You don't need to have a conversation out loud with someone else. If Angela had known how to use her emotions as a source of information to guide her decisions, she could have asked herself the questions I asked.

Next time you feel frustrated, pay attention to it. Take a moment to explore the frustration. Be curious. What situation has caused it? What values of yours are being overstepped? Breathe. Now consider how you might use that as a source of information. What's the powerful leadership decision you make then?

Emotions and horses

Being honest and transparent about your emotions can feel vulnerable. Remember, everyone has an emotion in every moment. When Angela owned her fear, it gave others permission to be more honest about theirs too. She was leading by example.

Throughout this book, I am transparent about the emotions I've had at different points in my story. I'll share with you where I used them powerfully in my leadership and where I failed to lead. Why? Because there is as much learning through failure as through success and because our emotions are a powerful source of information that often doesn't get enough attention.

Because horses operate primarily from their limbic or emotional brain, they are open and honest about their feelings. If they are in a hurry to come in for a feed in the evening, they don't pretend to be polite. They will jog at the gate and show they are in a hurry. I never let them push me around. I manage my boundaries. Instead of judging them as dominant and aggressive, I notice that they are in a hurry.

I recognise that they want something, and I empathise with their needs. I also have needs, and I make sure that I make those clear in return. Somehow we find a way to meet both of our needs – the desire for the horses to rush in and my desire not to be pushed over! As soon as I let them in, they relax again. They are not being difficult for the sake of being difficult; they are trying to inform me they want or need something. It's a form of communication.

People do the same. They communicate their emotions. That difficult person in the team is trying to tell you something. They don't get out of bed in the morning thinking they'll be difficult. Most people want to do great work. If you have someone in the team who is challenging, be curious. Understand their needs and work with them rather than against them. Telling them to put up and shut up won't work long term.

When I took on my first horse Kalle, she was difficult for me to handle. She was trying to tell me I wasn't strong enough to keep her safe, so she was taking charge. Now she's like a different horse. She is calm and relaxed all the time. If something happens in the environment, she may spook as the fear kicks in, but she recovers quickly because I pay attention and have learned how to handle her. I know she's not being difficult. I've learned how to stay calm and ask her to listen to me.

Fear is an emotional response, so it's ok to lead when you are scared as I learned to do with Kalle. Unfortunately, the fear signal is evoked in business situations much the same as it would if your physical safety were in question. Usually, you are not physically unsafe in business, so it's important to recognise fear as information. Examine the source of the fear and find ways to reduce it, either by getting help or reducing workload or responsibilities. Fear is your body's way of alerting you to the limit of your capabilities as a leader.

As a result of me taking time to understand Kalle and her emotional responses, I can now lead her in a way so she feels safer and can avoid going into panic. If you have someone on your team who is challenging, be curious. What is driving their behaviour?

How can you lead and inspire people to help them feel safe and comfortable?

People want to cooperate. They don't always know how.

Horses can show you where you trust fully and where you lack trust. With that awareness comes an ability to be more conscious about the choices you make.

Fear of failure

Fear plays a huge role in business, even though you might not want to admit it. Many of the leaders I work with are scared. They are afraid of getting things wrong and losing their job. If you think you're never scared, look again. Usually, the leaders who believe they are never scared are the ones who are too terrified to admit to it.

For fourteen years, I had a successful corporate career. Then it went wrong. I made a mistake and never recovered because I lacked the skills to know how to recover with a sense of dignity.

I spent fourteen years living in fear. Fear of not being good enough, not getting it right, thinking I would be found out for what I really was. I was afraid to show my true self, so I learned to conform, to play the game. I did it very well. I was excellent at my job, getting pay rises and promotions. I was a high achiever. I was respected by my peers, the people who worked for me (mostly) and the more senior management teams above me. What could go wrong?

My ego. Although I didn't consider myself to be ego-driven, I was. I had learned to conform to play a game where politics and game-playing were the norms. I had sold my soul.

Oh, you may judge me for this, consider me an egotistical person. The truth is you have done it too. You've said and done things because you think they are the "right" things to say and do. You think you'll be rewarded for it, so you do it. None of us is immune to the ego. It is constantly in play and needed too. It's the ego that provides passion, drive and commitment. Where would you be without that?

When I began my career, I was known for being direct and transparent. I was criticised for it, told I was naive and needed to play a political game. I learned to do that, although I continued to be more direct than most. I learned to conform to what I believed I needed to be to "fit in". I did it pretty well too because nobody seemed to notice. Even I didn't realise I was doing it at the time.

In November 2008, I went to the Women's International Networking Conference in Rome, sponsored by my company. One particular speaker inspired me. She had grown up in a remote village in the Philippines, and she decided that she wanted to do something for her community. She made beautiful shawls out of the stringy bits of banana skins, dyed them with raw materials grown locally and encouraged the women in her village to make them. She eventually brought Vogue to this remote village to do a fashion shoot, and her business took off, providing work for her local community. I was moved by this because community is important to me, and my first thought was that I didn't have a community. Then I realised that I was part of a global community of 400,000 employees! That's a pretty big community within which to make a difference!

At the time, I was considering my next role in the company. I went back to work inspired, and my boss asked me if I'd had any thoughts about what I wanted to do next. I said: "I want to make a difference in the community." He said: "That's nice, but what job do you want to do?" I realised he needed me to be more pragmatic so I held onto that vision and looked around for roles where I thought I could make the biggest difference.

I identified a role in a different part of the organisation as a Communications Partner. Morale at the time was low, and communication internally was poor, so I was convinced that I could make a difference here. I knew that people needed to be inspired and led, and I knew that creating effective dialogue would go some way towards doing that.

I got the job of course, and the first thing that struck me was that everyone in the team was operating from their ego. The communications team thought they were important because they were working with the board of the company. I didn't like this and I fought it, but found myself getting sucked into it and operating from that place too. I hated that, but I didn't know how to be in this new environment with no support, where people had little real understanding of the business.

I failed at the role. My manager genuinely seemed to have little desire to communicate with his organisation. In the whole year I did the job, he allowed me into his office to talk to him only twice, and both times he was doing emails at the same time!

I didn't stand up to him. In my desire not to upset him,

my desire to gain respect and not rock the boat, I failed to tell him exactly what I thought needed to happen. I continued to present to him as he failed to pay more than even cursory attention. He was not engaged. I was doomed to fail. And still I said nothing because I made up a rule that it was not my place to rock the boat, not my place to tell him that his organisation needed his attention, not my place to...

My downfall was conforming to what I believed was expected of me rather than what I wanted to say and do. I lacked the skills to influence the people I needed to influence. I wasn't leading.

If I had known then what I know now, I might have been able to influence the situation, and the outcome could have been very different. I lacked the courage to say what needed to be said to the right people. I lacked the ability to trust and find respect and gain it in return. I held onto a specific outcome, and I didn't use my energy powerfully as a leadership tool, finding myself bouncing between giving up and being more forceful in equal measure. I'm talking fine tuning here, as I will do throughout this book.

I believe that when we reach the limit of our leadership capabilities, we exhibit behaviours that we don't like and don't want to exhibit. Yes, you too. If you've ever moaned about someone or something, you've reached your limit of leadership ability and are failing to do something powerful about the person or situation. No doubt you have lots of reasons why, and you will say how valid they are.

It is my intention with this book that you consider how you can keep stretching into your leadership so that you notice more consciously when you are out of your level of expertise. Then you can find ways of expanding your leadership more consciously and fully.

I spent a year in fear of not being able to do the job effectively, and that is exactly what I created. It hit me hard. I'd never failed before. I felt worthless. I was afraid I'd never get another job. I'd gone from being highly respected and sought after to what I believed was a huge failure. I felt the tension of failure in my chest. The very thing I feared the most had happened because I lacked the skills to be courageous in my leadership and lead from my heart and soul.

For the first time, I'd entered a role with a deep desire to make a difference in the community, and it had failed. It was hard to take. I was also angry. I was angry that the person I'd worked for had only met me twice, and both times he had made it clear that he had no respect for either me or the role I was doing. He had no respect for the 9,000 people in his organisation who desperately needed more dialogue and communication.

I was angry that I failed to influence him and angry that all of his leadership team had failed to do anything to help, even though they had recognised that what I was trying to achieve was the right thing. They were afraid to influence their boss too. Without his commitment to communication, it was not going to happen. So I looked for another role.

Fear took a hold. I told myself I would never get a decent job again. Nobody would want me. I felt that everyone was judging me. Of course, they weren't, but the stories that we make up in these moments of self-doubt can be destructive to self-confidence. I looked around for other jobs and was offered three, so clearly they weren't judging me as harshly as I judged myself! Still, I felt bruised by the whole experience, and it took me a while to recover and regain my confidence.

How fear influences your leadership

Fear has a significant impact on business, and it is rife in every business I ever work with. Angela was afraid of the horses. She acknowledged that she got scared at work too and didn't know what to do. She had never used her fear as a powerful source of information before. She had always labelled it as weak and squashed it.

I did the same in the role where I failed. By squashing my fear, I allowed it to drive all my decisions. If I had used it powerfully as a source of information, the scenario might have gone something like this:

I'm feeling scared. What am I afraid of? I'm afraid of not being respected in this new job and not being able to make the difference I want to make. What do I really want? I want to transform the way we communicate in the company. What do I need to do that? I need the General Manager to listen to what I have to say. What if he doesn't? Then I can't be effective in the role, and I would be better off looking for something else.

If I had used my fear as a source of information, I might have recognised earlier that my success wasn't solely dependent on what I did but on how others worked with me too. I could have been more transparent and clear about what I needed. I didn't because I was afraid of being vulnerable, afraid of asking for what I needed in case I didn't get it. By not being transparent with the General Manager that I needed him to work with me, I didn't get his support. If you don't ask for what you need, how can you get it?

Do you remember the first presentation you ever did in business? Did your knees shake and your heart pound? When fear strikes, your body gets ready to fight, freeze or run away, in a similar way to your ancestors all those years ago in caveman times. Your brain works much the same way today except you don't need to fight or run away from a lion. You simply have a presentation to do! You need to stay so you can operate out of your comfort zone, collaborate through your differences and be resourceful when you do.

Fear can make you play small. You may have dreams, hopes and desires. You want things. Yet you continue to play small because you're afraid.

Fear is an emotional response to your safety being threatened. When you work with horses, you have to manage your physical safety. When you work in an office, you are unlikely to be physically harmed, but the fear of your emotional safety being threatened is real and strong too. Fear is a great source of information to indicate you are at the limit of your capabilities. For some people, speaking up about something you don't like is a perceived threat to your safety. What if everyone disagrees? What if you are misunderstood?

The key to mastering fear is to manage your safety or perceived safety. Find ways to feel safe, and the fear lessens. It requires significant trust in you and your capabilities too as well as the ability to ask for help when you reach your limits. Fear never goes away because the more you master it, the greater the challenges you are likely to take on! You are far more resourceful than you might think you are. There is nearly always a way out of some sort, either by asking for help or taking time out, and deciding whether or not you want to do something.

The future is unpredictable. How do you know how to handle it? You don't, and that's why it's important to hone your leadership skills, so that you can be resourceful in those moments of uncertainty instead of terrified.

The seven leadership skills in Part Three of this book are the antidote to fear. Fear is rife in business. The pressure to perform can be so intense that people live in fear of getting it wrong, losing their job, not being respected and so on. When you feel fear, it's a pointer that you are out of your comfort zone.

The more senior people become in business, the more deep-rooted fear is and the less you may realise when you are operating from fear. At the heart of fear is a lack of self-belief and self-confidence. That's why business leaders are not transforming business in the way it needs to be transformed. Fear holds them back. Clients demonstrate this when they work with horses. They are often terrified of leading a horse, in case they get it wrong. They judge themselves or are afraid their peers will judge them in the feedback.

The thing you fear the most is the thing you put your attention on and is the one thing you end up creating. I was terrified of not being respected in the Communications Partner role, and that is exactly what I created. Fear stopped me being powerful as a leader. I allowed fear to drive the decisions I made on what I said and did. It led to my failure in the role.

Let's imagine there is someone in the workplace that you find difficult to work with in some way. You are afraid of being in conflict with them, so you avoid having a conversation to air your differences. By avoiding conflict, you create it because misunderstandings develop due to a lack of communication. Notice where your attention is in business.

Are you focussing on what you want or the things you don't want?

Wherever your attention is, that is what you will create. Focus on what you do want, not on the things you fear. There will always be problems and challenges, and you don't need to fear them. When fear shows up, you lack courage and trust in your capabilities. By not respecting your ability and being attached to a specific outcome, your actions will be driven by fear rather than powerful leadership.

Fear is the number one inhibitor to success in business. People fear many things - getting things wrong, not being respected, not achieving, not being good enough, not being understood or listened to, being in conflict, not being in relationship, not getting people to do what you want them to do.

The seven skills in Part Three of this book are a foundation of powerful leadership. Each one of them is profound and has multiple layers. As soon as you think you've mastered them, you will discover new depths with each of them for you to stretch into. That's what leadership is: a continuous path of learning to inspire and influence.

Chapter 4

Building rapport

"Relationships are the foundation
of everything you do in business.
Take time to build your relationships
and especially nurture the ones that are difficult."

Jude Jennison

I approached Floozy tentatively. I was scared. I had no idea how to behave around a horse and no idea how she would respond. In my desire to get it right, I lacked confidence and self-belief. I was trying to be someone. I was trying to be who I thought she wanted me to be.

Floozy stood still, making no effort to engage with me. I felt rejected.

I wasn't a powerful leader in the interaction. I had more in me than that, but fear was getting in the way of me showing up fully. As a result, Floozy disengaged. She knew I wasn't congruent. She knew that beneath the fear, there was more.

Dave asked me what was happening. I explained that I was holding back because I was scared and didn't know how to be with her. He suggested I tell her. I went back up to Floozy. I stood beside her and said: "Be gentle with me. I'm terrified." As I owned my fear, it no longer had a hold on me. Floozy turned her head towards me, nuzzled my hand and walked with me.

By being honest, I had nothing to prove so I felt more confident because I was no longer afraid of being found out for being something I wasn't. The relationship was now built on congruence. She didn't mind me being afraid as long as I was honest about it. Fear is something horses recognise in themselves and others. As a prey animal, every time they run as a herd they are all frightened, and someone still has to lead. Floozy purely wanted me to be honest about it.

Many clients have a similar experience. They believe they need to meet the expectations of others, without knowing what those expectations are. As a result, fear gets in the way of congruent behaviour and causes a breakdown in the relationship. As soon as people own their fear, it reduces and creates the space for relationship to be built.

Saying hello

One of the first things we do when we work with the horses is say hello to them. Now there's nothing strange about that. You say hello to people all the time. The difference is that we do it in a way that connects the horses to us. It's about building rapport, beginning a relationship that sets the client up for success. We approach the horses in their environment and ask for their respect and trust. That's a big ask in the first few minutes of meeting them, so we meet them in a way they understand so they feel comfortable around us.

When horses greet each other, they put their noses out and breathe in and out together. They get a sense of each other's energy. Then they turn and walk away. It shows they don't feel threatened by each other.

As a prey animal, horses have their eyes on the side of their head. They are constantly on the alert for danger. They have almost 360-degree sight. The only place they can't see is immediately in front of them and immediately behind them. That's why when you approach them, they often turn their head so they can see you.

People usually approach a horse from the front and rub its nose. Most horses don't like that. A horse can't see directly in front of its nose so it will usually move its head away so it can see you. The nose is also a very sensitive part of a horse's body so touching it the first time you meet the horse is like going up to a stranger in the street and throwing your arms around them saying: "How lovely to meet you!" They are likely to stiffen and brush you off, wondering what on earth you want from them. That's the impact you have on a horse if you go straight to rub its nose when it doesn't know you.

In the same way as when you meet a person for the first time, the initial impression counts, as it does with a horse. If you behave like a predator, then horses (and people) may feel unsafe and will not want to be in relationship with you and will certainly not want to follow your lead. It's obvious, isn't it – yet how many times do we think of this when we meet people?

The best way to approach a horse to say hello is from the side. That way it can see you coming. Hold your hand out and allow the horse to sniff it. It's a bit like a handshake. You don't grab a person's hand when you meet; you both offer your hands, shake and withdraw your hands at the same time. It's the same with a horse, only hand to nose. You show them the back of your hand, allow their nose to come and sniff it, and then you move your hand away as the horse moves its nose away. This demonstrates that you are not a threat. Then you stroke the horse on the side of the neck, turn your back and walk away.

The reason you do this is to show that you are not a predator. Nothing about your behaviour can appear to be threatening if you want to build powerful relationships. Most people pat horses on the neck, but horses only pat each other in the wild to move each other around. They do stroke each other though. Think about it. Do you prefer to be slapped on the back or would you prefer a gentle stroke? Horses prefer to be stroked too although many of them have become accustomed to being patted, but if you watch them, you'll see that they don't soften when you do it. They disconnect rather than connect.

Walking away is the hardest thing for most people to do because they want to stay and hang around. When a predator goes in for the kill, it goes for the neck and stays. A predator will not give in until the horse is on the ground. By walking away, you show the horse that you are absolutely no threat to it. Usually, the horse will turn its head to watch you, then drop its head and soften. You've won it over.

If you say hello to a horse in a way that builds rapport and a strong relationship, you develop an opportunity for mutual respect, understanding and trust. When clients say hello to the horses in this way, they often notice the horses soften and become relaxed around them. It surprises them that these simple and quick interactions make such a big difference in the relationship. Imagine what it would be like to build all your relationships with people like that too.

Imagine you meet your new team for the first time. They don't know you, so they have some trepidation about who you are as a leader. They want to know if you'll respect and trust them. Will you be the leader they want you to be? They want to know that they are safe. If the first thing you do threatens the safety of the team, you will create a lack of trust. The team would be wary and reluctant to follow your lead. You might set yourself up for a lot of hard work regaining that trust and respect later. Helping people feel safe is crucial to building a solid relationship quickly.

How many times have you gone straight into a meeting or conference call without taking time to get everyone present and relaxed?

It only takes a few moments, and it's simple to do. If you spend time building rapport, you'll be rewarded tenfold by people who want to work with you rather than against you.

Do you make people feel safe when you meet them?

How might you build a better rapport with your team?

Relationships are the foundation of everything you do in business. Business is fundamentally about inspiring and influencing people to do great work together for the benefit of a greater good.

Whilst the human handshake is mere courtesy and business etiquette, the horse handshake is much more. It sets the tone for future interactions. It invites you to connect with the horse, to show you are not a threat, and to invite them to work with you. It's an invitation to you too, to connect, to leave behind your insecurities and fears, and to recognise that you are being met as a sentient being.

In my interaction with Floozy, I initially approached with the fear of not being who she wanted me to be, and

Floozy responded by not wanting to be in relationship with me. Why would she? I wasn't showing myself to be a capable leader in that moment. It was only when I was honest about how I felt that I could build a relationship that was congruent and honest. She was much more willing to engage with me on that basis. It's the same for people too.

Everyone has people in the team that they naturally work well with and others who think differently from you. It's easy to find yourself spending time with those people whose company you enjoy and less time with those people in your team that you find challenging. There is a reason why they are challenging, so take time to get to know them. Find ways to help them relax in your presence, and you'll find you start to relax in theirs too when you understand each other.

Chapter 5

Leading through uncertainty

"What do you say and do in those moments when you don't know what to say and do? You lead. That's all you can do."

Jude Jennison

The music was playing as Emma and I walked into the arena shortly after 6.30pm on Thursday 8th May 2014. The audience had paid to come and watch a demonstration of Leadership with Horses. It was our first live event, and it was a big deal for us. I had never worked with Emma or her horses before, and we had chosen to do it live in front of 100 people. No pressure!

I led Arqueiro, commonly known as Rchi (pronounced "Archie"). He is Emma's grey Lusitano and is a strong, powerful, playful gelding (a castrated male horse). Before we entered the arena, I'd wanted to connect with him and get grounded, but we were already running five minutes late, and sensing this, he dragged me into the arena. Being no match for his physical strength, I had little choice but to follow. Emma laughed and followed with her other horse Hermione (Hermi).

I wasn't as grounded as I would have liked, but I trusted I could recover. Meanwhile, Hermi was a rock. She's an 850kg part Clydesdale mare that Emma has had for 16 years, and they leaned into each other as they entered the arena. Not physically of course, but the relationship between them is solid, and Hermi provided a strength that Emma was able to feed off.

As we entered the arena, the soundman cut the music, and the crowd went silent. The anticipation was palpable. It was a professional live event, and people had paid to come and see us! Emma had asked me to kick off the evening. I felt the excitement of Rchi in my left hand as he mirrored the anticipation of the crowd and the pre-performance nerves that I was also carrying. I tried to get grounded while walking from one end of the arena towards the audience.

We walked the full length of the sixty-metre long arena in silence, and as we approached the audience, the tension built further. This was live theatre! We stopped in front of the audience, and I said: "Good evening, ladies and gentlemen." Before I could go any further, Rchi started to chew my headset microphone and tried to remove it from my head. No amount of planning prepares you for moments like these.

What to do? Without even thinking about it, I knew. I led instinctively. I knew what to do even though I didn't know what to do. I asked the soundman to cut my sound. Our horse handler was standing at the side of the arena, and I asked him to take Rchi. I managed to remove the microphone from Rchi's mouth and put it back on my head. The soundman instantly put my sound back on. Meanwhile, the audience were on the edge of their seats. They seemed more anxious than me at the way things were turning out. I felt them willing everything to be ok, similar to when you watch professional actors in a play. It was a reminder that people wanted us to do well. The crowd was behind us.

We had begun.

It wasn't the kickoff to the evening I'd planned and prepared, but we were live in front of a hundred people, and we needed to perform.

We needed to lead.

I'd planned a few words to kick things off, but these were gone from my head and no longer relevant. I spoke about how we never know what is going to happen and introduced the evening as an opportunity to observe or participate in leading through uncertainty. None of the words I spoke were planned. I don't know where they came from. I simply spoke to what was happening at that moment and used it to inform me of what to say to keep the evening going, without it turning into a major drama, and without looking like a bumbling fool.

I was completely relaxed about the whole process, leading instinctively and confidently. I trusted I could create something spontaneously that would serve the audience and the evening. That allowed me to be flexible and work intuitively. That's what the horses have trained me to do.

It was a perfect start to the evening. I was modelling leading through uncertainty and showing leadership as a place of vulnerability. It set the tone for the rest of the evening and allowed the participants to lead courageously out of their comfort zones in front of a live audience too.

Leading through uncertainty

Such is the magic of working with horses. You never know what is going to happen. When you lead a horse, it requires you to pay attention and work with it rather than against it.

That's also what it is like to lead people in business. No amount of planning and preparation prepares you for these moments. As business transforms faster than you can imagine, you are leading through uncertainty every day. How many times do you get to work and find everything works out exactly as you planned? Not many, I imagine.

Your ability to flex, to adapt to what is needed and to

lead is essential as a leader in the current business environment. When you've learned to do that with 600kg or more as your team member, you realise you can lead anyone in almost any situation.

When you lead a horse, you are leading through uncertainty. You cannot plan for every eventuality. Horses are authentic all of the time, and they will choose to play if they wish, regardless of what you might be doing. Be compelling in every moment, as the leadership changes in every moment.

It's the same with people. Your clients and teams will make decisions about your leadership based on every action or inaction, everything you say and do. People might be more polite than horses and stay around because they feel they should, but rest assured your leadership has an impact in every moment.

Mastering the art of leading through uncertainty is essential in today's global economy, where the speed of change is astonishing. If you try and stick to your original plan and are unable to flex, you'll get caught out.

How flexible are **you** *when leading through uncertainty?*

How do you lead?

As I handed over the lead rein with a horse on the end of it to a client, he looked at me terrified and said: "What am I supposed to do?" Some people even ask me: "How do I lead?"

My response to this is always: "I don't know. How do

you lead? I only know how I lead." I ask them to try. As the client stepped forward out of his comfort zone, he was vulnerable. This place of not knowing can be hard for most people, especially when their team is watching, poised to give feedback.

For those who've never led a horse before, they are faced with a huge animal and no knowledge or experience to use. It's a vulnerable place to be. It requires courage. Even people with horse experience feel vulnerable, which often surprises their peers. They may have led a horse before but not when others are providing feedback on their leadership skills. The desire to get it right raises expectations and increases the pressure.

Leadership isn't an "Insert letter A into B and get C" experience. Leadership is finding ways to inspire and influence others and navigate challenges in life and work. That requires more than knowledge. It requires sensing what's needed and an authentic approach where you show up fully. It requires the courage to try something new and different without knowing if it will work. It requires you to build relationships with others and collaborate with them. There are no right answers in leadership. You have to find your own way of leading, whether it is with a horse or a person.

Making an impact

Most people operate unconsciously most of the time. If people don't do what you need them to do, a good place to start is to understand your impact.

What impact do you have when you walk into a room?

When I ask clients that question, they usually don't know. Most people have never considered their impact. Some of my clients tell me they don't have one. I assure you that you do have an impact! When clients start to pay attention to the impact they have on different people in different situations, they are often surprised. You may have done intellectual forms of training that help you negotiate, manage projects and understand how people think. But how you show up, your presence and non-verbal communication also have a substantial impact on how you lead, inspire and influence others.

Are you getting what you want?

Are you inspiring and influencing in every situation?

Often you will know what you don't want. You don't like the way a meeting runs or the way someone interacts with you. The focus tends to be on the problem rather than the solution.

Often when clients lead a horse, if the horse stops and refuses to move, the client will turn back and face the horse, scratch their head and try to work out how to get the horse to move again. They are getting feedback on their impact in this moment. It's an opportunity to recalibrate and try something new. For those who are resilient and creative, they may find it easy to get going again. For others, they turn their back on the direction they were going and focus on the problem. The horse is now a problem rather than a team player. Relationship is instantly broken in that moment.

This is mirrored daily in the workplace too. That person you find challenging? You make them a problem, you see them as someone who gets in your way and sabotages your success. By focussing all your attention on the problem, you put your energy into trying to get them to do something differently. You exacerbate the problem by breaking the forward momentum and seeing that person as a problem.

Frustration can kick in easily at times like these, especially if you are under pressure. Instead, be curious about the needs of the other party, be clear about where you are heading and how you get there together, and the subtle shift in focus and energy creates a profoundly different result.

The same frustration that you have at work shows up when working with horses too. Some clients get frustrated more quickly than others. It's useful to know what your default response is to not getting the result you want.

Do you get frustrated or are you creative and resilient?

Most people consider themselves to be creative and resilient, and often the frustration they feel surprises them. When working with horses, we are more aware of our emotional responses, so it highlights what is happening at a deep level, enabling you to identify the emotions early on and use them powerfully in your leadership. Once you have done this with a horse, you can't unlearn it. It becomes a life skill that enables you to be more conscious of your impact in future.

Chapter 6

The comfort zone

"Leadership happens outside of the comfort zone.
At times, it's excruciatingly uncomfortable,
and at other times, it's effortless and easy."

Jude Jennison

In June 2014, my new gelding Tiffin arrived at the yard. He was the new member of the team who would replace Opus in the Leadership with Horses workshops, working alongside my mare Kalle.

Only four days after he arrived, we had a team booked in to do a workshop. I arrived at 8am to discover that Kalle was lame and needed veterinary attention. I called out the vet. The clients arrived at 9.30am and the vet arrived at 10am. I left the clients with my business partner Emma while I talked to the vet. She explained that she needed to sedate Kalle and perform surgery on the yard. We quickly agreed that Emma would hold Kalle while I led the clients.

I wasn't sure what to do as Tiffin was so new to me and had no experience of doing the work. My old gelding Opus was retired, and Kalle was undergoing surgery. I had a workshop to deliver and an under-performing team. On top of that, seeing my horse undergo emergency surgery was incredibly worrying for me. It was a lot to hold. I asked Opus if he would come out of retirement for one day and work with Tiffin as a handover. Opus was eager to be back in work. He puffed himself up and was fully prepared to boss Tiffin around the way he used to with Kalle (and sometimes still does when he has the energy).

Usually, clients begin the day by observing the horses loose in the arena. I couldn't do that as Kalle was having surgery next to the arena, and I didn't want to disturb her. Instead, I threw away the timeline, thought on my feet and decided to get the team of graduate leaders to lead each other blindfolded in silence around the arena. I explained to them what was happening and asked them to respect the fact that Kalle was under sedation. We needed to walk past her quietly as she was hardly aware of what was going on around her.

I also told them that I wanted to cry and go home, but

instead I was staying, and we would have a good day. They looked shocked. I was close to tears, and they expected me to be in charge and know what I was doing. I explained that this is leadership. My new horse had to work with clients four days after arriving at the yard, my old horse had come out of retirement, and my mare was being operated on only one metre away from the arena. No amount of planning and preparation prepares you for a day like this.

You are always being called on to raise your game, to lead through uncertainty, to say and do things in those moments when you don't know what to say and do! This was one of mine! When you know that you can lead through uncertainty, it gives enormous freedom to trust that you are fully resourceful and can navigate almost anything that life and work throw at you. This was proving to be another test for me. I felt vulnerable, scared and tearful, but no matter what, I was a leader, and I would lead transparently and with integrity. I modelled the power of vulnerability that day.

Despite everything, we had a great day. Opus allowed three people to lead him, and then he decided that Tiffin was such a natural at his new job that he could take a break. By lunchtime, Kalle was virtually breaking out of the stable wanting to be involved. She is a challenger, and she wanted this team to raise their game. She knew she was the horse for the job. We allowed her to engage with the team for a short time after lunch, and then Tiffin was on his own all afternoon. He was incredible. He simply behaved like a horse, cooperated, went with things and planted his feet if he didn't think they were leading powerfully. Brilliant! The new team member was a hit with the clients and a hit with me!

I was massively out of my comfort zone all day. I was working with a new horse, worried about Kalle and concerned that we were asking too much of Opus in his retirement. You need to stay in those awkward moments, dig deep, be transparent about what is happening, lean into others for support and ask for help. I asked the graduates to respect how difficult it was for the horses, and they showed enormous respect. I trusted that somehow we would navigate the day. There was no right or wrong way. I had to lead!

The comfort zone

Leadership happens out of the comfort zone. Your comfort zone consists of all the things you know how to do and feel comfortable doing. I imagine you can write, type, speak and eat. Most people can. You can most likely drive a car and find your way to work. Aspects of your job will be in your comfort zone. You can do it without thinking too much.

When you get to the edge of your comfort zone, it starts to get a little bit uncomfortable. It might be things you don't often do in your job that feel slightly uncomfortable. You know you can do them, but you're not sure if it's going to work or not. The edge of the comfort zone leads on to the learning zone.

Because the comfort zone feels comfortable, it's natural for many people to want to stay in it a lot of the time. Of course you want to be able to do some things without having to think about them, but if you remain in the comfort zone too long, you get stuck in it. If you never step out of your comfort zone, it will feel terrifying when you do. The more you practise stepping out of it, the more comfortable it becomes to have a stretch.

Where are you operating in the comfort zone?

How easy is it for you to step out of your comfort zone?

The learning zone

Surrounding the comfort zone is the learning zone. If you take a small step out of your comfort zone, you enter the learning zone, where you do something new or practise a new skill. For example, when you learn to drive, your driving instructor will help you develop your skills steadily, encourage you to increase your speed gradually and do more complicated manoeuvres. As you learn to drive, your comfort zone expands until you find yourself driving confidently without thinking about it. The more you practise being in the learning zone, the more your comfort zone expands and the more comfortable you will feel doing new things.

The more capacity you have to learn, the greater you are capable of doing great things. Leaders inhabit the learning zone the majority of the time. You're leading, making decisions, doing things you've never done before, saying things you've never said before, and thinking things you've never thought before. You get promotions and pay rises and develop your career by being in the learning zone.

Where are you in the learning zone?

Where might you stretch yourself further?

Children are excellent at operating from their learning zone. They pick themselves up quickly from mistakes and try again. As adults, we become less likely to do this. The fear of failure can cause you to hold back. The more you practise doing something new, the greater your chances of being resilient and robust under pressure. It also develops your creativity and flexibility, skills that are critical for building relationships, collaborating with others and leading business change.

Most people, when they work with horses, are operating out of their comfort zone. My role as the workshop leader is to help them find the learning zone so they identify their leadership strengths and learn to navigate the places where they get stuck, without getting to a place of overwhelm.

The danger zone

If you take a huge step out of your comfort zone, you could enter the danger zone. Perhaps doing a bungee jump, mountain climbing, doing a presentation or a public speech is in your danger zone?

For some clients, the thought of leading a horse is terrifying. They are at risk of entering the danger zone and being unresourceful. Those clients will recognise the feelings. They will most likely experience fear in different situations at work too, although they are probably used to shutting it down and pretending it is not present.

The danger zone is a place of overwhelm. It's where you go beyond vulnerability and fear into feeling terrified. If you become overwhelmed, you cease to make decisions effectively. If you've ever had a "rabbit in headlights" feeling, where you feel frozen to the spot, you've been in the danger zone. When people reach this place, they tend to retreat back into the comfort zone. If your heart is racing, you can be sure you are in the danger zone.

My role is to help those clients in overwhelm to manage

their fear and bring them back to a resourceful state. This happens surprisingly quickly. For these clients, the learning can be profound as they learn to manage their fear in other situations too. They learn not to shut the fear down, but to recognise it, find the wisdom in it and make conscious choices that move them forwards.

If people own their fear, the horses are soft with them and will provide a source of strength, just as other people will too. If you continue to push it down and ignore it, it gives off an incongruent message and the horses will mirror the fear by being more challenging and taking charge. This is similar to the workplace too. By being honest about fear, you can ask others for help, and colleagues are nearly always willing to provide it.

Everyone will enter the danger zone at times. That panicky feeling is useful information to remind you that you are not at your most resourceful in that state. If you spend too long in the danger zone, you may feel anxious, get panic attacks, feel work-related stress and anxiety and could end up on long-term sick leave.

If you find yourself stretching more and more in your work and you feel over-stretched constantly, you need to take time out to relax and recharge. When people go off sick with work-related stress, it's because they have felt as though they are constantly in the danger zone and have not felt able to take time out. Your adrenaline kicks in, your heart races, the palms of your hands may feel sweaty, and your legs or hands may shake. It's important to catch yourself if you feel like this every day. You will eventually hit burnout or work-related stress if you carry on.

Where are you in the danger zone?

What do you need to help you navigate this situation?

Find a way of getting support, take time out or do something to bring your heart rate back to normal. No career is worth burning out over. One person who was in the audience of a speech I gave recognised she was in the danger zone constantly and understood why she was exhausted. She emailed me later to tell me she had taken the following day off and felt much better. That self-awareness prevented her from burning out and saved her career.

Watch out for members of your team too. Often people will hide it differently. Some people will be open and honest about being stressed and in the danger zone. Others will stuff it down under the surface and try to maintain nothing is wrong. It's not cool to get stressed at work, and yet a substantial proportion of people are, primarily because they are operating so far out of their comfort zone on a long-term basis.

Everyone's comfort zone is different. Everyone's capacity to stretch out of it is different. There is no right or wrong, but it's interesting to notice what is true for you and where you are in the model in various situations.

Leading through change

In today's rapidly evolving business environments, innovation and collaboration are critical skills for leaders. The learning zone is the place of development and growth. If you fail to step out of your comfort zone, you'll fail to grow as a leader. Your career and the business will stagnate. Some people love to challenge themselves and step readily into the learning zone where others fear it, and it shows up as resistance.

Most businesses are undergoing substantial change. If you lead teams, you will experience change and have people in those teams who are in the comfort zone, the learning zone, and the danger zone. It is different for everyone. Some people embrace change and welcome it readily. They leave their comfort zone easily to step into the learning zone. For them, it breaks up the routine, livens things up and gives them new challenges in which to shine.

Some people love to challenge themselves to the extreme by being in the danger zone and creating learning from it. They find it exciting rather than scary and are motivated by it. Many others will avoid the danger zone at all costs.

For those who feel the pain and overwhelm of the danger zone, even a small step out of the comfort zone is massive for them. They resist change vehemently. Some will retreat within and resist quietly. If you've ever been asked to do a project or a piece of work that feels outside of your comfort zone, you may have dug in your heels and refused. It probably feels like the danger zone.

Nobody ever comes to work wanting to be awkward even though sometimes it appears as if they do. When people find situations too challenging and feel as though they have entered the danger zone, they are likely to resist change. If people don't like being in the learning zone, even one tiny step out of the comfort zone will feel like the danger zone.

Imagine you are asking a member of your team to do a piece of work. You think it's just a tiny stretch for them. You think it's an opportunity for them to develop. For them, it feels like a massive stretch. It's the danger zone. There is fear. This is a great time to be curious because if you're getting resistance, people are effectively trying to say: "It's too big a challenge for me, and I'm scared." Those people need help to navigate change and still feel safe.

One client who worked with the horses wanted to know what the process of leading a horse was before she picked up the lead rein. She found it virtually impossible to ask a horse to move without knowing how or being told the process. But there is no process for leading horses – or people! Instead, there is an opportunity to influence and inspire. This client's manager observed her being stuck and understood why she had met resistance from this person in the past. It was not because this team member was contrary. It was because she was afraid to leave her comfort zone to do something new without a process and the logical steps set out for her. She was terrified of change because it meant moving away from a known process into the unknown. Working with the horses helped her to understand this and practise building her confidence in doing new things.

It's important to explore how you can navigate change while reducing resistance as much as possible. People don't mean to be difficult. If they are resisting, there's a reason, and it's your job as a leader to get curious and look at how can you help them be in the learning zone.

Chapter 7

Teamwork

"Pay attention to the whole and
ask yourself: What's needed now?
Then go and do that."

Jude Jennison

I felt unnerved. I didn't like being in an arena with four loose horses charging around. I felt out of control. I said no. I was clear about my boundaries and this was a step too far for me out of the comfort zone. The other two people I was working with assured me it would be ok, and

I gave in, with significant trepidation. I didn't want to be the party pooper, and I trusted their capabilities, but I had major reservations.

The team decided to send the horses away to get their respect. The horses all charged around the arena and created a lot of energy. My fear increased. I felt unsafe, so I called a halt again. We were training as HorseDream Partners to gain a European accredited Equine Guided Leadership qualification. I was working with two people who were highly skilled with horses. I had gone from being scared of horses to being on a Train the Trainer programme within a few weeks.

Our task was to lead a horse over an obstacle course. There were four horses to choose from, and we could work with any or all of them, with or without lead ropes. The others were confident in their horsemanship skills. They decided that we would use all four horses and lead them all without lead reins over the course. I explained that I felt overwhelmed and needed to feel safer.

I did it confidently. I was willing to leave both the team and the arena if they refused because I needed to manage my safety. This wasn't working for me, and I was clear about what I wanted instead. I suggested that we work with two horses and have them on lead ropes instead of being loose. After some discussion, we agreed to work with all four horses on lead ropes. As there were only three of us in total, it meant someone had to lead two, and the others each had one.

We achieved the task in harmony. It was still ambitious

as there was only room for one horse at a time to navigate each obstacle. We worked out a way to do it by swapping horses over, with one person holding two horses while the other two people led their horses over the obstacle. It involved complex logic, working in harmony and sensing what we needed to do at any one moment, both individually and as a team.

After the initial conversation, we worked together effortlessly. We went over the obstacles in virtual silence, only speaking when we asked for or offered each other help. Each person in the team took responsibility for the team's success. We knew our roles, and we flexed between them as we recognised what we needed to do. We were completely in flow. As we reached the final goalpost, there was total silence and a deep connection.

This is the magic of working in a cohesive team. Few people have experienced the effortlessness that comes from cohesion.

3 Positions of Leadership

In the Leadership with Horses workshops, clients do a variety of different team exercises. We introduce a shared leadership model that horses use in the wild to work as a united team. Many of my clients have embraced and implemented the model into their business. The model is based on building relationships rather than a more traditional command and control style of leadership. The success of the team depends on every team member taking responsibility for leadership and changing their position within the team according to what they believe is needed.

The model is directly relevant to how a high-performing human team works. Many corporate teams I've worked with have identified weak spots in their teamwork and issues with their organisational culture. This has enabled them to explore how they enhance their teamwork and ability to drive results cohesively and in harmony.

The 3 positions of leadership model is adapted from an equine model developed by Klaus Ferdinand Hempfling. He observed that there are three different leadership roles in a herd of horses. Each member of the team is leading at different moments, and all are essential to the success of the team. We apply a similar model to how people work in business and clients perform team exercises to identify where they perform well in a team and where they get stuck.

1. Leading from the front - The alpha mare is the most dominant member of the herd and leads from the front. Her role is to set the pace, direction and destination. Since horses are a prey animal, they are on the alert for danger. Imagine a pack of wild dogs appears. The alpha mare will decide where the herd go, how they get there and how fast they go.

If the dogs are close by, she will set off at a gallop. If they are further away, she will set off at a walk. She will go as fast as is necessary to keep the herd safe. This way, the herd conserve their energy for when it is most needed. Many people in business are going at three hundred miles per hour constantly. That is exhausting, and more balance is essential to prevent burn-out and work-related stress.

In the workplace setting, the leader of the company and each team and department usually lead from the front. For example, the MD or CEO will set the strategy and vision for a company. A Project Manager defines clear goals and objectives for his project team. A leader of a team sets the vision and goals so everyone on the team has clear expectations.

If nobody takes the lead from the front or the vision and direction are not clear enough, the team gets diverted and disperses. This can ultimately cause conflict in the team and increase the workload as the team becomes ineffective. If you've ever sat in a meeting and listened to a discussion go round and round without a decision, you've experienced what happens when nobody is leading from the front.

One of the challenges of leading from the front is you can get so far ahead that you lose the team. It is essential to keep checking that all team members are coming with you and understand where they are going. A common mistake in organisations is to believe that the strategy and vision have been clearly communicated when they have not. If the team is not doing what you want them to do, the destination, pace and direction need to be clearer.

When leading from the front, the focus is in the direction you are heading. If you keep turning round and looking back, you create a stop/start behaviour in your team. It indicates doubt, a lack of self-belief and self-confidence. Leading from the front requires enormous trust in yourself and the team and a belief that people will execute the strategy you have set. Be purposeful, focused, committed and clear about where you are heading or the team may stall.

2. Leading from the side - the majority of the horses in a herd lead from the side and this is the least dominant position you can take. This is a coaching and democratic style of leadership. Every horse will ensure they work as one cohesive unit, with safety being threatened if one horse gets separated from the rest of the herd.

In a workplace setting, everyone needs to be able to do this role from time to time. That's why many organisations are implementing coaching for their managers. This style is useful for ensuring every team member stays on track and aligned with the vision and goals. It helps when people get distracted, perhaps by family or other external issues. It helps team members who lack the skills to do the role required. It also helps them develop their skills and understand the requirements, so they stay with the rest of the team.

If you have set a clear strategy and vision from the front and people still don't do what you need them to do, then it's a great idea to switch to leading from the side. Here you can be curious about what is not working, find out what support people need and make sure they have the skills and support to do the job and meet the goals and objectives set.

In human teams, it is common to blame or judge people who are misaligned in the team or not working fast enough. In a cohesive team, leadership is fluid. Each member of the team can lead the others at varying moments to ensure the team stays focused, moves together cohesively and collaborates effectively. If nobody leads from the side in a team, the team can feel as though they are being driven too hard, and their challenges and feelings don't matter.

One of the challenges of continually leading from the side is the vision can be less clear if there is too much focus on being democratic. Too much time is wasted trying to set goals collaboratively and keeping everyone aligned. I once worked for a manager who was so democratic that no decisions were ever made and we spent hours of excruciating debate about what to do and how to do it. If the direction is not clear, by switching to the front you can make a decision, communicate it and ensure you have the commitment of the team.

3. *Leading from behind* - this is the role of the alpha stallion and is the second most dominant role within the herd. The primary role of the alpha stallion is to exert pressure from behind to move forward. The alpha stallion works closely with the alpha mare to ensure the team follows her lead and moves forward in the direction and pace set by her. He uses as little or as much energy as necessary, moderating his energy accordingly. That might be as simple as him following the herd. The herd move forwards, respecting him and his very presence. If they don't or are not paying attention, he may bite them to get them to move more quickly.

The benefit of leading from behind is you can see everything that is happening in the team. You can steer to a small extent from behind by where you position yourself, but largely the team can choose its own way. For this reason, it is essential to have a clear understanding about the goal and the direction you are going.

In a workplace setting, this role is typically performed by Sales Operations, Finance Directors or Business Operations. Project Office Managers will lead from behind for their Project Manager. Leading from behind is useful when you are clear where you are heading and need an extra push towards the end of a project or deadline. It is useful to remind people of the commitments they have made.

Constant communication with the leader in the front is essential to ensure the pace and direction work for everyone and progress is being made. The leader at the back can advise the leader in front to slow down or speed up or modify the direction based on what is happening in the team. That's why it's useful to have a right-hand person when you lead from the front. If you have someone you trust who can let you know when things are going off track, you can modify the pace according to the needs of the team.

Leading from behind has a check and balance approach to it and requires as little pressure as possible to get a result. In human teams, the person leading from behind often exerts too much pressure too soon; for example, they may be coercive when people are doing the best they possibly can. If you regularly exert too much pressure from behind, it can have a nagging effect, and people will switch off. It is a good indication to lead from the front or the side.

When a horse leads from behind and nips another horse, it does so as assertive behaviour to get the other horse to pay attention. If you are leading from behind, raise your energy if you want to get someone to pay attention, but drop the energy again once you have the attention. Otherwise you risk being coercive and losing the respect of the team.

People often fall into the trap of raising their energy and keeping it raised. They don't lower it again because they assume that this level of energy is needed constantly. Horses are much more skilled in raising and lowering their energy according to what is needed at a specific moment, and we can learn so much from observing the way they lead from behind.

If nobody takes this role in a team, then the team can lose momentum and fall behind the leader in the front or go off track. One of the challenges of leading from behind is it can feel exhausting if the direction and pace are not already clear. If you find yourself getting exhausted, there is a good chance you are leading too much from behind, and more time is needed to clarify the vision, goals and objectives from the front.

What leadership position do you normally adopt?

Working in a high-performing team

As I stepped into the office at 10am, I felt the hum and excitement of success. This was a great team to be a part of. The cohesion, energy, togetherness, desire and drive were palpable. The office felt as if it were vibrating with excitement. I knew we would sign the deal. I had been invited to join a bid team to work on an outsourcing contract for a major bank. I had flown in to support a member of my team who was new. The bid team had been working together for several months, and we had a few more weeks to sign the deal. The team was working long hours and weekends, and the pressure was on.

As I walked through the office, I noticed everyone working together with the belief that this was a contract that was right, both for our company and for the client. We could not fail. Everyone in the team was focussed and committed. There was a clarity about what was expected from every person in the team, a desire to support each other, work through differences and make it happen. There was strong leadership that enabled this to happen.

It wasn't the first time I'd worked in a team like this. I was blessed in my 16-year long corporate career to work in quite a few high-performing teams – teams who came together with great leaders for short periods of time and didn't know each other, yet somehow managed to get off to a fast start and make things happen. I loved those moments.

I also led and was part of high-performing teams who had been in place for longer. The buzz of excitement had gone, but the drive, enthusiasm, commitment and teamwork were no less. These were teams that worked through their differences, came together in pursuit of a common goal, supported and challenged each other and made a difference. Trust and mutual respect enabled us to work through disagreements openly. It was fun, and it was challenging and frustrating at times too.

Everyone on the team was 100% committed to success. It meant they asked for help when they needed it, they openly discussed challenges and worked through them together, they helped each other out. They had courageous conversations, knowing that any disagreements were being ironed out for the greater good. There was flexibility and creativity that came from being in it together.

There were a few times when I worked in dysfunctional teams as well. They were difficult times, stressful, uncomfortable. There were differences of opinion, sometimes articulated and sometimes not, sometimes resolved and sometimes not. Individually, the people in these teams were some of the most talented people I've ever met. The knowledge, information and commitment were unsurpassed.

Somehow we didn't have the skills to relate to each other, to work through our differences. Leadership in these teams was missing, teamwork was disjointed, egos were in abundance, and it was painful. There was a lack of clarity, trust and respect; goals and objectives were misaligned, and judgment was in abundance. With the level of talent in those teams, it could and should have been different. While the individual talent was unquestionable, the teamwork and leadership was sorely lacking. In those moments, blame and judgment were rife because we lacked the skills to work in harmony.

Changing positions

Horses show us how to work in harmony and embrace our differences. They change position and roles if they believe the safety of the herd is in question. As a leader, you may find yourself operating from different positions according to the different situations and teams you are in. Your flexibility in moving from one position to another is critical to your agility as a leader.

For example, a Project Manager will lead from the front to set the goals and objectives. If he fails to do so, the team is likely to be unclear about what is expected of them, and the project will get off to a slow start, with chaos and confusion. Most project teams that lack clarity require more leadership from the front and will look to the Project Leader to provide the direction.

The same Project Manager will, at times, need to lead from the side with some members of the team. If someone in the team is new, or under-performing, they may need more guidance. A coaching style of leadership can be useful in these situations, where the leader works alongside the team member. Equally, the Project Manager may lead from the side with the whole team, when there are decisions to be made that need the whole team's input. He will need to step back into leading from the front once a decision is made, in order to make that decision clear and ensure everyone is aligned.

The Project Manager may need to step into leading from behind when a final push is needed on a project, for example, when a deadline is approaching. He may make it clear that the deadline is approaching and make it clear that it has to be met. At that point, he may identify certain members of the team who are falling behind. What many leaders do is exert pressure on those people and drive them harder. It's important to consider whether this is useful when there are two other positions that might obtain a better result. For example, if someone is falling behind a deadline, there is almost certainly a reason. If you exert pressure without understanding the reason, you create stress and frustration. You could try leading from the side instead, to understand what the issue is and find out how you can help that person navigate it.

Once you understand the subtle nuances of the different positions of leadership, it provides you with the agility to move from one to the other. You can even try this within the same meeting, depending on what is needed. Many of my clients have used this as a tool to help them navigate difficult situations. They ask themselves: "What is needed now?" and then change their position, to great effect.

Most people have a default style of leadership that they prefer. If you find yourself in a role that doesn't work for you, there is a high probability that you are required to lead primarily from a position that is not your default and not your natural style. It's useful to understand what your own default is and to practise operating from other positions so you can lead people in different situations and flex between the positions effortlessly.

For example, as a Business Operations Leader in my organisation I mostly led from behind, and my boss led from the front. He set the strategy for the team and communicated the direction and pace, making the goals and objectives clear. My role was to ensure everyone in the team delivered. Because I was leading from behind, I could see everything that was happening in every part of the team. If someone or something went off track, I would notice it first and communicate with my boss. We would decide what action was needed to bring the team back on track.

In order to have that conversation with my boss, I would step into leading from the front as I articulated clearly to him what the problem was, what I thought we needed to do and why. I was setting the new pace and direction. Once he agreed, he stepped back into leading from the front, communicated it to the team or team member, and I would step back into leading from behind. In this way, leadership was shared and allowed everyone to take responsibility for success.

Flexibility between the positions achieves the best result. It's important to feel what is needed in every moment for the team and step into it. Don't wait for permission. Some people focus so much on roles and make up rules about what they can and can't say and to whom. Leadership is about leading, inspiring and influencing people at all levels of the organisation as well as your clients. That means taking full permission to do what you believe is needed to lead and create success in any given moment.

When something is not flowing, consider which position you are in and reflect on which one you think might be more useful. For example, if the team is prevaricating and discussing at length, but no decision is being made, lead from the front, make a decision and set the direction. If someone is not doing what you need them to do, you might want to have a conversation to explore how they stay on track with the rest of the team. That is leading from the side. Alternatively, if you've been very clear about what you want and people don't do it, you might need a sudden push from behind.

Be careful not to do all the work though. Structure your team to cover all the positions and allow everyone to operate cohesively, knowing what their responsibilities are. This is about choosing the right style for the situation and people you are working with.

If you find a particular position harder than others to adopt, make sure you build a team around you who can take the different positions. Don't use it as an excuse for not stepping out of your comfort zone and trying a new position!

While there is a hierarchy of sorts, and everyone in the herd understands it, the responsibility for leadership is shared. No matter who is in the lead and setting the direction, other members of the team (herd) always have an opinion and move forwards as a single unit.

If one horse within a herd separates, it is likely to be eaten by the pack of wild dogs. For this reason, it is essential to work as one team, one unit to maintain their safety. Of course, in the workplace you're not likely to be eaten by wild dogs! But your project may go off track if you are not operating consistently as one unit. If any of the positions are missing, it is the role of everyone to notice and step into it as soon as you notice.

When working with horses, it quickly becomes apparent what your default leadership position is as well as the pitfalls. Many clients learn how to embody each leadership position effectively and often implement the model in their organisation.

PART THREE

7 Leadership Skills

In which I introduce the equine teams,
share my leadership successes and failures,
and explore seven foundation skills we can learn
from horses that are at the heart of
every interaction in business

Chapter 8

Meet the equine team

Early in the morning
My team greet me
With a soft nicker
Calm, gentle and nurturing
Powerful, majestic and imposing
They wander over to the gate
I gulp. I'm ready to raise my game

Jude Jennison

This book is only possible because my team of three horses have taught me so much about the subtle nuances of leadership. When I took on my first horse Kalle, I had no idea how to care for one. Some suggested that was crazy, but we all have to start somewhere. I put Kalle into a livery yard where other people looked after her for me. I wanted to do the sensible thing and learn from others because I knew so little about horses. I did learn a lot in the six months she was on that yard but mostly about how I didn't want to look after her.

I now rent my own land, with arena, stables and workshop facilities so that my horses are kept in an environment that works for me, them and our clients. I try to keep my horses as naturally as possible, with as much time out at grass throughout the year. The horses only come into their stables overnight between December and February each year, due to the mud. The rest of the time, they are free to graze as a mixed herd 24/7.

As a novice horse owner, I've not done the usual British Horse Society training, and my methods may appear unconventional to most horse owners. I've learned by listening to my horses. They know what they want. They have trained me to pay attention at a deep level, to a flick of an eye or an ear. I take the time to understand their wants and needs, and we decide between us how we do things, in a way that meets both our needs and desires. I don't care if it meets the rule book. I do care whether it meets their needs.

People and horses are communicating non-verbally with us all the time. We mostly tune it out. That's why we have conflict and grief in society. It's why horses go lame.

We sometimes have to get to a point of frustration before we can get people to listen. If you have someone in your team who is not co-operating, trust that there is a reason and be curious. My horses aren't always easy, but when they play up, there is *always* a reason. It's the job of a leader to pay attention, much more than we actually do.

The horses have certainly taught me to do that. I never use force with them. If they stop at the gate, I get curious about what is happening for them. That doesn't mean they always get their own way. It means I seek to understand them and negotiate. I have been misunderstood by others for being weak with my horses because I don't lead them with a strong hand. I invite them to follow and give them a long lead rein, so they have a choice. I always suggest to my clients that they lead with a smile in the lead rope, and that they do the same with people too. Leadership is an invitation to join you.

Many people are afraid of giving a horse an opinion. I understand that. They are, after all, spirited and physically stronger than us. As a result, most of the horsemanship manuals will tell you that you need to dominate a horse and be clear that you are the boss or else you are unsafe. I think that is the old style of command and control leadership that's still common with horses and people. We miss out on deeper levels of connection and understanding if we fail to move forward into a place of shared leadership and collaborative working. The same is true in business.

Instead, I teach my horses that having a loose lead rein

isn't their cue to rush on ahead without me. If they do, I stop, ask them to wait for me and work with me. This way, they learn to collaborate with me as much as I do with them. It's more challenging to lead like this, but this is leadership. The alternative is command and control. I choose to invite my horses to work in harmony with me. As a result of the relationship we have built, I can now lead two of my horses (Kalle and Opus) without a lead rein as we use the relationship to work together. Tiffin is still learning, and I trust that in time, he will have the same level of freedom too.

We can learn much from how horses lead each other and apply the same ways with people too. I'm lucky that I get to practise this on a daily basis! Each of my horses has had to learn that when I give them an opinion, that doesn't mean they get to call all the shots! I still have an opinion too. We work together with both of our opinions, equally. They soon learn this and recognise that I manage my boundaries and won't be pushed around, any more than I would push them around.

When I invite my clients to lead a horse with a long lead rope, it's the relationship and connection that brings the horse with them willingly. *That* is leadership. I don't believe that paying attention and inviting someone to come with you is a weakness. It is often more challenging than pushing and pulling someone into doing what you want them to do short-term, but it's rewarding to see the willingness to engage. I do wish I'd been able to listen and observe at such a fine level when I worked in a large corporation. Although I had a fantastic career and achieved some great things with my teams, I know I could be a much better leader now than I was then, thanks to the horses, and my deeper sense of listening.

Meet the horses

Allow me to introduce you to the three leaders who have been and continue to be a joy and delight to work with. They are my teachers, my guides, my challengers. They accept nothing less than my best leadership in every moment and ask me to raise my game on a daily basis. I'm honoured to have them in my life and delighted to share them with as many people as possible.

When I first decided to get a horse, I asked people for advice. Everyone told me to get a sensible cob. I come from the city of Nottingham, where a cob is a bread roll! I had no idea what a sensible cob was in horse terms. I was also told by everyone to get a gelding because they are easier. I duly asked around for a sensible gelding.

The fifteen-year-old daughter of my friend Paul suggested I look for a mare. When I asked why, she explained that you can connect more easily with a mare. I instantly knew that I would take on a mare because I wanted a horse I could connect with. My first horse was Kalle; she wasn't a sensible cob and she wasn't easy in the early days, but she certainly did connect! I have never met a horse before or since that connects in the way Kalle does. She looks deep into your eye and gives you her heart and soul. She only asks that you do the same in return. I was ready and willing.

Kalle

On Saturday 17ᵗʰ December 2011, Kalle came into my life. She is not a novice horse yet somehow she saw something in me and I in her that brought us together. Perhaps it was my willingness to connect at the same level that she does. Thankfully, her previous owner Julie also saw it and allowed me to take on her horse that she adored. Julie was forward-thinking enough to recognise that Kalle could have a different role in life from the originally planned riding and breeding one. She was also instrumental in making sure I didn't give up when things got challenging!

Born in April 2000, Kalle (original name Holme Park Krystal) is a 16.2 hands black Trakehner mare. Trakehners are a German warmblood that are half Arab and half thoroughbred and known for being spirited. Not a sensible cob then! Kalle was 12 years old when she came to me. She is strong, powerful, spirited and opinionated. She is also sweet, gentle and kind. When she gets scared, she runs first and thinks later (sometimes). She requires a powerful leader who connects deeply and builds a strong relationship with her. Once you've done that, she will do almost anything you ask of her.

Kalle teaches clients how to be in relationship in a way that enables both parties to have permission to be fully themselves. She is an incredible example of how to stand strongly in your power and connect deeply with such gentle sweetness. She has a massive range of leadership skills, is highly intuitive and knows exactly which buttons to press, so you get the maximum learning from her. She will head-butt those clients who don't show her respect and be incredibly sweet and gentle with those who are afraid. Many who work with her are moved to tears by the depth of connection.

I describe Kalle as raw horse because although she is well handled and willing, she is used to living in a herd and often responds as a horse would in the wild. Most of my leadership lessons have been from Kalle. She accepts nothing less than my highest leadership in every moment, whilst forgiving me of my mistakes with such grace. Many of the stories and learnings in this book are drawn from my experiences with Kalle.

Opus

On Monday 2nd July 2012, Opus joined the team. Opus (original name Steel Grip) was born in New Zealand in October 1988 and is a 16.1 hands high dark brown thoroughbred gelding. He was bred as a racehorse, coming from a line that goes back to Northern Dancer, one of the most influential racehorses of all time. Opus was injured when he was two years old, so he never made the track. Instead, Opus was re-trained as a riding horse and competed with his owner Laura in almost everything you can at an amateur level. He has lived in New Zealand, Australia, Bahrain and the UK, so he's well travelled and confident in his own skin. Nothing phases him. He came to me on loan in his retirement because he had become stiff when ridden.

I describe Opus as the MD of the company. Horses don't come much more experienced than him. Nothing gets passed unless it has his approval, and if you want him to move his feet, you better have something good and you better be compelling in how you ask it of him! It is easy to enter into a power struggle with Opus because he never lets go of his opinion. You always have to work with him on it. He senses what you need to learn the most and raises the bar just enough to stretch you into it.

I found Opus challenging to connect with at first. Many clients did too. He doesn't need to be in relationship with you as much as you do with him, so he can take you or leave you. For the two years he did the Leadership with Horses workshops, he particularly enjoyed giving senior leaders and executives a hard time. He knew that they were experienced, and he expected them to be compelling leaders. He would not accept command and control. There is no controlling Opus. By contrast, with graduates and inexperienced leaders, Opus was gentle and sweet and gave people such incredible confidence in their leadership. He knew which buttons to press so you got the maximum learning. He was a joy to watch at work.

Although I loved him dearly, it was sixteen months before we had a breakthrough. That moment came in November 2013 when I stood in the field with the horses, and Opus unexpectedly gave me a back massage for twenty minutes. He had never done anything like this before.

It was a sunny day, with frost on the ground, and the horses were standing, resting in the winter sunshine. I went up to each and checked them over as usual, not wanting to disturb them from their peacefulness. I stood still with them for a few minutes, enjoying being with them and watching their breath in the frosty air, blowing in and out gently. As I stood there, content in their presence, I felt a sense of joy in the life I had created for myself. As I stood enjoying the moment, Opus nudged me with his nose. In the past, he had done this to push me away. This time he turned me round gently until I had my back to him. I was curious. This was unexpected behaviour from Opus.

It felt different, so I allowed him to move me to where he wanted me. He put his nose in the middle of my back, and I felt pain shoot up my back. He gently nuzzled it with his mouth and chased the pain round my back for a full twenty minutes. I stood, tears rolling down my face. How did he know? And what a generous thing to do. Meanwhile, Kalle stood next to him, pulling faces. It was as if she was telling him what to do and how to do it. Out of the corner of my eye, I watched her flicking her eyes and ears at Opus, and he would respond by moving where he was massaging me.

That was the moment I learned to communicate with the horses too. Since then, we've been deeply connected, and I understand him and his needs more than I ever did before. I don't confess to be an animal communicator, but I often sense their needs. It's one of the reasons why I don't like to be on a big yard because I feel the pain of horses and sense the unmet needs. I believe I get it wrong more than I get it right, but I learned in this moment to pay attention at a deeper level. We can learn to do this in business too, and it's one of many key areas of learning for people in our workshops.

Somehow, Opus and I opened the channel of relationship at a deeper level. This moment with him was certainly surprising. Whilst he is a gentle horse, he had previously never shown a soft, nurturing side in this way before. Perhaps he recognised that I was open to learning something new. His biggest lesson is his strong, masculine presence. How do you lead powerful, opinionated people by matching them in strength and power without getting into a power struggle? And how do you stay soft and gentle with such people (or horses) too? This is what he teaches us.

We are on and off the knife edge of assertiveness every minute of every day. One degree to one side and you can become slightly passive, giving in or going along with someone else's opinion. One degree the other way and you enter coercive behaviour where you are in control in a command and control style of management. Neither of these are leadership yet we all do both of these when we get to the limits of our leadership capability. Some of the stories in this book demonstrate that. Opus, meanwhile, demonstrates it on a daily basis. He is a wise old soul who

I love dearly.

In March 2014, Opus retired from the Leadership with Horses work as he no longer wanted to work, but he continues to play an important supporting role in the background for both me and clients. When Kalle and Tiffin are working, I bring Opus into his stable, and he has a ringside view of the proceedings. He lets out a big sigh or snort every time a client lands a powerful learning, and he chunters or kicks the stable door if he thinks I've missed something important!

Opus is very clear. On one occasion, he nearly broke down the stable door to come out of retirement to work with a particular client who was working on an issue she had with her MD. Opus gave her the learning she needed, and ten minutes later, he was back in his stable, happily munching his hay, and leaving the rest of the work to Kalle and Tiffin!

Opus continues to enjoy life, despite ageing gracefully. He recently overtook Tiffin at a gallop, and when Tiffin tried to match his speed, Opus went up another gear. He showed the young boy what he is capable of. He is after all the great-grandson of a famous racehorse!

Tiffin

Tiffin (original name Tippin' Around) is a 14-year-old Irish thoroughbred. Standing at 16.3 hands high, he is the tallest of the herd. He was born in Ireland as a racehorse in April 2001, and he has done team chasing and hunting. He was never placed higher than fourth in racing and when you watch him gallop round the field, it's obvious why! He's not the most gainly racehorse and with a name like Tippin' Around, what can you expect? At twice his age, Opus will overtake Tiffin at a gallop with ease.

Tiffin has been ridden hard and looks older than his years. With each week he spends with us, he looks younger as he relaxes more and more into his new life and realises he does not have to be ridden. I think at some point he has taken a tumble onto his face because it is misshapen.

Tiffin joined the team in June 2014 when Opus retired from the work. For two months, he was a dream to handle. He was so much easier than either Kalle or Opus, and I was delighted to have such a gentle horse on the team.

Whilst Tiffin would spook more than Opus, he would quickly regain his composure and listen to me. As he relaxed into his new environment and his new role as an equine leader, he became more opinionated. Opus handed over the role of alpha stallion, and like an unskilled leader in a new job, Tiffin threw his weight around, pushing Kalle and Opus around and trying to do the same with me. He became aggressive for a while, trying to chase me out of the field.

One day, Tiffin rushed at me with his head and neck flat in line with his back, charging like a stallion towards me. I checked my escape route over the fence, but I wanted to try and stop him first. I stood my ground and sent all my energy towards him, yelling at him as loud as I possibly could to stop. He pulled up three metres away from me, dropped his head, turned and walked away. Phew! I had gained his respect, although I was very close to leaping through the fence for safety. Since then he has been sweet and gentle as he realises I'm allowed an opinion too!

A few months later, Tiffin started to recall some of the trauma of his racing days. He went through a period where anything I did that reminded him of racing would send him into a blind panic, and he was completely unreachable in those moments. This included things like grooming, putting a fleece on his back and tying him up briefly (and loosely) on the yard. He reared up, his eyes were wild with fear, and he snorted and danced around.

Tiffin now recognises that I am seeking to understand him, and we are working closely together to build the levels of trust. He is learning that he can have an opinion without being a bully and is encouraged to express himself gently whilst respecting that we all have opinions too. Meanwhile, he does great work with clients. He has taken over from Opus in requiring clients to be strong and compelling before he pays attention. He also has a softer healing side, often putting his nose on parts of the body where people have pain.

Tiffin calls us forth into our leadership, and he heals the pain that gets in the way of being your best leader. I'm excited to see how he progresses.

Other horses

I have had the privilege of working with a number of other horses in my work, including riding horses from Warwickshire College, retired racehorses from Moorcroft Stables and some ponies in Devon. Every one of them has willingly shared their wisdom and teaching and helped me grow in confidence around horses that I don't know.

Hermi and Rchi

Hermi and Rchi, who have been mentioned already, are owned by Emma Taylor, my business partner. They are our regular co-leaders when we run Leadership with Horses Live Events and workshops. Hermi brings power, timeless wisdom and grounded energy, whilst Rchi brings play and youthful exuberance, and much more. They are a powerful combination!

The Horse Trust

Emma and I have been privileged to work with some of the horses at The Horse Trust – a charity that provides retirement care for horses from the police force and military. I was particularly fond of Aurora, a former riding horse of the Queen, and Sam Slick, a thoroughbred from the Household Cavalry Regiment of the British Army. Both of them had massive wisdom to share with us and our clients.

Chapter 9

Courage

How do I lead
Through the murky terrain?
My soul is alive
My heart full of love
I falter and fall
I'm willing to fail
Yet I <u>want</u> to succeed
With Kalle, March 2012, inspired by Okokon Udo

As Kalle's front legs came back down onto the ground, she threw her head up and span round me on the lead rein, snorting and terrified. I mirrored her fear, feeling out of my depth, not knowing what to do. My legs were shaking; I was overwhelmed and felt unresourceful. I looked around for help, but there was nobody in sight or earshot.

I was leading Kalle back to the field from her stable. As we walked through the gate, she sniffed the electric fence, giving us both an electric shock. Kalle reared up in front of me and ran round me in a circle as I hung onto her lead rein.

As a novice horse owner, I was terrified. My safety was severely in question. When a horse rears up, and you are hanging onto the end of the lead rein, you are vulnerable. My fear of horses began when two horses reared up in front of me in a field. In the split second as Kalle reared up, the old trauma was reinstated, my heart was pounding, and I had no idea what to do.

Vulnerable. In danger.

In an instant, my survival instincts kicked in. When there is nobody else to help, you find a way to dig deep. These moments call for leadership. The previous day I had read about a natural horseman called Klaus Ferdinand Hempfling. He would allow his stallions to rear up and let them burn off steam as long as they did it out of his face, so he remained safe!

It was the only thing I knew to do. I could be seriously injured with 700kg of snorting bouncing horse on the end of a lead rein and no ability to manage it. Drawing on what I had read about Hempfling and the way he worked with wild stallions, I decided to send Kalle away to create safety for both of us. We were in a small paddock so I realised I could invite her in again, once we had both calmed down. Terrified at how she was snorting and charging about me, I unclipped her lead rein and sent her away. My heart rate instantly dropped a little although my legs continued to shake.

As with people, control over a horse is counter-productive, especially if you are forcing the horse to remain in what it sees as a danger zone. By sending Kalle away, I showed respect for her survival instinct and allowed her to regain her safety and self-control. As she rushed around me in the small paddock, I worked with her energy, so she could burn off excess energy and fear. When she started to slow down, I raised my energy to keep her moving, so I was influencing the position of her feet and the speed she was going. In doing so, she was paying attention to me, and we created mutual respect. Once you have created mutual respect, the horse comes in to your side because it trusts you to act appropriately to keep it safe.

To make matters worse, people on the yard came out and started yelling instructions to me across the paddock. Suddenly my vulnerability was of a different kind. My physical safety was handled, but both my mental safety and emotional safety were now in question. I was scared I was being judged for what I was doing because I knew I had a different way of working with my horse to everyone else on the yard. They didn't approve of my gentle approach. They mistook it for being weak. They had never seen anyone send a horse away like this before and didn't understand the value of it. It was impossible to tune them out and focus on my relationship with Kalle.

I had done this exercise as part of my training and had practised it a couple of times with Kalle in an arena, but I'd never done it under such severe pressure before. It took her longer than usual to calm down and regain an attitude of respect. At last I invited her to return to me. She came nervously, and I clipped the lead rein back onto her head collar.

Whilst Kalle appeared to trust me, I was not yet back in my comfort zone. I felt judged and still doubted my ability to keep both of us safe. The judgment of others kept me from trusting myself, and my legs continued to shake uncontrollably. Of course, Kalle sensed this and became agitated again as soon as she was back on the lead rein and by my side. I opened the second electric gate into her field and managed to get her in and turn her loose. I felt shaken and close to tears. Not for the first or the last time, I longed for support and experience.

I went back to the yard, and people said that Kalle was naughty, and I should have slapped her. I heard similar comments repeatedly in the following weeks. Whereas I was respecting Kalle in her moment of fear and vulnerability, the people on the yard did not afford me the same respect. They tried to control me by telling me what to do and being exasperated when I didn't do it. I felt as though I was constantly in the danger zone of self-doubt and vulnerability.

Vulnerable and scared: the two often go hand in hand. I was seriously out of my comfort zone. I felt vulnerable because my safety and reputation were threatened. I didn't trust myself and wasn't respected by others. In retrospect, I wasn't giving myself enough credit: in this particular moment, Kalle was scared and hard to handle, but would have been for many an experienced horse person.

I handled it to the best of my abilities. Somehow I remained resourceful. I trusted my instincts and followed natural horsemanship ways I'd read in books in order to keep us both safe. The course of action was clear in the moment, and I took it.

On the other hand, I let self-doubt overwhelm me because I felt unsupported. I questioned my abilities. I worried I was out of my depth with a strong, powerful, scared horse, and I was putting myself in a precarious position. I was afraid of being hurt again. I was well aware that horses are dangerous beasts if you don't know what you are doing, and I certainly felt as though I didn't.

In the first six months of caring for Kalle, I frequently questioned whether I should continue. Even as I considered giving it all up, I knew I was doing the work I was born to do. It felt effortless when Kalle and I worked with clients; Kalle was brilliant, and feedback was incredible. I dug deep and carried on. I looked for support – the right kind of support – and I found a way to make it work.

At the time, I never considered myself to be courageous. I felt vulnerable, scared and an incompetent wimp!

Vulnerability and fear

Vulnerability. It's uncomfortable. Most people avoid it at all costs.

It's a vulnerable place to be leading a horse when you have no idea what you are doing and how she will react.

It's a vulnerable place to be standing on the edge of a cliff on a windy day. Your safety is threatened. There is a risk that the wind will whip you off, and you'll fall over the edge.

It's a vulnerable place to be sitting in a job interview wondering if you can explain who you are and what you do. You need to stay in those moments of vulnerability. Your physical safety is not threatened yet the fear can kick in and feel the same as it does when you stand on the edge of a cliff.

Vulnerability, fear and courage go hand in hand. When you find yourself in a vulnerable place, your survival instincts kick in to keep you safe. That's what fear does. There is a need to weigh the balance between risk and reward. If the reward for being courageous is higher than the risk, it's a good time to stay. That balance is different for everyone, even when faced with the same situation. It is personal. For some people, doing a bungee jump gives them a sense of achievement, and the high is worth the risk and the fear. For others, the perceived risk is far too great, and they have no desire to do it. For some, something as simple as driving to work a different route feels risky. Recognise that risk is different for everyone.

As a leader, you have choices to make.

Is this a moment to step back from the vulnerability and fear, or to dig deep for courage and keep going?

In the first six months of owning a horse, the risks felt enormous. I kept digging deep and finding the courage to continue because I knew the work created incredible results for my clients. It's the hardest thing I've ever had to do. The risk and vulnerability were worth the challenge and emotional pain of achieving the results. I was doing something bigger than myself. Having goals and desires in service of others in the world enabled me to dig deep and be more courageous.

We work in a global economy where things are changing faster than ever before. Your ancestors were probably vulnerable much less often. Things were more defined and more predictable. When they were vulnerable, it was a matter of life and death. In the industrial age, people followed a process. Perhaps you do today in your business, but it's not enough; in a global fast-changing world of work, you need more than processes. You need to inspire and influence clients and teams without having a process for it. You need to lead. It makes you vulnerable and requires courage.

Every time I lead a horse, I feel vulnerable. I am aware

of my physical safety and make it a priority. If it is threatened, I turn the horse loose and send it away. Often my physical safety is not threatened, although I might feel as though it is. It is mostly mind over matter. Sometimes you have to dig deep to find your inner strength and courage.

There is a misconception that being vulnerable is a weakness. We focus so much on "knowing stuff". Knowledge is power, and information is king, but you can't know everything. You will never know everything. There is too much to know! The days of knowing the basics, progressing to the next level and building on what you know, so the person at the top knows everything, are gone. If they ever existed at all!

That's why leadership is increasingly important in business. Every day you go to work, you are vulnerable. Leadership and courage are your allies. If you never feel vulnerable, you're probably not leading to the best of your capabilities.

*Where do **you** feel vulnerable?*

Where do you hold back because it's uncomfortable?

Don't hold back. Dare to dive in. Dare to live. Dare to show up fully. Leadership is about being courageous in every moment of every day.

What is courage?

Courage is the ability to find the confidence to step out of your comfort zone and try something new without being reckless or under-prepared.

It takes courage to be a leader in business in the 21st century. With the current complex realities of business and a highly competitive global marketplace, you need to have a greater capacity to leave your comfort zone than ever before. When you forego the safety of what is familiar and enter the unknown, you may feel vulnerable, but you open up to creativity, innovation and transformation.

Courageous leaders need a strong sense of self-belief to enable them to be more creative, innovative and effective in transforming people, business and society. Never before has this been so essential. Business and society depend on your ability to develop a culture of courageous leadership.

When I overcame my fear of horses, people told me I was courageous to leave my well-paid corporate job, set up my own business in the middle of a recession, with horses I'd previously been afraid of and had no experience of looking after. At the time, I didn't consider it that way. Perhaps I was naïve, I don't know. I simply felt aligned, and it felt right, obvious and easy.

Since then I've overcome enormous challenges, both in running a business and looking after horses. I've needed to dig deep to stay and continue to do what I do. Telling myself that I was courageous helped me do what I needed to do. Every time I considered giving up, I knew the work I was doing mattered. I needed to get over my insecurities and fears to carry on providing the service I provide to clients. Because I know it is needed.

It's important to have a goal bigger than yourself. I'm not working purely to earn a living. I do the work I do because I want people to live and work in harmony with each other. We are rarely trained to work in harmony, and I want to change that. I find the courage to overcome challenges because I'm doing it for the sake of creating more harmony in work and life, for making a difference in business. If I get stuck in fear, I remind myself why I do what I do. If I can't find the courage to do it for myself, I can nearly always find it for the sake of others.

Congruent action

Courage feels different to everyone. It's a subjective, felt experience. Courage can feel terrifying, or it can feel effortless and flowing, or it can feel anything in between the two. What some people believe is courageous is natural and organic to others.

When I set up my business in 2011, I asked 30 people to describe me in three words, any three words of their choice. More than half of them said I was courageous. Really? I'd never considered myself to be courageous. I noticed where I got scared a lot and wimped out when it was difficult. For those looking on, the willingness to embrace vulnerability and step out of my comfort zone was courageous. Most of the time when I demonstrate courage, I'm doing what feels right, even if it feels uncomfortable. It's congruent action where the action is based on what feels right emotionally as well as intellectually. That's why it is usually the obvious option, even if it's not the easiest.

What makes someone enter a burning building and rescue someone they don't know? Courage. Why does someone take the courageous option and act in the way they do? They are willing to take a risk because they know they could potentially save a life. If you're not stretching into courage, you probably need to have more exciting goals and objectives. Find the passion that helps you come alive.

Here are some of the feelings I have experienced through courage:

1. Alive with excitement - Whenever my business partner and I do a live event with horses, we feel alive. It is exciting. We invite members of the audience to lead the horses. We never know what will show up as we don't know who is in the audience and what they will do. We've had to call a halt when someone was dragging a horse, and stop a horse from falling over because it was bored and fell asleep. We've had a whole lot in between too. It is courageous to collaborate with participants like this in front of a live audience, and it's fun too.

We trust that we can deal with whatever shows up and create from the possibilities. You know you are in the learning zone when you feel alive with excitement. You push aside risks and fear. There is fun to be had, and any obstacles can be overcome. I like this kind of courage a lot!

2. Effortless and flowing - When I was 19 years old, the French girl who I lived with in Grenoble asked me to be a skiing instructor for five-year-olds. I agreed even though I'd never been on skis before. I was willing to step in. Was that naivety or was it courage? I'm not sure, but it felt effortless and flowing. In these moments, it often doesn't feel like the courageous option. If it feels effortless and flowing, you are in the learning zone and are confident about being so.

Most children are confident in the learning zone and do so with effortless ease. If you've ever watched five-year-old children on the ski slopes, they are fearless. They whoosh down the mountain without thinking about it. Rest assured they are operating from the learning zone. They embrace new experiences and are courageous in doing so.

Adults need to dig deeper in their courage to make the learning zone be effortless and flowing, but the more you practise being in the learning zone, the more comfortable it becomes.

3. Uncomfortable - When I asked my boss if I could have a voluntary redundancy, everyone said I was courageous to give up my job and start a new business in the middle of a recession. I hadn't considered it as being a courageous option. Yes, it felt uncomfortable stepping out into the unknown, but the pain of staying in a career I no longer loved felt more uncomfortable.

It feels uncomfortable publishing my first book. What if nobody buys it? What if you the reader think it's a waste of effort? It takes courage to do it and work with the discomfort. This is the kind of courage it's easy to wimp out of. It's easy to play safe and stick with the status quo. Courage helps you break free and do the things you want to do.

4. Terrifying and crazy - I regularly considered my sanity in the early days of running my business and working with horses. I wondered if I should give up. It felt crazy to continue when I was so far out of my depth. I realised if I wanted to continue with the work, I needed to get the right kind of support. It spurred me on to ask for help and be clear about what I needed in order to feel supported. I knew I was courageous. When you have to dig so deep to keep going, you know you are on the brink of the danger zone, and the willingness to continue and persevere is a courageous act.

Courage is specific to you. It doesn't look or feel a particular way. These are examples of where I have felt courageous or where others have deemed me to be courageous. Courage is subjective. I have a friend who is happiest when she is doing crazy things like a bungee jump or extreme sports. People say she is courageous. For her, it's the oxygen she needs to feel alive. For others, changing job can feel a big stretch. Whilst most people would not consider it to be courageous, it might be for someone who likes a routine.

Courage is the authentic option. Courage is saying what you want to say and doing what you want to do. It means having those courageous conversations, being willing to work through the consequences and handle the impact. If you find yourself holding back, you are hiding behind a mask.

When children are born, they are authentic, open and honest. As you grow up, you learn to conform to what you believe is expected of you. You wear masks that keep you safe. Your masks stop others from seeing you deeply, break connection and prevent you from being rejected. They help you fit in and conform to what you believe others want of you in any given moment.

To lift the mask is an act of courage. When you do, people see congruent behaviour. They have the chance to see the real you. That can be vulnerable. Both the fear of rejection and not being good enough, or the fear of being too good and standing out, can prevent you from allowing yourself to be truly seen by others. The authentic you is much more compelling than any mask you may wear.

What mask are you hiding behind?

Change and courage

Change and courage go hand in hand.

Business requires every ounce of courage you have, and then a bit more. It takes courage to make people redundant. You probably don't want to have those conversations, but they may be needed for the sake of the business long-term. It takes courage to tell people in your team they are not performing at the level you want them to perform. Those conversations are needed to help guide people to perform at their best in line with the organisation's objectives.

It takes courage to implement new projects and have bold conversations with clients. It takes courage to make decisions on a daily basis, knowing the impact of them is wide-reaching. Leadership happens out of the comfort zone. It requires you to go to places you've never gone to before and do things you've never done before. That requires courage and practice.

Olympic athletes don't turn up on the day and hope to get a gold medal. So too, leaders can't expect to lead and inspire without regularly practising. If you want to be the best leader you can be, you need to fine-tune your leadership to develop your capabilities and skills, similar to an Olympic athlete. Every day you have the opportunity to lead, inspire and influence. It requires courage to stay when it's uncomfortable and challenging. You hope what you are doing matters and makes a difference. If it doesn't matter or make a difference, then for goodness' sake have the courage to stop wasting your time and energy on it and do something else instead!

Changing your job is an act of courage. You may have all the skills and experience on paper; the interview may go well; you may get a feel for the new company and the job. It's only when you change and start doing the new job that you know if it was a good move or not. That takes courage. You weigh up the risks and are willing to try.

Many people aren't. Many people stay in the same job or company, too afraid to make the move. What if it doesn't work out? What then? You are resourceful and can work it out.

It's more painful to hold yourself back and not get the result you want than it is to go all out and not get it. At least you know you've tried your best. If you hold yourself back, you may wish you'd gone full out.

Where are **you** *holding back from being courageous?*

Missed opportunities

When courage is lacking, opportunities for innovation, creativity and joy are missed.

I recently walked Opus out of the yard and down the drive towards the main road. I'd never done it before. I was too scared. I never realised I was afraid until Christmas Eve 2014 when Opus stood at the gate looking longingly down the drive. I opened the gate and led him through it. I felt my heart rate increase slightly, then I found my courage, relaxed and soon enjoyed myself as I realised how happy and confident Opus was.

If you had asked me previously, I would have said I didn't have time to do it or Opus wasn't bothered. On Christmas Eve 2014, I found the courage, opened the gate and off we went. We didn't go far, only 10 minutes down the drive and back, but it was a moment of connection, being together, and it brought me tears of joy. I wondered why I'd taken so long to do it. In hindsight it's not a big deal to walk a horse out of a gate and down a drive. What's the fuss about? I went through all my excuses, but the bottom line is I lacked the courage to do it before because it was new. I hadn't realised it before, so I'd never given it a thought. Now we do it daily; it's a moment of connection for both of us, and something he loves to do in his old age.

What experiences are you missing out on because you lack courage?

All of us lack courage at times. It shows up in the conversations you want to have but don't, the missed opportunities because you are not sure if they are right, so you stop yourself from trying. What seems courageous before you do it often seems easy afterwards, and you wonder why you didn't do it before. The stories you make up about how difficult something is often don't turn out to be true once you are in the moment.

You lack courage if you stop yourself from changing your job or setting up a new business when you've had a great idea. No doubt you have all the perfect excuses. You convince yourself why you should stay in your current job. Your negative inner voice takes charge. It tells you that you need the money to pay the bills, it's too risky, the new job/business might not be any better and so on. The real reason you don't do it? You lack courage. It sounds harsh, but it's true. It's ok. Go easy on yourself because courage takes courage! And we all have our limits.

I've lost track of how many times in this last week I've failed to be courageous. I failed to have conversations I wanted to have because they felt difficult. I wasn't sure how to articulate what I wanted to say, so I put it off until later. I failed to walk Kalle or Tiffin out of the gate because I'm too scared they might panic, and I won't be able to handle them. I didn't ask others for help because I didn't want to take up their time. I tell myself I don't want to lead Kalle or Tiffin out of the gate, but that's not strictly true. I would love to do it. Does that sound like courage? Definitely not! If you've ever held back in a meeting, wanting to speak up but remaining quiet, you lacked courage in that moment.

Courage is a work in progress. It takes practice on a daily basis. Sometimes the little things require courage so we can experience those moments of pure joy, as I did when I led Opus. These things are easy to wimp out of. It doesn't matter if I take Opus or not, except the shared joy and connection was magical and worth the minor stretch.

The more courageous you are, the more you develop your capacity for courage in the future. Children don't think the learning zone is scary because they operate from it daily. It doesn't feel courageous because they are used to not knowing how to do things. Look at what children do. Many children are bold and fearless.

When courage is missing on an individual level, you will find yourself stagnating in your comfort zone. You only do the things you know how to do. Learning and growth stop.

Identify what stops you; notice where your focus is. If you focus on what might happen if it doesn't turn out as you want it to, then you will hold yourself back from being courageous. Children focus on trying and are not attached to the outcome. They see the learning zone as a place of play and trial and error. Adults are more likely to look for the risks. You stop yourself from skiing in case you break a leg. You stop yourself from climbing a tree, even though the views would be magnificent, because you fear falling from the tree. No doubt you think you have no desire to climb a tree. When you lack courage, you create a story to make it ok. You tell yourself you don't want to do things, but if you dig deep and are honest, a lack of courage is the biggest inhibitor.

Most adults are risk averse and seek to get things right first time. Business rewards getting things right and employees live in fear and lack courage. I'm afraid business today requires more from you. If you are following a process, you are managing – not leading. What happens when there is no process? It takes courage to lead and inspire and influence others, not knowing where you are going, how to get there or if it will work out or not.

What happens when you enter uncharted territory?

Who leads then if not you?

Few organisations have a culture of courageous leadership although many would like their leaders to be bolder. Fear of failure is the biggest inhibitor to trying something new. If your organisation has a culture of fear (as so many do), it will lack the courage to lead transformational change and have a major impact on your bottom line. A fear culture will influence you too as you create rules about what is allowed or not allowed. You'll wait for permission instead of taking it. How do you know unless you try?

When courage is missing at an organisational level, innovation cannot thrive, and there is no opportunity for collaboration. Collaboration is different people coming together to co-create new things. It takes courage to navigate the differences of opinion that prevail whenever there is something new to do, to embrace the ideas of others even if you don't know if they will work.

Organisations can and must generate a culture of having a go if they are to develop courageous leaders who can transform business results.

How do you develop courage?

As with all the other skills in this book, courage is a felt experience. You don't wake up one day and think you've got courage handled. It's much more complex. Courage keeps growing and growing the more you practise it. You develop courage by continually stepping out of your comfort zone and into the learning zone. Practise, practise, practise.

I'm sure there are some situations where you are courageous or have been in the past. What enabled you to take the courageous option?

Most people I work with consider themselves to be confident leaders, and they appear to be, but it can be based on a shaky foundation. Often people's confidence and self-belief is based on external factors such as being rewarded with a pay rise or promotion or being told they are doing a good job. When they work with 600kg or more of sentient being with a strong opinion, self-confidence and self-belief can be shaky under those circumstances.

Once people realise their confidence and self-belief are shaky, they dig deeper and find their true inner confidence and self-belief, based on their self-worth rather than an external view of them. When they've embodied the feeling, they find it again in the workplace.

Most MDs and Chief Executives I work with lack self-confidence and self-belief when you take them out of their comfort zone. None of them would admit it before they arrive because they don't realise they do, but many admit it once it shows up around the horses.

Courage means believing in yourself, beyond the job you do. It goes hand in hand with your self-worth. You are far more resourceful than you can ever imagine. Try new things each day. Drive a different way to work. Have coffee instead of tea, or vice versa. Challenge yourself every day to do something even a little bit courageous. Make doing and being different your new normal. The more you do, the more you step into the learning zone and the easier it becomes.

If you like to do new things, stretch your boundary of

courage. Do something bold. Make your heart pound. Say what you want to say, do what you want to do. The more proficient you become at stepping into the learning zone, the wider it grows. Once you've developed the ability to expand your comfort zone with ease, the actions you take will seem obvious to you and courageous to everyone else.

That's how I found myself running a business with horses. The more I stepped out of my comfort zone, the more I realised I was resourceful and capable. It gave me the courage to try more new things to the point where little of what I do feels courageous any more.

Along the way, I also learned where I hit overwhelm. I learned where my danger zone is, how to recognise it and what happens to me when I step into it for too long. That's where you become ineffective as a leader, so it's important to step into it briefly so you know where the boundary is for you. It's also important not to spend all your time in the danger zone. Sometimes the courageous thing to say or do is to stop, take time out to recharge or ask for help. If you stay too long in the danger zone, you risk getting burnout, and it will take much longer to bounce back and be effective.

The boundary of the comfort zone is different for everyone. Learn what feels right for you and the people you lead, so you can continue to expand and grow without causing stress. Also, find where you challenge yourself too much or too little.

Where are you operating out of the comfort zone?

160

Where are you hitting overwhelm?

Case Study

Many clients show enormous courage when working with the horses. It's a courageous act to lead a horse. You can't force a 600+ kg horse to move. You can only invite it to come with you willingly. Most of my clients have never led a horse before. Some arrive at the stables terrified of horses, as I once was. Others are excited about the possibility of doing something new. All of them feel vulnerable to a point. They are out of the office, in a field with a horse and workshop leader they don't know, and they get feedback on their leadership skills doing something they've never done before. That's courageous, and the benefits of doing it are enormous.

Rachel was in tears with fear. I talked to her to keep her calm and explained she didn't need to do anything she didn't want to do. Unusually, whatever I said didn't help her fear reduce. After everyone else had led, I asked her if she wanted to stroke a horse. She said she wanted to lead one. She chose Kalle. She asked me to walk beside her to keep her safe and I did. She then led with such confidence and poise, built a strong relationship with Kalle, provided clarity, intention and was purposeful about her leadership. Her tears dried up; I stepped to one side, and she was leading alone.

Rachel said she had never stepped out of her comfort zone before, and it was a massive deal for her to do this. She often worried about situations she was not sure of. She would get scared and stop herself from having a go at new things. This time, she had been willing to be courageous in front of the whole team, stepped out of her comfort zone in a big way and realised she could do it again.

Six months later, she reported stepping out of her comfort zone on a regular basis because she had learned she was a competent leader even when she was in a new situation. It gave her the confidence to do it repeatedly, and, as a result, she was promoted to a senior level within the company. Her HR director could not believe the transformation. She asked me if it was because of working with the horses. I said we can never know, but I'm almost certain it was. Why else would Rachel have stepped out of her comfort zone regularly and taken bold actions in her leadership?

Putting it into practice

Where are you prevaricating or stalling as a leader?

What fears get in the way?

What rules do you make up?

What if you broke the rules and created new ones? What might the new story be?

What will you do to be more courageous in your current situation as a result of this awareness?

Chapter 10

Compassion

In the stillness of a frosty November morning
The sun comes up over the horizon
Opus turns me round with his nose
Chases my pain until I am free
In the moment of giving and receiving
A heart to heart connection is created
Nothing will ever be the same
With Opus, November 2013

I gasped inwardly, but I did nothing, and I said nothing. How could that be? Was I frozen in fear too? I felt sick to my stomach and still do today remembering the event. I do know I was completely out of my depth as a leader at that moment. I'm uncomfortable sharing this story. I'm uncomfortable at the lack of leadership I demonstrated, but it's an important example of what can happen when we are unskilled.

I had had Kalle for about six weeks in my care when the farrier came to trim her feet. Kalle doesn't have shoes; she's barefoot, so it is like having your toenails cut. The morning the farrier came, the yard owner had told me to wash Kalle because she had rolled in mud and was dirty. She said Kalle was rolling because she was itchy and being dirty would make her itch more. I wasn't convinced, but I was a novice horse owner, so I listened to the advice. Against my instinct, I hosed Kalle down with cold water in the wash box.

You can imagine even on a warm March day being hosed down with cold water is not much fun for anyone and Kalle put up a bit of a fight. I started by hosing her feet and legs to get her used to the cold water, but the yard owner thought I was taking too long. She insisted Kalle was naughty and needed to learn to get used to these things. She took over from me, made Kalle stand and was fairly forceful in doing so. Kalle was not impressed, but it was quickly over. I led Kalle out to the grass around the stables to let her graze in the sunshine while we waited for the farrier to arrive.

Kalle was agitated and obviously cold, even in the sunshine, and was pretty intimidating to handle. I noticed a gelding on the yard was grazing loose on the same grass around the stables, but when I checked with his owner, she said: "Oh, he'll be fine. Don't worry about him. He's only interested in the grass."

I carried on. Suddenly, the gelding spotted Kalle and rushed at her. Kalle threw her head up and tried to run. Of course I was holding the lead rein, so in her desire to balance being kind to me with trying to escape, she span around me. I was terrified and called for help. The owner of the yard wandered over slowly to help.

Once again, she said Kalle was being silly. I led Kalle back to the stable. She was dancing on her toes and uncooperative. Not only had she been scared by a cold shower, a gelding had chased her whilst she was on the end of the lead rein from me and unable to escape.

I put her back in the stable and a few minutes later the farrier arrived. By this time, my heart was pounding with all the drama of the morning, and Kalle's heart was pounding too. I took Kalle back out of the stable for the farrier. She came out on her toes, her head up high, snorting and difficult to hold. Kalle was genuinely frightened, and I was frightened trying to hold her. My instinct was: "This is not a good day for her to have her feet trimmed." If you ask a horse to lift her foot, it puts her in a vulnerable position because she can no longer run from any danger. To put a horse in that situation when they are already frightened is arguably madness. But that's what we did.

My intuition said: "Put her back in the field; she can

have her feet done next week. It's no big deal." I didn't listen to it, and that was my first major mistake. Instead, I listened to the knowledge and information of the yard owner who was an experienced horse handler. She said: "Kalle's naughty, she's badly behaved, she's got no manners and she needs to learn." She pinned Kalle against the wall. I don't know if you've ever tried to pin 700kg of horse against a wall. It's not an easy thing to do, and Kalle did put up quite a fight although not as much as you might think she would.

I stood by, and I said nothing.

I'm not proud of it, but it was what it was. Kalle stood there, terrified and rigid in her body. The farrier came up from behind her, grabbed her back foot and lifted it. My first thought was: "What about coming to the front and saying hello first to a scared horse? What happened to building relationship? What happened to being conscious of your impact? Where is the compassion for the horse in all of this?"

I said nothing though, and as the farrier grabbed Kalle's foot, she kicked her leg back out to free her foot. She had no intention of kicking him; she was purely trying to release her foot to feel safe. The farrier belted her four times in the rib cage.

The yard owner took a firmer grip on Kalle, so she had no way of moving her head, and the farrier grabbed her foot again. This time he held on forcefully, determined to win. Kalle was so scared and put up quite a fight until she lost her balance. With the farrier hanging onto her leg, she fell onto her knees. As she collapsed, my knees buckled beneath me too as we mirrored each other. I hung onto the bales of hay behind me to stop me falling to the floor.

I felt as though time stopped. As Kalle and I mirrored each other in the horror of the situation, we looked each other directly in the eye. At that moment, we had a deep soul-to-soul connection, and as we shared a moment of emotional pain, I silently said to Kalle: "I don't know how to stop this. I'm really sorry. I promise I will never let it happen again."

It never has, and it never will. I'm now much more conscious of what the needs are of my horses, and I will not allow anything on my yard to impact their emotional or physical wellbeing. I went home and sobbed for an hour. It was one of the most distressing moments of my entire life. The feeling of powerlessness in a moment when Kalle desperately needed me to stand up for her rights is a hard lesson to bear.

Unskilled behaviour

The farrier showed exactly what can happen when you get to the limit of your skill set. When you become attached to a specific outcome, it's easy to lose sense of the humanity of the people preventing you from achieving it. In this case, the farrier was attached to doing his job of trimming Kalle's feet that day. He wasn't able to recognise she needed a more gentle approach. He wasn't able to listen to her and be in relationship with her in the way she needed. He wasn't aware of any of this. He single-mindedly focused on getting the job done.

This is what happens with people too. "I've got to get this job done. Never mind everybody else who is in my way, I'm going to push them all aside." Of course, you're not consciously thinking those words when you do it, but it is the outcome of being focused on the task and not being conscious of your impact on others in the process. When you reach the limit of your skill set and no longer know what to do, you may give in and leave the job to somebody else or push your way through. That's passive aggressive behaviour, and it's not leadership.

When you fail to lead, people and animals get hurt. Hopefully nobody in your office is ever going to be beaten in front of you, but people do resort to coercive behaviour. Most of us have at some point raised our voices and been slightly more coercive when we have been attached to something being done a particular way. When you use coercion, it's unskilled behaviour and is what can happen when you get to the limits of your capabilities.

That's why it's important to be gentle with yourself and to have compassion for yourself. There will be times when you will get to the limit of your skill set and don't know how to handle a situation. That's why I forgave the farrier because in his world horses have to stand still, and if they don't, they have to be told. Sadly I didn't have that conversation with him because I didn't feel able to at the time. That's unskilled behaviour, too. I avoided a seemingly difficult conversation. The default when we get to the limit of our capabilities is fight or flight. Avoid the situation or push your way through it.

What conversation are you avoiding because it is difficult?

Two years on, I would certainly have the conversation now. I'm more skilled than I was then. Whatever happens, you can learn from it. You need to pick yourself up, learn from it and recover because that's what leadership is. It's about recovering from your mistakes and carrying on.

It's why we need to have compassion for ourselves. I have compassion for myself and for the mistakes I made that morning that have resulted in a painful memory and story. If I didn't, I'd probably spend the next thirty years feeling guilty and beating myself up over it. That doesn't benefit me and creates negative energy. Instead, I chose to learn from it, move on and tell my story in the hope you will be inspired to be more compassionate to yourself when you make mistakes. Furthermore, be compassionate to those who have different opinions from you and appear to be getting in your way, too.

Forgiveness

To this day, I don't fully understand how I completely failed to lead at that moment. I only know I reached the limit of my capabilities as a leader that day. I was so far out of my comfort zone and into the danger zone, I hit overwhelm and did nothing. In the process, I became completely ineffective as a leader. I froze when I was needed in a crisis. It's uncomfortable to admit.

I forgive myself. That might sound odd, but I was doing my best. Was it enough? No, it wasn't enough to stop Kalle being beaten, but it was the best I could do that day in that situation. I live at peace with it and accept we all have our limits, and this was one of mine. For whatever reason, I felt unable to speak out at that moment. That's why it's important to be self-aware and aware of your impact on others, so you continue to grow and develop and be more resourceful in future situations.

I forgave myself, and I've learned from it. I was in the danger zone, and I brought myself back into the learning zone and said: "How can I learn from this? This can never, ever happen again. No horse will be beaten in front of my eyes, and no person will either." Now that's a bold statement, and somebody said to me the other day: "How can you be sure?" I said: "As sure as I know how to ride a bike now, that's how sure."

I also forgave the farrier instantly. It might sound odd. You might expect me to be angry with him, but he was at his limit of knowing what to do too. In his mind, "I've got a job to do. I need to trim this horse's feet and get out of here."

What mistakes are you currently making because you are at the edge of your skill set?

I've made lots of mistakes. I've made more in the last three years running my own business than I ever allowed myself to do in my corporate career. I hate making mistakes; it's uncomfortable, but it's real. It's what we do as leaders. If you are going to step into the learning zone, you're going to get things wrong. You are leading through uncertainty, and you don't know how to do things.

It's important to keep learning and be gentle with yourself and others along the way because everyone is doing the best they can do. Even when the farrier didn't look as though he was doing his best, he was. That was his best on that day, and it's your job and my job to say there's another way. Instead of judging him as a bad person, we can show people how to have a different impact.

Who do you want to forgive?

Forgiveness is very different from delusion. If you think you're not making any mistakes right now, you're deluding yourself. We all make mistakes all the time. The person in your office that you find difficult? It's because you don't know how to work through your differences with them. It's ok. Leadership requires you to notice your impact and continue to grow and develop to expand your range. You can work on increasing your skills, so you can work in harmony with them. Forgive yourself for being at the edge of your limits and try something else. Forgive them too.

What will you forgive yourself for?

What is compassion?

Compassion is the awareness of the suffering of others and the desire to relieve it. It is the ability to listen to all points of view, empathise with them and develop solutions to meet everyone's needs, including your own. Having compassion for others reduces stress and enables you to work more harmoniously as a team.

You need to have compassion for yourself as a leader too, allowing yourself to make mistakes, to take time out when needed and to be human. If you fail to have compassion for yourself and manage your stress, you will eventually burn out.

A high volume of change requires you to influence others and bring them with you. Compassion is not airy-fairy fluff and nonsense. It is the foundation of all relationships and is sorely lacking in many organisations. The desire to achieve can cause you to focus on the result and overlook the humanity of the team in the process. It is people who deliver the business results. Business needs more compassion, to prevent burnout, reduce stress and encourage collaboration. See every person as a human being, trust the team has the skills they need, develop them if they don't, and your business results will improve as if by magic.

Compassion is not weakness and being soft on people. It's building powerful connections, being curious and seeking first to understand and work collaboratively with others. Compassion is a strength. True compassion implies a willingness to engage with a person as a whole and shows vulnerability with enormous power behind it.

When people work with the horses, they very quickly learn whether they are compassionate or not. Some clients, by their own admission, say they are more interested in getting the job done than bringing people with them. The pressure on them in business is so great they overlook the importance of the relationships. The horses will often give these people a hard time, either by taking charge and dragging the client around the arena, or by refusing to move until the client builds the relationship.

Horses simply won't tolerate a leader who doesn't afford them an appropriate level of compassion in the process. People are more likely to go along with a leader who doesn't show them compassion, but they do it begrudgingly. These clients begin to see the true value in building relationships. They learn that they achieve the task more quickly with a cooperative team, and that it is more enjoyable too when you take the time to build a relationship.

There are times when you get to the limit of your skill set. What do you do in those moments? Do you become more coercive? Do you sit back and ask others their opinion? What happens when nobody agrees? Do you take a stand?

What's your default behaviour when you reach the edge of your capabilities?

If you've ever found yourself speaking from a place of

frustration, you lack compassion at that moment. You've stepped over a line into coercive behaviour. There is such a fine line between passive and assertive behaviour. When there is conflict, however minor the disagreement, there is a tendency to push your own opinion or give in and say nothing for the sake of a quiet life. Look what can happen if you do! It's important as a leader to stretch your abilities continually and remember to have compassion for those around you.

Employees genuinely want to do a good job. They honestly don't set out to hurt others. When you go beyond your skill set, you leave the comfort zone, and if you stretch too far, you enter the danger zone and are no longer fully effective or resourceful.

Being compassionate isn't a doing activity. It's not about sending flowers to someone who is ill. Compassion is something you need to exhibit in every interaction – in everything you say and think and in every action you take. This seems to be the hardest thing for people to find in our busy modern-day world. The attachment to doing and achievement leads to overlooking the people who get the job done.

In the agricultural and industrial ages, management was done in a command and control way. There was a clear hierarchy where everyone knew their place, and the lower ranked people did as they were told. They had little choice. The alternative was to lose their only chance of a job and live in abject poverty. Conforming was a basic need for survival. There wasn't a lot of compassion for workers in the industrial age.

Thankfully, we've moved on. We live in a global economy, a time where the internet gives you access to work all over the world, often from the comfort of your own home! If you lost your job, you would find another one or you could set up your own business or collaborate with someone in another continent. You only need to search for headhunters and agencies on LinkedIn, and you would have a job in a matter of weeks. Treat your employees with compassion, or you could find they look for another job.

Where do you want to have more compassion?

If you repeatedly push employees to their limits and beyond, they develop work-related stress and anxiety. If you don't pay attention, or you ignore the signs, employees may go off sick. Once they do, it can take months for them to recover, and some never do. The perceived shame of going off sick with work-related stress is enormous. Employees will persevere under severe stress for as long as they can before they admit to needing time out.

In addition, if people do not feel cared for they won't hang around for long. The days of a job for life are long gone. If you fail to treat them compassionately, you will have a high turnover of staff. If this is happening in your business, consider how you show up.

What is causing people to leave? What could you do to help them stay? Staff turnover is expensive. I worked with a client who considered himself to be compassionate. He cared about his team. However, they had no idea he did because he showed up as dominant and coercive. This is such a common problem. If you fail to show your team you care, they won't see you as compassionate, and you may as well not be.

When compassion is lacking in the workplace, people don't feel heard and understood. They may feel put upon, and you may experience resistance and negativity as a result. Employees who feel put upon will eventually stop going the extra mile. It can lead to a silo mentality where people only do what serves them and no longer consider the bigger picture. This reduces collaboration and innovation.

Compassion is not about being nice to people in order to get what you want. That is manipulation. Compassion is genuinely caring for the needs of the business, other people and yourself, and *showing* it. It doesn't always mean everybody is happy. Most people, when faced with making someone redundant, will do it with compassion. Those one-off events are easier because you consider them carefully and plan them. But what of the everyday conversations with people who you find challenging? How compassionate are you towards those people? Do you allow frustration to kick in and let the conversation become more heated? Or do you recognise that everyone is doing their best and treat them gently, even though they may not be doing what you want them to do? Compassion isn't always taking the easy option. It is making a powerful choice in service of a bigger picture.

Uncertainty

The challenges in business are greater than ever before. High workload and expectations, misaligned goals and objectives and a high-performance culture all contribute to work-related stress and discord within teams. With constant change and the need to lead out of the comfort zone, differences of opinion can escalate into tension and even conflict, causing a reduction in productivity.

In a global economy, hierarchies are flattened, and you work in a meritocracy where the leader is identified in every moment on merit. When project teams come together, the leadership is fluid. It's ever-changing. The way business is done is changing, largely driven by what employees will and won't tolerate. They want to be engaged, inspired and led. If you are stuck in the old ways of "I'm the boss, do as I say" you won't have engaged employees, and you will have a high turnover of staff. It is expensive for the business.

Employee engagement is one of the biggest challenges for the 21st century. Senior management teams need to change and recognise that the newer generations coming in want more than a job with a monthly salary. People don't leave their job or their company, they leave their manager. If you are a manager of people, then that's an issue for you. It is time-consuming and expensive to recruit, and project work is at risk while you find someone. You need to keep the team engaged.

People want to make a difference, not only in their job but also in society. They want to know you care. Not by asking them how their cat is for the sake of it. Really care. Not simply by asking about their personal lives and pretending to be interested because you think you should. Really care. In every moment. Care about their workload and whether they feel overwhelmed. Care enough not to shout when something goes wrong.

Take the executive who is trying to sell a multi-million dollar deal to an existing client. While he is in the office negotiating with the client, a major issue arises with the existing work performed for this client. The client is unhappy. The executive is attached to selling the multi-million dollar deal, and he gets annoyed and frustrated. His quarterly results depend on this deal. It's important. His bonus is at stake, the holiday he promised his wife and kids. He fails to see that it is an error. He forgets everyone is talented and doing the best they can do. He gets frustrated, calls a meeting and makes it clear this deal is critical, and this issue needs to get sorted. He raises his voice. He may even bang his fist on the table (I've seen this more than a few times). Not only is he interested in the solution, he's interested in who caused it in the first place, not because he is mean but because he is scared.

That is right. Fear. He is terrified he'll lose his job. He may not realise it, but he is. The minute fear takes over, compassion gets left behind. Business is tough. Competition is high in most sectors. Businesses are undergoing massive transformation, and along the way mistakes get made as people transition and change the way they do things.

Compassion is needed now more than ever before. Yes, the multi-million dollar deal is important for you personally and for the business. Yes, you need to make sure the team understands the commercial realities, and you need to rally them around. Engaging your employees is equally important in the longer term. They are the ones who will deliver the deal. You need them on your side, so it makes good business sense to build the relationship with them through compassion.

Those employees are human beings too. They are human beings doing their best work every day, earning a living, wanting to make a difference, wanting their company to be successful and wanting to live and work in harmony with each other. A mistake is not deliberate sabotage.

The problem is people don't know how to be compassionate towards each other. When you get to the limit of your leadership skill set, you give up or get coercive. It is normal. The challenge is to notice it, catch yourself, pause, breathe and dig deep. Understand what is important to you and articulate it clearly, openly and compassionately.

Where are you at the edge of your skill set?

Equally, when clients lead a horse, fear can kick in if the horse doesn't do what they want it to do immediately. People are terrified of getting things wrong and being judged. In those situations, clients either become passive and try to get the horse to co-operate by being nice, or they become coercive and try to drag the horse. You can never win a tug of war with a horse! Horses will not move unless you show compassion, but it needs to come from a place of strength, not faking being nice.

I've never seen any of my clients shout at a horse the way I've seen people shout in an office. Often, those clients who lean towards being coercive under pressure in an office feel powerless when faced with an uncooperative horse. These clients are much more likely to show compassion towards a horse than they do to their fellow colleagues. In the process, they learn that caring about others in those moments of discord helps them get a resolution much more quickly.

Frustration

Have you ever felt frustrated at work?

Frustration is a great source of information. It's a normal emotional response to not being able to do something you want to do. It's a reminder of being unskilled, and a reminder that compassion is needed instead for both you and your team.

As a leader, you need to manage your emotions. You can't spray them out when they arise and hope people will cope. Leadership requires you to manage your emotions and use the information they provide to make powerful choices.

Have you ever felt frustrated with someone because

they didn't do what you asked of them? You probably think you've articulated what you want, but if they are still not doing it, they either didn't understand the request or didn't know how to do it. The problem is one of communication or unskilled behaviour. Being frustrated with someone is not going to help improve the communication or build their confidence in doing something different.

The emotion is real though, so don't squash it down and pretend it is not happening either. Notice your frustration. Be curious about it. How does it inform you? Then decide what you can do differently to get the result you want. Suppressing your emotions or exploding them is not leadership and doesn't get results. Instead, use them to help you decide what is important to you and what you can do to achieve it by trying a different way.

In May 2014, my mare Kalle had a foot abscess and spent a week in the veterinary hospital. When she came out, I had to re-dress her foot daily for a week and then every other day for a month. It was exhausting. My other work didn't stop. I still had my business to run and two other horses to look after. It took up a lot of time. In addition, she didn't like having the dressing changed. She would dance around, and it was tough to get her to stand still. She didn't like it being done, and she refused to cooperate.

I didn't like doing it either. It was physically hard work to hold her foot in the air in one hand, unwrap the old dressing, wash the foot clean, re-pack the holes made through surgery and re-wrap with three different layers of wrapping, the final one being a waterproof one. All the time I had to stop her putting her foot down on the dirty ground otherwise we had to start again. Remember, I'm a novice. The whole time she would want to remove her foot from my hand. She is 700kg and strong, and of course I'm no match for her if she does decide she's not cooperating. I was unskilled in doing this.

The first time I did it she snatched her foot away. I washed it clean, and we started again. By the third time, I found myself feeling frustrated. I had to stop short of yelling at her, shouting and screaming. The frustration of not being able to achieve something you know you need to do can be immense! I knew I had to do this for her health and wellbeing. I couldn't afford to call the vet out to do it on a daily basis for a month at £80 a day. I had to find a way to do it myself.

When I got frustrated about changing Kalle's foot dressing, it was initially directed at her. She was not cooperating, and I felt frustrated. Except you have to own your emotions. You can't blame other people for them. I was at my limit of capability. I had to learn fast and get her on my side to cooperate with me. I also knew frustration was not going to help either of us. Forcing her would not work. For sheer size and weight, my money would be on Kalle to win a power struggle every time! I had to find a way to inspire her to lift her foot, engage her and make her understand this was a necessary, temporary moment of discomfort we needed to go

184

through together. I also had to self-manage. Now was not a good time to get frustrated with her.

When I first felt myself getting frustrated with Kalle, I walked away from her until I calmed down. I sat out of sight and regained my composure. Quickly. There is no value in being stuck in an emotion once you've got the information you need from it. I knew I was unskilled and needed to find a way to get her to work with me. I went back to Kalle and explained to her what I was doing. I had to continue to appeal to her sense of nature and the strength of our relationship. I had to ensure she understood what I was doing and why. Of course, she didn't understand the words, but she understood the intent, which was: "I'm doing this. I need you to cooperate. It's in your best interests and mine to do this quickly, so please help me." She felt the energy of my request. She cooperated. Mostly!

If you have such massive respect and trust with your team, they will do almost anything for you when a crisis hits. Not through fear but because they want to. In order to cooperate, they need to understand your opinion and why it is important. They need to know you are all in it together for the sake of the common good, even if you don't like what you need to do. In this case, neither Kalle nor I liked changing her dressing, but she learned to go along with it, and I learned to do it. We didn't like it, but it was a necessary part of getting her back to health.

I learned to manage my emotions in the process. I had to have compassion for me as I was unskilled in what I was doing. I allowed myself to make mistakes and not get frustrated. I put them down as part of the learning and the process. I also had to have compassion for Kalle, who had to endure this process daily even though she didn't want to. Every time she resisted I dug deeper for compassion for us both and released my frustration. It wasn't easy, I can tell you! That's what it is like in business too. Sometimes you have to do things to get the business back to health, even though you might not like doing it. Sometimes you have to dig deep!

Perhaps you get frustrated with yourself more than you do with others? Every time you get frustrated it's a sign you are at the limit of your skill set. As a leader, you need to keep expanding your range and finding new ways in those unknown situations. Nobody wants to follow a leader who is frustrated. Use the frustration as a source of information. What do you want to happen? Recover quickly, let the frustration go, accept you are at the edge of the learning zone and are leading through uncertainty. Ask for help.

If what you are doing is not working, try something else. When something doesn't work when people work with the horses, they often repeat it over and over again. It can be as uncomfortable to watch as it is for the person trying to get the horse to move.

Where can you be more creative to resolve a frustrating situation or relationship?

Increasing the pressure on others through coercive

behaviour does not work long term and often not short term either. It breaks trust and respect and damages a relationship. My instinct when Kalle wasn't cooperating was to get cross with her because I was unskilled. That would not have helped, any more than it helps you in the workplace with your team or helps a toddler learning to walk. When you direct your frustration outwards at other people, you are blaming them and making them wrong. Instead, look at what you can do differently to achieve a different result.

Blame and judgment

When compassion is missing, it is replaced with blame and judgment.

Have you ever lain awake at night wishing you had done or said something differently? Beating yourself up for mistakes adds no value to what you do in the present or the future. Of course, it's useful to learn from your mistakes, but the beating up bit adds no value. What is in the past is done. If you assume you were doing your best under the circumstances, that's all you could have done. If you regularly beat yourself up for getting things wrong, you lack compassion for yourself. Give yourself a break and let go of the past. Focus on the learning and move on.

If you blame either yourself or someone else for something not working out as planned, you lack compassion. Similar to beating yourself up, blame and judgment indicate a right/wrong, black/white approach. If you are leading out of your comfort zone, the outcome may be unexpected. If it isn't what you want, try something else. Behind your blame and judgment, there is a request. There is something you want someone to do differently. What is it?

What is the request you have behind your blame and judgment?

What is the outcome you want?

Every day when I lead a horse, we rarely walk in a straight line from A to B. Horses don't walk in a straight line naturally. They move based on where they see the next tastiest piece of grass. If I lead a horse without a head collar, we can expect to meander. I need to stay focussed on the relationship and the destination we are headed, and I need to inspire the horse to come with me, avoiding distractions along the way. Leadership is surprisingly much the same. Even if you focus on where you are heading, you will encounter distractions and unforeseen circumstances along the way. People go off track when they notice something critical or interesting. You need to be able to navigate distractions and circumstances without making yourself or anyone else wrong.

People blame and judge each other every day in the office. There is a sense of right and wrong. If you are right, then I must be wrong or vice versa. Most people's egos can't cope with the concept of being wrong, and the obvious thing to do is to make the other person wrong so you can be right. I'm sure you believe you are. Consider the farrier in the story earlier. You might judge him as violent and out of control, or you can respect he had passion and commitment for his job and respect he was out of his depth and beyond the level of his skill set.

Blame and judgment create fear. They imply there is a right and a wrong way of doing things. They stifle creativity and prevent people from trying new things. A corporate team who judged and blamed each other a lot came to work with the horses. Each person was terrified to lead a horse for fear of getting it wrong and being judged by the rest of the team. They held themselves back, wanting to know how to do it "right" before they tried any of the exercises with horses. They were terrified to step out of their comfort zone because they feared being judged. They judged themselves as much as they judged each other. It inhibited their ability to get creative. It stopped them being courageous. Imagine the impact on business.

If you want innovation and creativity to transform your business, you need to create a culture of openness where being vulnerable is the norm and respect for each other is a given.

Who are you blaming and judging?

What if you had compassion for them instead?

How do you develop compassion?

Whenever you feel frustration building, be curious about what the source of it is. Is your frustration directed at you because you can't do something, like mine was when I didn't know how to dress Kalle's foot? Are you frustrated with someone else because they won't do something you want them to do, as I also was when Kalle wouldn't cooperate?

Remember your frustration is a source of information. Don't let it get a hold of you. Pause. Breathe. Whether you direct your frustration at yourself or someone else, let it go. You are doing your best, at the limit of your capabilities. Would you shout at a toddler when they fell over while learning to walk? Then don't get frustrated with yourself or your team when things are not working as you would like. Be gentle with yourself and them. Everyone is doing their best all the time, even if it looks as though people are being difficult.

Nobody intends to sabotage their success or yours. People do their best, and if it is not up to the standard you want, they may be at the edge of their skill set, or they may not understand what you need and why. They need your help and guidance.

Don't squash the frustration. It has useful information. If you squash it, it will escalate until you lose your temper. Instead be curious about the information behind it and think creatively to find a solution. If the first way doesn't work, keep tweaking and trying new ways until you get a result. Let go of needing to get it right first time. Remember you are in unskilled behaviour, and your team is too. Having compassion for both of you is essential throughout the process. Notice what you are doing, how you are doing it and the impact it is having. No doubt it's not the impact you want to have. That is ok. It is useful information.

When I felt myself getting frustrated with Kalle because she wouldn't stand still, my instinct was to get cross with her for not cooperating and cross with me for being useless. Neither of these was true, and it's certainly not leadership. Instead, I took myself away from her and the situation and got curious. I was frustrated I couldn't change her dressing without her putting her foot down. I was frustrated with her for not standing still, and I was frustrated with myself for not being able to do the job I needed to do.

When I understood that, I found a way to stay calm, accept that she was doing her best and persevere in trying to persuade her to work with me.

Case Study

Often clients find it easier to be compassionate with a horse than they do with people. Why do animals enable people to be kinder in their approach? Do people know they won't be judged for being weak with animals? Clients learn compassion is a strength, not a weakness. They learn compassion is a foundation for building relationships, and they learn to be kinder to people as well as horses.

Roger led Kalle around the arena. He was an experienced senior leader who was confident in his leadership. It showed. Kalle followed, happy to be with someone who was clearly competent. Throughout, Roger showed a gentle compassion, and Kalle leaned into it gratefully. She needs a strong relationship with gentleness too. The rest of the team were taken aback. They had no idea Roger could be so kind. He was known for being demanding and not caring about people's feelings. The team saw a new side to Roger, and he learned he didn't need to hide behind a front. He could show how much he cared, and it was compelling and engaging. It was a strength rather than a weakness to show his compassion.

Roger explained he didn't want to appear weak, so he had never shared his softer side before. He had always focused on the tasks and where the team was going. Once he realised his softer side and compassion were engaging, he showed more of it and took more of an interest in the people in his organisation. His team is now more relaxed and works better together because they recognise he cares.

Putting it into practice

Who are you frustrated with? (You, someone else or both)

What do you want to achieve and why?

What is getting in the way?

What do you want someone else to think, say and do?

What can you say and do to bring more compassion to this issue?

Chapter 11

Mutual respect

*"If I respect six hundred kilograms of sentient being
and its opinion, and I respect me and my opinion,
how do we stay in relationship when we're poles apart
and want completely different things?"*

Meeting JohnJo, March 2011

I was working with a corporate team on a six-month long transformational leadership programme called Challenge the Status Quo. We were inviting them to face their fears and be courageous in their leadership. I wanted to lead by example and be willing to overcome my fear of horses.

After a short phone call with David Harris of Acorns 2 Oaks, he agreed to spend a couple of hours with me, helping me overcome my fear.

On 17th March 2011, I went off to meet Dave in Windsor, and I got far more than I had anticipated. Dave introduced me to two of his horses, JohnJo and Floozy. He explained JohnJo had been shipped over from Ireland, and the groom who had travelled with him wasn't gentle, and JohnJo kicked him and broke three of his ribs.

Dave was about to apologise because he realised I'd also broken ribs around horses. As I stood there, my heart was pounding. I turned to Dave and said: "Oh, I get it. I'm not meant to be afraid of them; I'm meant to respect them. If I respect five or six hundred kilograms of sentient being and its opinion, and I respect me and my opinion, how do we stay in relationship when we're poles apart and wanting completely different things?"

This is an important question I continue to be curious about today. How do you stay in relationship when you disagree with someone? Unresolved differences usually end in conflict and relationship breakdown. That is unskilled behaviour. It's not leadership. Yet we all have our limits. Our innate response to conflict and difference is fight or flight. It's why tribal villages fought one another when their differences were a threat to the safety of the existing tribe. That's what happens in business because your brain mostly works in the same way. The default is to run away or push through, but business needs more from you. Business needs you to practise staying through differences so you can collaborate effectively. Mutual respect is a foundation to help you to stay.

Not only did I overcome my fear of horses in the first five minutes, but I also learned about mutual respect in more detail than ever before. I specifically learned: how do I stay in relationship with someone I find intimidating, whether it's a person or a horse? I learned how to respect myself, my own opinion, needs and desires at a deeper level than ever before. At the same time, I learned how to respect the opinions, needs and desires of others and how to co-create together through those differences, so the real needs of both parties could be met. In all my years of corporate leadership, I'd never truly understood how to inhabit this place of mutual respect at such a deep level.

I entered the arena where JohnJo and Floozy were standing. Whilst my fear had dropped significantly, I can't say I was comfortable. It was a new experience for me to be in an arena with a loose horse. JohnJo was curious because I was a new person. He is confident in himself, and it showed. He came right into my personal space, and I felt uncomfortable. I asked Dave how to send him away. He showed me, and I sent JohnJo away by waving my arms. JohnJo responded to the request by moving away.

Instantly, I felt awful. I thought I was mean sending him away. Dave explained JohnJo wasn't bothered. He was still watching us from a distance, and he still felt connected. I understood and made the connection with work too. When you send someone away, you are not saying: "Go away. I don't like you. I don't want to be in your space." You are saying: "Please give me some space right now." The two have completely different energies and impacts. The first is a personal rejection; the second is being clear about your boundaries.

I wasn't being mean to JohnJo. I was protecting my personal space because I felt uncomfortable with him being too close. I was clear about what I was willing to tolerate – and having a large horse in my personal space was too crowded. I wanted space. I needed to manage my boundaries. That is one of the ways you create respect. If I had let JohnJo in close when I felt uncomfortable, it would have been disrespectful to me because my needs would not have been met.

I realised JohnJo didn't mind being sent away because my intent had not been done with frustration, coercion or any other negative emotion. It came purely from managing my boundaries and being clear about what was ok for me and what wasn't. JohnJo respected me. I respected him for complying with my request. We were building relationship even though I was sending him away. Who would have thought it was possible?

Through this small interaction with JohnJo, I thought: "There's another way. There's a way where I can hold onto my opinion and needs and respect myself and also respect you, your opinion and your needs. How do we create something from our differences?"

We spent the next two hours exploring the relationship in different ways. I learned that being clear about my needs helped me generate respect from JohnJo, as it does with people too. The more confidently I respected myself, the more I could ask for respect from JohnJo. I respected him in return for standing strongly in his own self-respect. At no point did he get annoyed with interactions. He engaged based on what I was doing and what he wanted too.

I learned not to resort to the fight or flight response, but to stay and be in relationship, even with people or situations that I found intimidating. If I can respect people and situations, I can remain in relationship with them and continue to engage harmoniously without being scared. It's simple on the face of it and sounds obvious, but the application of that learning means virtually nothing scares me now. As a result, my ability to be in conflict situations has grown exponentially.

What is mutual respect?

Complex business environments with high volumes of change can be motivating and overwhelming at the same time. The era of competition is being succeeded by an era of collaboration, and this requires a fundamental shift in leadership style.

Mutual respect means you consider the opinions and needs of everyone including yourself and hold them in esteem. This creates an environment where others respect you in return. Mutual respect begins with self. If you fail to respect yourself, you will be unable to gain it from others.

Historically, people respected those above them in rank. Doctors, the police and other working professionals were respected for the job they did. Respect is no longer about hierarchy or one person being better than another. It involves respecting everyone you meet as a human being regardless of whether or not you agree with them or have anything in common with them.

Can you respect a homeless man on the street as much as you do a CEO?

Can you respect the challenging person in your team as much as the easygoing one?

Genuine respect focuses on who someone is rather than what they do. Mutual respect involves working in partnership, letting go of judgment, blame or criticism and embracing different points of view, with everyone at all levels of the organisation. You develop it through open relationships, collaborative communication and clear boundaries, needs and opinions.

With a sound basis of mutual respect, you reduce resistance to change. Instead, you create an environment where people collaborate harmoniously, feel included and willingly work with you rather than against you. Conflict reduces, and you create an open dialogue.

Human beings are naturally tribal and gravitate towards those like themselves. That no longer works in today's business. Now you need to embrace differences and create mutual respect with everyone so real collaboration can flourish with ease.

When my gelding Tiffin arrived at the yard, he respected Kalle and Opus. He accepted that Kalle was the alpha mare and Opus was the alpha stallion of the herd. He slotted quite happily into the middle of the herd, and there was instant harmony. That's what happens when mutual respect is at play. As Opus was ageing rapidly, he handed over the alpha stallion role to Tiffin. Tiffin was unskilled in leading the herd, and he quickly started to throw his weight around. He would toss his head and neck from side to side, using his size and weight to push Kalle and Opus around.

In his new role, he lacked respect for both of them. Although they recognised his role as alpha stallion, they didn't like him, and they took themselves away from him, avoiding him as much as possible. If you throw your weight around (metaphorically speaking), you are more likely to be feared than respected, and you will alienate people.

For the next few months, Kalle was unsettled in the herd. She accepted Tiffin's lead, but she didn't like it. Tiffin was also dominant with me. He had always been on large yards, following a routine set by someone else where all the horses knew their place and had to fall in line. Now he had an opinion, he was expressing it fairly strongly and disrespecting everyone else's opinion.

I didn't blame Tiffin and judge him for this. I knew he was learning to take a leadership role without knowing how. As I encourage my horses to have an opinion, he was learning how to express himself and recognise that we all had opinions too.

I had to stand my ground with Tiffin and make it very clear that I would not allow him to push me around. I had to manage my boundaries actively, or I might have been unsafe around him, due to his size. I respected that he was learning to integrate into a herd that he didn't know or understand, and he needed my help to do so. I continued to be clear about what was acceptable to me, as well as allowing him to express his own opinion. It was an intricate balance, and I don't know that I always got it right. But mutual respect is about finding a way to be in relationships where everyone has an opinion and a right to their wants and beliefs.

Mutual respect requires you to be curious about the needs of others, as well as managing the boundaries on your own. It requires you to listen to what other people are saying – non-verbally as much as verbally. Have the courage to articulate what you want with compassion; don't create a right/wrong approach but an open dialogue where everyone can express themselves fully without fear of retribution or ridicule.

Respecting self

The first step to creating mutual respect is to respect yourself and to accept yourself fundamentally as a leader of your own life. If you don't respect yourself, how can you expect anyone else to respect you?

Respecting yourself means you accept who you are, you recognise the mistakes you make, but don't beat yourself up over them. If someone criticises you, it doesn't make you any less of a person. Respecting yourself means you accept your opinion for what it is, believe in it and understand why it is important to you. You don't let your needs be superseded by what someone else wants and you don't allow yourself to be pushed around.

When I took on my first horse Kalle, I had no idea what I was doing. Other people on the yard criticised me regularly and always told me what to do. I felt uncomfortable. I tried to fit in. I lacked the self-respect and self-confidence to be truly myself. Why would you want to fit in and conform? Conforming is over-rated. I know because I spent years doing it. I spent sixteen years in a large corporation trying to fit in. When I finally realised I was more compelling without the masks I hid behind, I became far more influential. Sadly for me, I had had enough of my career and was on my way out. It's not too late for you. You can show up fully, vibrant and compelling without your masks. I assure you people will love you for it.

The difficulty is we have no idea we are conforming when we are in the middle of it. Whenever I did a presentation, I learned to stand still. My tendency is to throw my arms around and move about a lot. I was taught it's not professional to dance and jig up and down. I'm not supposed to laugh too much or too loudly. I'm supposed to point at the screen and be calm and confident. Deep down, I was playing a role. The role of a professional presenter. I learned to be still and graceful because I thought people expected it. I had no idea I was doing it until I discovered that when I danced up and down and threw my arms around wildly, people laughed at me a lot! Some people were even a little uncomfortable watching me. That was their stuff, not mine. I was more compelling, but it was edgy for some people to watch.

When you believe in what you are doing, you can stand up for your rights. Managing your boundaries shows you respect yourself. Be clear what you will and won't tolerate and make sure you stick to it. Mean what you say and honour your promises. When I met JohnJo for the first time, I was still terrified of horses. I respected myself in the fear. I knew I did not want him to come too close to me, although he was trying to because he was curious. Out of respect for myself, I initially sent JohnJo away (with the help of Dave, who showed me how to do it).

Manage your emotions and admit mistakes. Mistakes don't make you a lesser person. They show you are real, out of your comfort zone and daring to live boldly and courageously. I was honest about my fear. Respect for myself showed I wasn't a lesser person for being afraid. Your emotions are real. Respect yourself no matter what emotion you are feeling. Remember it is purely information on your current situation.

When you respect yourself, others are much more likely to respect you too. When I sent JohnJo away because I didn't want him too close, he did as I asked. He respected my request and moved away from me. He was able to respect me because I was clear with my communication, and my request came from a respect for me and my boundaries.

If you find other people don't respect you, the first question to ask is where are you not respecting yourself? Are you clear with your communication? Are you managing your boundaries? Are you asking for respect with your non-verbal signals? If not, you won't be respected. It has to start within.

Where are you not gaining respect?

How can you respect yourself more in this situation?

Horses have complete respect for themselves. They never apologise for showing up. If you are too polite because you want the horse to like you, they won't respect you because you don't respect yourself enough. Instead they plant their feet or drag you around the arena.

When Opus is in a hurry to come through the gate for his supper, he doesn't cough politely and say: "Excuse me." He makes it clear he is in a hurry. He may even be pushy at the gate. It's his way of being clear. He respects his own opinion and is unapologetic about it.

If I ask him not to push me out of the way, he respects me too. It's my job to be clear about what I want, so we can create a result together. If I fail to respect myself, I allow myself to be pushed around – by people as well as by horses.

Respecting others

The other part of creating mutual respect is to respect others. That means respecting everyone you meet, whether you agree or disagree, regardless of the job they do, their race, religion, gender and so on. Respect everyone for the choices they make and the actions they take because everyone is doing their best.

In order to respect someone, take time to understand them. Listen to them, hear what is not being said as much as what is being said. Be curious about their opinion. Don't try to change it, and don't instantly agree or disagree with it. Accept it as their opinion and seek to understand it.

Can you respect everyone you meet, regardless of who they are or the roles they do?

We all want to be respected. Horses do too. Horses are much more clear than people about respect. When people lead them without respect, the horses will plant their feet or engage in a power struggle. They will not accept being pushed and pulled around out of disrespect. People are more likely to tolerate this behaviour but will do so grudgingly.

Do you want your team to follow you out of respect or fear?

Which are you getting currently?

The former is leadership, the latter isn't. Be honest with yourself.

Typically, you may respect someone for being good at their job. Mutual respect goes one step further and is about being respectful in every interaction, with everyone. It happens in those short moments of conversation, in everything you say and do. I've learned some of the finer points of mutual respect through working with horses because they are incredibly clear about what they want.

For example, in the morning when I feed my horses I wait until they have finished eating their breakfast before I change their rugs. Why? Because it's not respectful to do it then. Changing the rugs while they are eating would speed up the process and get the job done quickly, but it's not respectful. Would you like someone to change your coat when you are eating? No – so why would I do that to my horses?

Thinking in this way has made me consider the impact I have on people too, with the small things I say and do. Am I interacting with everyone in a way that is mutually respectful? Does it honour my needs and the needs of others?

You could argue that when I feed the horses my needs are to get the job done quickly and get out as quickly as possible, therefore the quickest thing to do is to change their rugs when they are eating. But longer term, I'm building a relationship with the horses, based on mutual respect, and that encourages them to return the favour and be respectful towards me too.

It's hard to measure, of course. If I did change their

rug when they were eating, would the relationship be any the less for it? Who knows? But I don't want to ask anyone, horse or person, to tolerate something that I would not like.

Interacting daily with the horses in this way has led me to be mindful of how I work with people too. Nowhere is this needed more than when you are in conflict. Conflict often brings out the worst in people, and mutual respect is one of the first things to be forgotten.

I once sat in the office of a senior business leader in Norway with my boss. The Norwegian leader was banging his fists on the table saying, "You don't ****ing understand my business." He knew the English swear words quite well! He was seriously angry. I was new to the team, and my boss was up for a fight. I sat back and watched the two of them arguing while I sat there passively, withdrawing, and thinking: "This guy is livid. What have we done to make him so angry?" I didn't have the confidence to ask him. Instead, I let him and my boss have an almighty fight that nobody won.

Of course, it achieved nothing. It led to them not respecting each other, not trusting each other, and never wanting to work with each other. It made doing business in Norway onerous for our team.

Throughout the fight, I lacked respect for my opinion. I didn't want to fight the Norwegian leader because I wanted to understand him. I was curious and had lots of questions for him. I feared making my boss angry with me, so I sat quietly saying nothing. I felt intimidated by both of them, so I withdrew and disassociated myself from the conversation. Fear stopped me engaging, in case they both turned on me instead. At the time, I didn't believe I was afraid. I stayed detached and allowed the two of them to have their fight while I watched on the side.

Throughout the argument, I did respect both my boss and the Norwegian leader. I recognised they were both passionate about the work they were doing, and both of them wanted to get the job done. If I had had the skills, I might have been the peacemaker who could help them meet each other in the place where they were both aligned. They both shared a desire to do the best job they could do. Their difference was in the execution. My boss and the Norwegian leader, however, lacked respect for each other. Their desire to be right and make the other wrong resulted in a serious argument and achieved nothing. That lack of respect broke down the relationship, and it was never rebuilt. That's the impact a lack of respect can have.

Both of them were afraid. My boss was afraid that she would not achieve the targets set for Norway and that this Norwegian leader would get in her way. The Norwegian leader was afraid that she was going to tell him what to do and how to do it and that he would lose control of his business. Fear prevented them from recognising that they both wanted the same result.

Business is about people, whether it is your clients, your team, your peers, the leaders above you. Your role as a leader is to work collaboratively, to achieve great things together with others. Respecting others is a foundation. If you lack respect for other people, they will respond by lacking respect for you, resulting in relationship breakdown.

Relationships break down in business all the time. When you reach the limit of your skills as a leader, you become coercive or withdraw. That is a normal response. Business is full of people who are fighting each other or avoiding conflict. It's uncomfortable.

Consider how you show up in meetings. Do you sit quietly and reflect and wait for other people to respond? Or perhaps you dive in with your opinion and try to persuade people to your point of view?

What's your default when there are differences of opinion?

You have different ways of engaging or disengaging depending on the circumstances or who you are with. In the situations where you feel confident, you might be more coercive. Perhaps in those situations where you are less confident, you hold back. Both of these lack respect for others and are driven by fear. To truly respect another person, you need to understand them. Find out what is important to them. What are their needs in this situation? How can you meet their needs and yours?

Finding the balance of respect

Conflict arises out of a lack of respect. If you lack respect for yourself and don't stick up for your rights, you won't get your needs met. That leads to internal conflict where you play out in your head what you wish had happened. Or you run through the conversations you want to have but don't because you lack the courage to ask for what you want.

If you fail to respect yourself and your own opinions, you may find people walk over you, push you around or ignore you. You make the other party more superior and more important.

If your energy is too soft, your voice too quiet, or you lack gravitas and presence when entering a room, you lack respect for yourself. When you truly respect yourself at a deep level, you can own your space and stand in it powerfully. You don't need to apologise for showing up.

If you fail to respect someone else, you make yourself more superior or important. In both of these scenarios, mutual respect is lacking and leads to relationship imbalance. When mutual respect is missing, the needs of everyone are out of balance, and relationships break down. People may perceive you as aggressive and domineering. I'm sure it is not your intent, but if you ride roughshod over other people's needs, you lack compassion and respect. Both are needed in harmony to build strong relationships and make a difference in business.

Many people who work in organisations complain about other people and the culture of the organisation. That implies blame and judgment, a right and a wrong way of doing things. It lacks respect for others and the organisation. In blaming and judging, you make yourself right and others wrong. That indicates an imbalance in respect. It's not leadership. Blame and judgment create negativity and pain. They are driven by fear rather than love.

Frustration is an indicator of a lack of respect, whether directed towards yourself or others. When you don't hold yourself or others in equal high regard, relationships break down. Teams don't work cohesively together unless everyone has equal respect for each other and themselves. It's one of the reasons why being self-aware can make such a huge difference to your leadership and your impact.

It would have been easy to be afraid of Tiffin when he first joined the team, to get frustrated with him and to judge his behaviour. He was dominant and at times bordering on being aggressive. Every day, I had to find a way to keep myself safe when he was challenging my leadership. Instead of judging and blaming him, I understood that he was learning a new way of being in a team and that he needed my help to find his leadership style.

I also recognised that I was learning too. Tiffin was new to me, his behaviour was new to me, and I had to find our new way, without being passive and without being coercive either. Even though he was unskilled and aggressive, I didn't have the right to reciprocate with similar levels of force and aggression. Now, six months later, he is sweet and gentle. He has learned to express his opinion without being aggressive, and he understands that I am trying to listen and pay attention to his needs as well as my own. He is still no pushover, but then neither am I!

How do you develop mutual respect?

The days of being respected for the job you do are largely over. It's not enough to be a partner in a law firm or an executive in a large organisation and expect your team to respect you. You need to earn respect. How do you do that? By being congruent in your behaviour.

You create respect for yourself by being clear about your boundaries. Articulate what you want with compassion, and be open to having a conversation about what is needed.

Embrace being vulnerable when you don't have all the answers. If you fake it, you demonstrate incongruent behaviour that people see through and won't respect.

When clients work with the horses, the balance of mutual respect is very clear. There is such a fine balance of passive, assertive and aggressive energy. If you focus too much on your objectives, you may be seen as self-centred and uncaring; focus too much on the needs of others, and people may regard you as a soft touch.

Leadership is a delicate balance of skills, and mutual respect is the most challenging of these to find the balance. The horses clearly show when a client is a minor degree out of balance, either dragging the client around or refusing to move. When the client does find the delicate balance of mutual respect, they learn how to recreate it in different situations, and it becomes repeatable in the workplace.

Case Study 1 - Respecting others

Some clients focus on getting the job done and forget to respect the opinion of the horse. The horses pick up on this and either refuse to engage until they feel respected, or they fight to have an opinion, and a power struggle can quickly ensue.

Richard was a strong leader. He was focused on where he was going, and he was determined he and Opus were going to get there. They did, but they entered a power struggle all the way round the arena. Richard kept a tight control on the lead rein; Opus kept fighting for his head and head-butted Richard a few times along the way. The more controlling Richard became, the more Opus fought for his opinion and the more he head-butted Richard. They achieved the goal, but it was uncomfortable to watch. One member of the team said he thought Richard had that impact on everyone. Richard was surprised. He had no idea.

I asked him to hold a loose lead rein so Opus had an opinion whether to come with him or not. I then asked him to lead Opus without pulling him. This time, it was smooth and effortless. Richard could not believe how easy leadership could be!

Richard had previously been unaware of his impact. He knew he got resistance, but he thought other people were being difficult, and he saw himself as someone who got a difficult job done. He did get the job done but at the expense of the people on his team. He also learned that when he gave people more of a free rein, they would come with him more willingly. Afterwards Richard said work didn't seem as much of a fight as it had before, and he had built better relationships with his clients as well as his immediate team.

Case Study 2- Respecting self

In their desire to be nice, some clients give the horse too much of an opinion, and the horse takes charge by refusing to move or dragging them around the arena. The client may respect the opinion of the horse but lack respect for themselves and their own opinion in the process. This is quite common for women, in particular.

Jane was a director in a large company. She led Tiffin and started off well. Then Tiffin decided to wander over to the gate. Jane followed him. Tiffin stood looking out at the grass beyond the gate. Jane talked to him for quite a while, but she could not get Tiffin to pay any attention to her. Eventually, she found a way to get Tiffin's attention and carried on.

Jane realised she had spent her entire life being nice to others. In her desire to be liked, she had lost all sense of herself and focused on the needs of others. She was seen as a collaborator and a peacemaker and was effective in this, but she became frustrated when she was not always listened to in meetings. She realised she was softening her energy in her desire to be liked and was not clear enough about what she wanted and why.

Jane learned she needed to stand up for her own rights and needs as well as others, and she could be the powerful leader she was without being coercive. As a result, she now has conversations she previously avoided. Using all her skills and not playing herself down showed her how much she could achieve for the benefit of the company. She is now much more confident at work, clear about what she thinks and wants, and is more actively engaged in team decisions. She feels she is being more respected than ever before.

Putting it into practice

Who do you struggle to get respect from?

How do you know they don't respect you?

What values of yours are not being honoured by this person?

If you were courageous, what would you ask of them?

Who do you not respect? (*A good place to explore is where there is conflict or disagreement*)

If you were to respect that person and their opinion and still respect your own opinion, how might you find some common ground?

Chapter 12

Trust

Lying on the ground
I sit beside you
A promise made
To be by your side when the time comes
It's an honour and a privilege
Though I dread the day
Thank you for trusting me dear friend
With Opus, Sept 2013

I led Kalle and Opus out to the field. We were halfway down the track with a hedge on our left and a fence on our right. I held Opus's lead rein in my left hand, and Kalle's in my right. Kalle went to put her head down to eat grass. I knew I needed to stop her, or I'd never get them going again. With my attention on her, Opus stepped behind me and playfully nipped her on the bottom. Kalle kicked out and did a massive buck. As I stood – thankfully – next to her neck, I saw her back legs go right above my head.

I was terrified. I knew I was in danger. The two of them span round to face each other. Both lifted their heads and flattened their ears back against their necks with their nostrils flaring as they prepared to fight. Horses can do this in play, so it's not necessarily serious for them, but for me it was. I was right in the middle of the two of them holding them both, their heads at least a foot higher than mine. We were on a narrow track where there was no room for anyone to move out of the way of kicks.

My instinct kicked in. I grew as tall as I could and screamed at them: "Stop it! We all have to be safe! Stop this behaviour now and walk properly with me!" I never shout at my horses, so it got their attention. I'm not sure what Plan B would have been, but thankfully they responded, dropped their heads and walked calmly with me to the field without incident. My heart continued to pound. That was a close one!

Afterwards, I continued to explore this. I'd gone to a place of yelling, and I questioned whether I was out of control and aggressive. In discussing it with others afterwards, we came to the conclusion that this is leadership – making a decision in the moment for the greater good of the team and managing its safety. If you need to raise your voice on occasion to get the desired result, then it's a leadership action, similar to yelling at a child that is about to put its hand in the fire.

What I learned from the experience was I can handle two huge horses of 600kg each, even when they are having a fight and I'm in the middle. It led me to realise there is virtually no situation I can't handle. I finally understood it's my job to keep me safe by the actions I take in any given moment. I felt good about the way I'd handled this and, of course, the next test was in human form to see if I had landed the learning.

I was working with clients and horses a week later. I had booked the arena all day. We had just finished a tea break, and I went back to the arena with the clients to find someone giving a riding lesson. I didn't want to shout across the arena, so I entered it and walked over to the riding instructor on the ground, and I asked him how long they would be. I explained I had the arena booked. He turned, walked towards me, puffed his shoulders up and made himself as big as he could, and then yelled: "We'll be as long as we want to be!"

He was standing with his face about 9 inches away from mine, and I felt him spit on my face as he yelled. I stood calmly. I felt my energy surround me (see the chapter on energy for more on this). I felt my full power and stood assertively with no fear and an open heart.

I said: "I've booked the arena all day, and I've got clients waiting to come in and work with me. If you need a few more minutes, we can wait."

His anger increased. For a split second, I calmly thought he might hit me. I felt no fear. It was just an observation as I remained totally grounded and calm under pressure. I had complete trust in myself and my ability to manage my safety, and I also trusted he would not want to hit me in front of his client and mine! If he had reached to hit me, I am sure I would have been ready to respond.

He yelled: "We'll be as long as we want, and the longer you stand here talking to me, the more you are a distraction and the longer we are going to be!"

I stood completely grounded and held his gaze with compassion. I saw how he was attached to completing his riding lesson. My focus was on providing a powerful day of learning for my clients. I let go of the outcome of how it might happen. I trusted it would. I said to the man: "What do you need?" I think the question disarmed him because it turned me from being his opponent to a potential ally. He yelled: "We'll be as long as we want!" and stormed off.

I calmly said: "Ok, we'll give you a few minutes to finish."

My heart was completely at peace at that moment. I wasn't angry, only compassionate towards him because I realised he was at the limit of his leadership skills. He felt the need to fight for something important to him, even if he had no right to be there.

I went back to my clients, who had observed and heard this interaction, and I said: "Let's go to Plan B."

I led them from the arena to a different place in the yard. As we were walking, I was thinking: "What's Plan B? What's Plan B?" I honestly had no idea what I was going to do next, but once again I trusted I could work with whatever did happen and create a powerful experience for the clients. When you work with horses, you learn to trust in your resourcefulness because the unexpected often does happen, and you need to be able to deal with it, just as you do in business too.

We walked a few metres away and stood overlooking a field of horses, and as we walked one of the clients said: "I can't believe how you handled it! I would have punched him!"

There was my lifeline. There always is one. You need to trust it will come. I said, "I could have done, but who knows where it would have got me." Would it have helped? Probably not. Would I have got the arena? He might have retaliated and flattened me. Aggression is never the answer. Somebody later said to me, "Were you not worried what the client was going to think of you?" I said, "That didn't even enter my mind." The important things were: How do I keep myself safe? How do I keep the man safe, so he doesn't feel the need to punch me? How do I keep my clients safe and provide powerful learning? That was my focus. Anything else would have been fear-fuelled.

We stood overlooking the fields of horses and had the most incredible conversation about: What do you do when faced with that level of aggression? How do you stay calm under pressure? How do you keep your heart at peace even when you have differences of opinion? How do you trust you are ok and things will turn out ok? How do you manage your safety when it is threatened? Having seen the situation, the client had also thought the man might hit me. For thirty minutes we talked, and the clients landed some incredible learning that day, by observing a situation and discussing it.

Safety

I achieved my goal of keeping us all safe and providing a powerful learning experience. Trusting myself enough to know the outcome would be perfect for the client gave me the ability to be flexible in the moment. As a result of not being attached to having the arena and turning someone else out, I achieved my goal in a very different way to the one I'd expected. When you trust you can create from any situation, it gives you more scope for possibilities to open up. The more you do this, the easier it becomes to create in the moment from whatever is in front of you.

My ability to be in conflict has grown exponentially since then, and I'm truly grateful to the man in the arena. It doesn't mean I enjoy conflict. I still don't like it. It is gut-wrenchingly uncomfortable at times, but I do know I can navigate it peacefully and achieve a great result for everyone in the process.

We have an innate desire to be safe. Trust you are capable of managing your safety. It's a matter of survival. It's one of the things we share with animals.

When I shouted at Kalle and Opus when I was leading them, I did it out of a desire to be safe. I trusted they would respond accordingly. I didn't shout because I was losing my temper. It was an act of love, not fear. I trusted I could keep them safe, even if I was scared in the process. They paid attention because they understood the intent of keeping safe.

Where do you feel unsafe?

When I stood in front of the man in the arena, I trusted myself enough to know I could keep myself safe. I also knew the reason he was aggressive was his desire to keep himself safe. He feared being made wrong and sent out of the arena, so he became the aggressor as a defence mechanism. It doesn't make him a bad person. It showed he was at the limit of his capabilities at that moment.

A breakdown in trust often occurs as a false way of creating your safety. In the office, you are unlikely to get hurt physically. If you think someone might hurt you emotionally or get in the way of your success, you are more likely to put up a barrier against them as a form of protection. Ironically, it has the opposite effect. Whenever you put up barriers, you cease to be open and authentic. In those moments, you are hiding behind a mask and unreachable. That exacerbates an environment of mistrust and causes relationships to break down.

Trust you can keep yourself safe. Trust you can be resourceful in these uncomfortable moments too, without needing to resort to being passive or aggressive, which is the innate response to conflict. Keep practising, and it will get easier. It's another leadership muscle to develop.

What is trust?

Staying in the comfort zone feels safe.

Trust is the confidence and belief in the integrity and ability of a person or thing. That includes you. Trust is something you feel, not something you do. It requires you to be open-hearted, honest and vulnerable, without suspicion or fear.

When you trust yourself, you can be more courageous and step out of your comfort zone more readily. Trusting yourself enables you to lead with confidence, even with people or situations you don't know well. When I stood in front of the man in the arena thinking he might hit me, I trusted myself to handle the situation. It gave me enormous confidence and prevented him from treating me badly. Trusting yourself actually keeps you safe and creates a positive outcome.

Whenever there is change or a new situation you are not familiar with, there is resistance due to a human desire to hang onto the old familiar way and stay within the comfort zone. Unforeseen circumstances (like the man in the arena) can and do happen, and you need to hone your skills to be able to deal with them. If you ignore the resistance, tension and mistrust get created.

Once you recognise resistance is a normal response to change or new situations, you can handle it sensitively and prevent it escalating and leading to a breakdown in trust.

Imagine you've been asked to do a presentation in front of a large audience. You trust yourself to do a good job. You trust your material is interesting and relevant. You trust the audience will gain some value. When you show up with trust, your confidence inspires and convinces others to trust you in return. If you walk with authentic confidence (not faked) onto the stage to present, it shows you trust yourself and your material, and people will trust you have something good to say. Your presentation is much more likely to go well than if you were a gibbering wreck. No doubt you've seen people present who didn't trust themselves or their material. No matter how good their presentation is, they are not compelling when they lack trust in themselves.

When you trust yourself, the self-confidence and self-belief you exude is compelling. It enables you to push the boundaries and do things you've never done before because you know no matter what happens, you can work with it. Trust creates safety. Mistrust breaks down relationships and reduces your safety.

When you trust others, you can embrace change, lead teams effectively, influence clients and create harmony, especially when there are differences of opinion. Trust starts within. You can only trust others when you trust yourself.

High-performance cultures have led to competition, stress and a mindset of fear. Ironically, this is the time when trust is most needed and often most lacking.

You need a different culture – one of trust, respect and harmony. Create an environment of clarity, openness, honesty and integrity. Trust yourself, and the rest will follow.

Trust and mutual respect

Trust works in balance with mutual respect. When the man in the arena was yelling and spitting in my face, it would be easy to disrespect him. That's a typical response when faced with anger or unreasonable behaviour. Instead, I respected the man. I recognised he was at the limit of his capabilities and had compassion for him. I respected his passion for what he was doing. His desire to stay in the arena was so great he was willing to yell and spit in my face. I was able to trust him because I respected both him and me, and the respect kept me safe.

Leadership requires us to make choices in every moment to serve the greater good – in this case, a powerful experience for the client. In trusting and respecting myself, I felt grounded and comfortable in my skin.

The way you build trust is the opposite of the way you create respect. You build respect by doing what you say you will do, and being clear about your boundaries, what you will and won't tolerate. With a horse, this might show up as not allowing them to push you around or run ahead of you when you lead them. You need to raise your energy and be clear with an active "I won't tolerate any nonsense" kind of energy that is bordering on a pushing away energy.

Trust is created by drawing people in. It has a softer energy than respect. Have you ever tried to persuade a scared animal to come towards you? You use a soft tone of voice; your body language softens, and the animal gradually comes in. A horse will only follow you if it trusts you. If it is not sure, it will plant its feet or take charge and drag you around.

Most people are good at creating respect or trust. Few people have mastered the ability to create both, and yet trust and respect need to be in balance in a harmonious relationship. Too little respect and people will ride roughshod over you. Too little trust and people will keep their distance and not open up in front of you. You need to be able to balance the energy of both simultaneously. When clients work with the horses, the balance between the two is evident. I've yet to find another way of seeing the impact of a person's energy so clearly as it shows up in this way with horses.

Trust and respect need to be continually re-created in relationships. You can lose trust and respect as quickly as you gain them. You need to ask for both on an ongoing basis. One client learned she created respect instantly. Once she recognised she was respected, she created trust. Then she assumed her job was done, and she didn't pay attention to it anymore. What happened was people often treated her badly, or didn't do the job she had asked them to do. It always took her by surprise because she thought she had created respect and trust. Of course she had, but in not paying attention to it on an ongoing basis, she lost it as quickly as she developed it in the first place.

Respect needs to be created before trust. Often people do it the other way round, and it leads to confusion. Trust is transient without respect. When clients build trust with a horse without respect, they can get the horse to follow them without a lead rope. This is an incredible experience for many people. If they have not gained respect in advance though, what happens is as soon as a noise occurs in the environment, the horse will wander off, and the trust is broken.

You must have respect first before you can create trust. The same thing happens with people too. Have you ever trusted someone and then they treated you badly? That's what happens when you create trust but not respect. One client didn't understand why she was always pushed around by people she trusted. It's because she had trust but not respect.

If you create trust before respect (with a person or a horse), they are then shocked when you get clear on your boundaries and have a tougher energy. It scares people away. This is why so many people are afraid to create respect because they fear alienating people. By trying to create respect after you have created trust, you break the trust and do alienate people because they think you are not as gentle as they once thought. It causes confusion.

If you create respect first, you make it clear you are not going to be pushed around by being assertive. When you set your boundaries and communicate with clarity, people understand where they are in relationship with you and can respect you. Once you have respect, you can soften your energy and create trust by bringing people in. It's important to maintain the boundaries and continue to be clear about your needs and wants throughout.

There is a delicate balance to find between trust and respect. If you find people moving away, create more openness and transparency and draw them in to create more trust. If you gain trust and lose it again, be clearer on your boundaries and set expectations up front to create more respect.

Internal and external conflict

When you lack trust in yourself, you suffer internal conflict. When you lack trust in others, you create an environment for external conflict.

If you fear the worst case scenario, you lack trust in yourself. You create negative stories of what might happen for fear of not creating the outcome you want. Trust requires you to open up and be vulnerable because you don't know the exact result. You don't know how a scenario will play out, so you can either trust it will or trust it won't. Whatever story you make up is simply that - a story! Equally, you don't know how somebody will treat you, so you can either trust them or not. If you lack trust in someone, they will lack trust in you, and you create a cycle of mistrust.

When you don't trust someone, there is almost certainly a trigger. Did that person do something to lead you to believe you can't trust them? Did they sabotage your success? Oppose you in a discussion? Be curious about how the mistrust arises. Often once you have lost trust in someone, it begins a downward spiral of mistrust. You can break the spiral, but often people fail to recognise it. Mistrust is usually based on stories you make up. If you must make up stories, please make up good ones!

In my corporate career, a relationship with my boss turned sour and began a spiral of mistrust. It had a terrible effect on the whole team. My boss was on holiday when her boss decided her role was too big for one person, and he wanted to divide it in two. He decided how the job should be split and offered me half her job. He had done it behind my boss's back. I suggested we wait until my boss returned from holiday and agreed it together. He said there was no need and announced me in the new position while my boss was out of the office!

When my boss returned, she was understandably furious! She accused me of going behind her back and went around telling people I could not be trusted. I had a great reputation, and people understood how this had happened, so they sided with me because she was vindictive with her words. I lacked the confidence to have a conversation with her to explain. She was great with words and good at twisting them. I believed I wasn't good at thinking on my feet, so I feared having a conversation for fear of being cornered. I lacked trust in my ability to have the conversation, so I ignored it. Every time we met up, I didn't trust her because she had been going behind my back saying awful things about me. She didn't trust me because she assumed I'd persuaded our boss to push her aside.

Assumptions were rife. Neither of us sat down and challenged those assumptions. We lacked the courage. We were afraid to engage in conversation. Instead, we believed our assumptions to be true and acted accordingly. We were a virtual team who met up once a month. Every time we met up, there was an atmosphere. She went to my boss's boss and told him I was not capable of doing the job. I believed she was going to do everything she could to cause my downfall. I don't know that to be true. It is an assumption I made.

As a result, I feared her, and it must have shown every time we met. The rest of the team thought I'd been treated badly and sided with me. In fact, we were both victims of a circumstance because our boss feared having an open conversation with the three of us and had made the decision behind my old boss's back. Eventually, she left the team for another job in the same company, which is a shame because she was brilliant at her job.

Whenever there is conflict either internally or externally, there is mistrust. Have you ever worked in a team where there is disagreement with someone on something? You don't trust them because they typically have a different opinion from you, so you make up assumptions about the person and how they show up. You convince yourself you are right, and they are wrong, and a spiral of mistrust is created and a broken relationship is the result. This is what happened with my old boss and me.

Nowhere is trust needed more than in conflict. When I trusted the man in the arena not to hit me, he would have felt the energy, even if he didn't understand it. My firm belief in him doing the right thing helped keep the situation calm. If I had believed he might hit me, I would have exhibited all the behaviours to show him I was expecting him to hit me, and he probably would have done.

When I met him again a few days later, he was guarded. I think he expected me to be angry with him. Instead, I recognised it as being in the past, and I met him as I did everyone on the yard, with a warm smile and a hello. I chatted to him about his horse. He apologised for being angry and said he'd had a bad day. Trust was restored. It was easy. I needed to trust him and show it. It could easily have gone the other way if I hadn't.

When you lack trust, you become more guarded and cautious in your approach. If you play a political agenda, manipulate a situation, insist on your ideas or hold back to avoid conflict you lack trust in yourself and others.

Trust starts within. Trust you are doing your best, and that is good enough. If you lack trust in yourself, you are more likely to be anxious about end results or how things might turn out. Fear arises from a lack of trust. In writing this book, I had moments of wondering if anyone would read it. If they did, would they think it is garbage? That is a lack of trust. It creates fear and anxiety. The decisions you make from a place of fear and anxiety are never going to be powerful. You'll play it safe, lack the courage to be bold. Every time I lacked belief in my material and my reader, I dug deeper and wrote even more from the heart. I trusted that what I had to say would reach the people who most wanted to hear the message.

How do you develop trust?

Honour your values. Speak and act with integrity. That means knowing your values, living up to them. Speaking from the heart in love and truth. Be kind and compassionate towards others and yourself too. This is a courageous act.

Don't make assumptions about other people. If you do, test them out by having open and honest conversations with people. If you must make up assumptions and stories, make up good ones. When clients work with the horses, they sometimes make up judgments about what the horse is feeling or thinking. A client might say: "I think he's bored and doesn't want to move." It's a way of justifying why you don't get a result. If you trust a horse is willing to engage and show all the signs of a compelling leader, they will come with you. If you believe they don't want to move, they don't! People are the same. If you trust you are worth following, people will come with you.

Be honest and open about your wants and needs. Have

open, courageous conversations with people. Iron out misunderstandings early. Don't avoid them because they will spiral downwards and become a much bigger problem than they need to be. When I first had Kalle, I didn't trust myself to lead her because she spooked easily. When she did and was hard to handle, I lacked faith in my capabilities. That caused a downward spiral of mistrust. I lacked trust in me, so she did too.

Trust yourself to do your best and know it is enough. If it isn't, ask for help. Get support and guidance, so you can achieve the result you need. Trust that people (and horses) will follow you, and they will. Often when clients lead a horse without a head collar, the horse looks at them wanting to follow. If the person doesn't believe the horse will follow, they create a more static energy, and the horse stops too. You create the results you get by how much you trust. Believe you are worth following as a leader, and people will follow you.

Respect others. They are doing their best. You might not know what challenges they are having in any given situation. Offer to help. Listen to what people want and work with them to meet their needs, as well as yours.

Some people think you have to earn trust, and you can't trust someone you don't know. They believe trust is earned by being credible and by how you behave. I disagree. I think you can use trust as a baseline in all your interactions, and it starts by trusting yourself.

Many of my clients who are scared of horses overcome their fear in the first few minutes. How do they do that?

They trust themselves. They tell me they trust me to keep them safe even though they've only met me thirty minutes earlier. They can't categorically know I will, but the trust they have in themselves and me enables them to be courageous. When clients work with the horses, it quickly becomes apparent who creates trust easily and who doesn't. A horse will not follow you unless you create trust. It is an essential building block for them to be in relationship with you. It is for people too.

Consider driving to work. Every day you trust that the cars coming towards you will stay on their side of the road. You take a risk. You don't know the drivers, and you can't know they will stick to their side of the road, but you trust they will. Otherwise, you would be in a constant state of anxiety about everything in life. Life is about taking a risk. Trust is something you create on a daily basis with people you meet and in new situations. You trust that the person at the checkout in the supermarket has charged you the correct amount. You trust your team will do what you want them to do.

Trust is a foundation to living and working in harmony. Without trust, there is fear, worry and anxiety. Every time you are worried about something, you lack trust. Notice, be curious about what you are not trusting, decide where you want to trust more and do it! Remember, this is a learned behaviour. If you have learned not to trust and to live in fear, it may have become the standard practice for you. You can change it through awareness and by trying to trust yourself and others more.

Where are you holding back and not trusting?

Ultimately, you are credible. You have shown yourself time and again you can achieve great things. You have shown you can recover when you get things wrong. Let go of any fear and worry. Instead, trust yourself. It's the greatest gift you can give. Trust is simple to create and elusive too! At its core, it is a felt experience. Think about the places where you trust other people or yourself in certain situations.

What enables you to trust?

Next time you feel yourself holding back, trust yourself, trust those around you and trust the situation. Give it a go! You are capable of making decisions to keep you safe. If you don't make the right decision in the moment, that's ok. Forgive yourself, have compassion and try again.

Case Study 1 - Creating trust

Sarah found it easy to gain respect. She was clear with her communication, articulated her boundaries and had a strength of energy, showing she would not be pushed around. She was able to establish an excellent relationship with Tiffin instantly based on respect. He was interested in her and wanted to follow. When she stood beside him, he nuzzled into her. She remained open, established good rapport and was happy to be with him. When she invited him to follow, he stood still. He watched her leave and almost moved, but he wasn't sure.

Sarah came back to him, re-established the relationship and tried again. And again. Each time Tiffin watched her, wanting to follow but not sure he should. Sarah explained she didn't believe he should follow her. "Why would he?" she asked. I said he looked as though he wanted to, but he needed more clarity from her. Each time Sarah returned to his side, she looked relaxed and connected to him, and he leaned into her. Each time she left his side, Sarah looked unsure of herself and didn't believe Tiffin would come with her.

She didn't believe in herself. She didn't trust herself as a leader and therefore didn't want him to follow because if she didn't trust herself, why should he? Months later, she told us this had repeatedly happened in her career, and she had become much more aware of it when it did. In other exercises with the horses, she had repeatedly demonstrated she was a competent leader who was worth following. She had used the embodied memory of these examples later to help her find a way of trusting she was capable.

Case Study 2 - Team trust

A team led Opus without a head collar or lead rope. He started off paying attention and going with them over an obstacle course. One of the team thought it was a fluke, and Opus didn't trust them. The instant he thought it was a fluke, Opus stopped. The team didn't understand why. They kept trying. The harder they tried, the more frustrated the team became and the more they didn't trust themselves to bring Opus with them. Opus stood there waiting. He was willing to go, but he needed everyone in the team to have faith in their abilities before he joined them.

I suggested the team change places, so they were fresher in their roles. Having a renewed focus enabled them to trust this reform of the team would work. The moment they believed it, Opus followed, and they led him effortlessly over the remaining obstacles.

A month later, I visited them in their office, and they said in the past, they had repeatedly found it difficult to work as a team. Something seemed to nearly always crop up to delay projects they were working on, and they assumed it was normal. They also got frustrated and had a sense of "Here we go again" and believed all their projects would be difficult. It was draining. Now they assume their projects will work, and they trust they can work it out when something happens.

One of them said: "If we can lead a loose horse over some obstacles, I'm sure we can find a way to lead each other through our work challenges!" Now when something delays a project, the team reforms and discusses the issue. They all decide to do something different, and they trust they can get the project moving again. Projects still have challenges, but the difference is they trust they can get them moving again whereas before they believed once it was derailed, it was unrecoverable.

Putting it into practice

Who do you not trust?

What fears get in the way?

What stories do you tell yourself about this person?

What if these stories were not true? What if the opposite were true?

What if you trusted this person? How might your relationship be different?

Where do you lack trust in yourself? (*A place to look is where you are afraid something might not happen the way you would like it to*)

Where can you increase trust today and be bolder?

Chapter 13

Energy

Like the gentle breeze
Your soft, warm breath
Whispers against my neck
You lighten up the dark
With your power and strength
You are all this and more

Kalle, January 2015

Kalle spooked easily, and when she did, she threw her head up high above mine and danced around on her toes. I got scared too. I didn't know what I was doing, and most of the advice I was given was contrary to what felt right. Every time I got scared when she spooked, she mirrored my fear back. Against all odds, I persevered and learned to stay calm under pressure, keeping my energy soft and relaxed, so Kalle could mirror calm instead of my fear.

After six months of owning Kalle, I took on Opus. My confidence with Kalle was at an all time low, and it was a tremendous act of courage to persevere with the Leadership with Horses work. Taking on a second horse was my commitment to making it work. I wanted a horse who would give me confidence without being too much of a stretch for me. I went to see Opus several times before I took him on, and he was easy compared to Kalle. He did everything I asked of him, so I thought he'd be a great addition to the team. He was a 24-year-old thoroughbred who had competed in most competencies and was confident in every situation. He did help me increase my confidence, but he was not going to do it by being a pushover!

His owner moved him to the new livery yard I was going to work from, and he settled in with no problems at all. He calmly walked off the trailer and into his stable as though he'd been there all his life because his owner was there, and he trusted her.

On the first day, I led him from the stable to the field on my own. He took one look at me, realised I knew nothing and then bounced along like a two-year-old racehorse about to go on a racetrack! He was hard to handle. I was taken by surprise. What had happened to the sweet, easy-going old gentleman I had met when his owner was around? My heart started pounding, and adrenaline surged through my system again, as it used to with Kalle.

With Kalle, I was still learning to drop my energy and stay calm and soft through fear. I tried dropping my energy with Opus, and he became dominant. He ran rings around me, spinning around me as I held on to the lead rein. The more I dropped my energy, the more he took charge. He wasn't scared; he was dominant because he thought I wasn't up to the job!

This went on for about five days until I got frustrated, and I shouted: "Stop it! Walk properly because I know you can!" He dropped his head and walked quietly beside me. Phew! Now *I* was in charge. I think he was relieved as well. I kept my energy strong, powerful and raised. If he rushed ahead, I would stop, shout at him, then wait until he dropped his head and came with me. It seemed to work for a while, but I knew it wasn't leadership. I was stroppy. If I needed to be stroppy to stay safe, I was willing to do it. I also knew I wanted more. I wanted to be in relationship with him. I wanted to lead and inspire without being coercive and stroppy.

I did feel safer, so for the next few days I continued to be stroppy, and he continued to be easier to handle. If I'd been an unconscious leader, I might have continued like this, as many people leading horses do. I wasn't particularly mean, only slightly coercive in approach, indicating I was at the limit of my leadership capabilities once again. Each day, I tried to find the balance, and I did finally find a way to keep my energy strong and soft, all at the same time.

My challenge came when I introduced Kalle to Opus. They were an instant hit! Within five minutes of turning them out together they groomed each other, and they have been inseparable ever since. Here was my next challenge. I had spent a week trying to learn how to lead Opus and six months still learning how to lead Kalle and stay safe. Now here I was with two horses who refused to move without each other! If I took Opus out of the field first, Kalle went crazy, charging round the field neighing and stressed. When I went back to get her, she would want to run on ahead to get to the stable where she knew Opus would be. It was terrifying. If I tried to move her first, she planted her feet at the gate and refused to move at all.

I called my friend Wendy for help, and she said: "There's nothing for it. You'll need to lead them both together."

I said: "I can't. I'm struggling to lead one of them at a time. I can't possibly lead them both. Also, with Kalle I have to be calm and soft, and with Opus I have to be strong and powerful. How will it work when I lead them both together?"

Wendy insisted: "I know you can do it. I'll come down with you every day and help you until you feel confident doing it on your own. If it takes six months, I'll be here every day." Of course, she knew I'd master it sooner, but back then I had no idea and was eternally grateful for the offer and her support.

For a novice like me, mastering opening a gate with one horse in the hand is difficult enough. Turning the horse around to close the gate and turning around again to move forward adds further to the challenge. Many horsey people make it look easy, but I found it very difficult. Now I had to do it with a horse in each hand onto a narrow track barely wide enough for all three of us to walk down. I wished I had a third hand to open and close the gate.

In addition, Opus is playful and would take every opportunity to nip Kalle on the backside, which would result in her either squealing or spinning round. It was a dangerous situation for a novice, but I knew I needed to overcome the challenge, so I persevered. I also knew from previous experiences with Kalle that my safety was paramount.

On the first day, Wendy opened the gate for me and closed it behind me. We wanted to make the challenge as easy as possible. It was still difficult. I led Kalle and Opus from the field to the stable. We got halfway down the track when Kalle spooked at something and nearly pushed Opus and me into the hedge. I raised and grounded my energy with her, keeping it calm, even though my heart was racing. She recovered but continued to dance along beside me.

Meanwhile, I kept telling Opus I wanted him to be sensible and to keep us all safe. He did. He was incredibly supportive those first few weeks. I kept a strong energy with him as if to say, don't mess with me, we have to be safe. We got halfway down the track, and my heart was racing. I could feel myself becoming overwhelmed. I was right at the edge of my capabilities. Wendy was following behind us, and I called her to help. She took Kalle, and we walked together to the stable calmly and without incident.

The same thing happened on day 2. By day 3, I knew I had to break the pattern of being scared when Kalle spooked and then giving up, so I persevered, knowing Wendy was there to step in at any moment. It gave me the confidence to stretch further out of my comfort zone and be more confident in my ability. I was able to lead both horses to the stable. Phew!

Within a week, I was doing this alone without Wendy. It felt massive the first time without her. I no longer had a safety net. I had to manage my horses on my own. It was an enormous stretch. I had to psych myself up in order to do it. I would ask Opus to be sensible, and I spent the whole time we walked together talking to them. The words helped me stay grounded, but I think the horses got the intent.

Each day it got slightly easier, except when Kalle spooked again, and we would slip back for a couple of days before I regained my confidence. Throughout this time, I was continuing to grow my confidence, to trust I was capable and resourceful.

What is energy?

Your energy informs people about your thoughts and emotions and has influence on everyone and everything - either positively or negatively. If your energy shows you have confidence in what you are saying, people will sit up and listen. If not, then you won't have the impact you want. The strength of your natural energy has an impact on you and others. Compelling leaders have presence as soon as they walk into a room. You sense it, feel engaged by it and get drawn in. Their energy creates that response.

Finding the right balance of energy creates trust and mutual respect and builds powerful relationships. You may need to raise or lower your energy according to the situation and people you are with so you align with them and bring them with you. If your energy is too passive or you hold back, it becomes much harder to gain respect. Too strong and you could be perceived as overbearing or aggressive.

School teachers are great at working with their energy. Imagine a class of five-year-old children running riot. The last thing you want to do is start yelling at them. It only increases the energy and would lead to chaos. Teachers drop their energy and make a request in a soft, low, clear voice in order to restore a sense of calm. Similarly, when a class of 15-year-olds are bored and apathetic, they need to be inspired and engaged.

Teachers will raise their energy and enthusiasm to do this.

Leading two horses with two different energies required me to master the use of mine. With Opus, I showed I would not be messed about, and he needed to be sensible. He responded well to the strength of my energy. Kalle needed me to have a strong energy to make her feel safe when she spooked, but it had to be balanced with softness to bring her own energy down and match mine. It was a delicate balance of the two. I continue to fine-tune when I lead two together because their energies are so different, and what they need in a crisis is different also. This is the challenge of working in teams, where everyone has different needs to be met.

Few people understand the impact of their energy yet it's one of the most powerful leadership tools you have. Even fewer know how to modify their energy. This takes practice and won't come straight away. Become more conscious of your energy, and you increase the power of your impact. Successful businesses need an organisation of vibrant, compelling and courageous leaders who work in harmony. You can feel it and sense it. Who wouldn't want to do business with that kind of energy? Are you vibrant, compelling and courageous? If not, it's time to shift your energy.

Personal energy field

You have a natural energy field extending all around you. To find the extent of your personal energy field, stand up and put your arms out to the side. Turn the palms of your hands face down with your fingers stretched out comfortably without over-stretching. Keeping the rest of your body still, swing your arms horizontally around you to make a full circle. Raise your arms above your head and back to the side. This is the extent of your energy field around you.

Drop your arms back down. Notice if your posture has changed. Usually, when you inhabit your full energetic field, you are taller, straighter and have greater access to your leadership power. If you've ever taken a deep breath before doing something, you'll know the impact of expanding your chest and growing into your personal space. Confident leaders don't apologise for their space. They own it by fully inhabiting it.

Now hold your arms out to where you think your energy field is currently. Don't judge it. Simply notice it. Are you projecting your energy beyond the natural energy field? If so, you probably intimidate people on first meeting them. If your energy is too strong, you can alienate people. It is a defence mechanism to keep people away. You might think it keeps you safe, but in reality you are preventing people from being in relationship with you.

Having too strong an energy prevents trust from being built. It causes you to create fear rather than respect. It creates an energetic barrier between you, the world and everyone in it. Perhaps you get the job done, but consider what is at stake in the process. This is the energy of aggression. I'm almost certain you won't see yourself as aggressive. I'm talking about fine-tuning here, and often people are unconscious of the impact of their energy. When people work with the horses, they are shocked to find their energy is coercive and over-extended. They had no idea.

Conversely, perhaps your energy is well within your energetic field and not extended as far as your arms can reach? If so, you are probably not creating mutual respect with those around you. I don't mean you don't gain respect from others at all. I'm talking about fine-tuning so you can maximise your leadership potential. If your energy is too soft, you are more likely to be over-ruled, not listened to or go along with what other people want. Perhaps you are trying to avoid conflict?

Some of the situations causing a collapse in energy are when you are in conflict, when you are not well (physically or mentally) or when you are tired. Have you ever had a duvet day where you curl up into a ball on the sofa with a duvet and don't want to be bothered? Or you collapse onto the sofa at the end of a day, exhausted. You're not going to make your best decisions at these times because your energy is collapsed.

Think about a situation or person you are in conflict with. Notice what happens to your body. Does it tighten and get smaller? If you collapse your energy in conflict as most people do, you probably do it as a form of protection. You do it to keep yourself safe so you can't be hurt. Paradoxically you are much more likely to be hurt in those moments because you are no longer inhabiting your full leadership power. You are at your most powerful as a leader when you inhabit your full space – no more, no less.

Mastering the use of your energy will enable you to do more, step out of your comfort zone more and do bigger things than you've ever dared do before. You can be more courageous when you strengthen your energy. It's important to raise your energy with a softness too. Otherwise, it can be too overbearing. Try playing with it and notice the impact you have.

This shows up subtly with the horses as they can show you exactly what you are doing with your energy at any given moment. If you want to have influence in any situation, then it is essential to master using your energy to support you.

Raising your energy is commonly misinterpreted as being more energetic. It can be, but it's often more subtle. Often when I ask clients to raise their energy, they increase their energy upwards into the head and can become frenetic.

Have you ever seen anyone get quite manic because they are attached to a specific outcome, and they don't know how to make it happen? That's one way of doing things, but it's not the most powerful. If you want to create forward motion with a team, then you need to project your energy in the direction you want to go – that's forwards, not upwards. It's important to stay grounded in the process too.

Being grounded

The natural tendency in a crisis or critical situation is to raise your energy. Your heart may race as your adrenaline kicks into your body to invoke the fight/flight response. That was fine in the days when we needed to fight or run away from a roaring beast, but now you live in a global economy, often working in global teams with different people and opinions. You need to be grounded under pressure and *stay* to collaborate. It's not an innate skill, so it's one you need to learn in order to lead effectively.

It is essential to keep your energy grounded at all times. Most people spend a lot of time in their head analysing and working things out. You may have to do this for your work. If so, you may find your energy rises upwards and becomes ungrounded. Most people have no idea they are doing this because it's not something they are asked to focus on. If you raise your energy and it becomes frenetic, it won't have much more impact than a lower energy, and it will quickly exhaust you.

Perhaps you already feel exhausted? If you do, then you are probably projecting your energy beyond your energy field and not from a grounded place.

Notice where your energy is in your body right now. Don't judge it; simply notice it. Is it in your head? Or your chest? Stomach? Or perhaps you can feel it in your shoulders as a form of tension? Notice also how far your energy field extends, as described earlier.

Stand with your feet hip distance apart. Lock your

knees until your thighs feel tight. Unlock them again to make them soft and release the tension in your thighs without bending your knees. Make sure you do this within your own body's capabilities. This is not about pushing beyond your limits. If it hurts, stop.

Bring your shoulders forward and slightly drop your head. Breathe in, bring your shoulders up to your ears and bring your head up to a normal position. Breathe out and rotate your shoulders backwards. Don't lower them; just feel them rotate. Continue to breathe out as you lower them back down. Do the whole process again, and this time be careful not to arch your back as you do this. You should now be taller and straighter.

Notice where the energy is in your body now. Has it moved, or is it in the same place? Has any tension in your body changed?

Imagine you have roots going into the ground like a tree. Whilst a tree is rooted, it can still bend and sway in the breeze. This is true for you as a leader when you stay grounded in this way. If you stay grounded, you are more able to make powerful leadership decisions without being off balance.

Practise doing this every day first thing in the morning and last thing in the day. Do it throughout the day if you can. Once you have done this a few times, you'll be able to find it without needing to rotate your shoulders or even stand up. If you combine this exercise with expanding your energy outwards, you'll be fully in your energetic power in a grounded way.

Mastering personal energy

You have a default level of personal energy. You naturally show up with a certain level and type of energy in different situations. Some people have a high energetic presence, and some people have a naturally low energetic presence. It's important to know what your default is and the impact of it, so you can use it to change what is happening around you.

Do you project your energy out or do you collapse it in?

When I was leading two horses together, I had to keep my energy strong to establish respect. If I collapsed my energy, one or other of the horses would take charge. I had to make it clear I wanted them to stay with me, and the use of force was not going to achieve that with a 600kg horse in each hand.

Expanding your energy to inhabit your full personal energy field is the easiest way to create respect from others. Exuding a sense of confidence and competence is compelling. Expand it too far, and you will intimidate people. That may cause them to keep their distance, and they will most likely respond through fear. If you collapse your energy in, you will lose respect from those around you. This is the fine balance between passive, assertive and aggressive again. Knowing your natural energy helps determine what to do to create mutual respect more easily.

When people work with the horses, they quickly see the impact of their default energy, noticing when the horse won't move and when the horse gets into a power struggle. Your energy also has an impact on people although the response is more subtle than it is with horses. Notice what your impact is next time you walk into a meeting. Do you naturally increase the energy in the room or do you lower it? Do people relax as you enter, or do they look on edge? Perhaps you get something else?

How you show up energetically is a learned behaviour, and you can learn to do something different. Because it is not normally an area of focus, people often are not skilled in changing their energy, but it can have an enormous impact.

People often think energy is about being enthusiastic and fast paced. Energy is much more multi-faceted. Verbal communication doesn't always match the non-verbal signs; for example, you can look calm and serene on the outside, but inside your stomach can be churning and your mind racing. This is a common scenario for a lot of people, and it's easy to miss work-related stress when people are internalising their emotional energy.

The strength of your energy is different from the pace you go at, although often they are closely linked. If you are working with someone with strong energy who works at a fast pace, you have a choice to either match them or slow things down. It depends on the task at hand as to which way you decide to go. If you think someone is going too fast and might miss some of the detail, you might want to create a slower pace to make sure everything is covered. You can do this by softening your energy without collapsing it in. Some people are naturally driven, will work at a fast pace and achieve a lot in a short space of time. Others will need to go slower. You need to be flexible in your approach to work with people and get the best from your team.

You also need to look at the bigger picture. Does one person in the team dominate the conversation? Are they over-extending their energy? You may need to create a space for others to feel comfortable sharing their information and ideas. Do you need to slow things down for the benefit of the whole team or do you need to encourage the rest of the team to speed up? Either way, your energy is a useful tool for doing this.

Emotions also have an impact on your energy. Anger, frustration, fear, anxiety, enthusiasm and excitement often show up as high energy. Reflection and curiosity often show up as lower energy. Your energy will be different from anyone else's.

With the speed of change in business, you may need to respond quickly to varying scenarios. As a leader, you will almost certainly be out of your comfort zone a lot of the time. If so, notice if you collapse your energy when you are unsure of what you are doing. It is important to inhabit your energetic space fully and use your full power.

External energy field

As well as your own personal energy, the energetic field

in your environment also has an impact. If you've ever walked into a busy bar, you will know immediately what the atmosphere is. You hear the loud music and talking. You have an emotional response to it. You might get excited about a party atmosphere, or you might feel disappointed that you won't be able to have a conversation with someone because it's too noisy. Either way, you notice the atmosphere and make a judgment. Similarly, if you enter a part of town and it feels dangerous, you sense the atmosphere and make a decision about your safety.

Imagine walking into a room where someone has had an argument. You can feel the tension in the room. Nothing is being said; perhaps the body language has relaxed back down. Nevertheless, you can feel there has been tension of some sort. That's the external energy field.

Are you an energy shifter or an energy colluder?

Don't make yourself wrong. Notice what your default pattern is, and decide if you want to continue to adopt it, or whether something else might serve your leadership better.

Most people are energy colluders. They are influenced by the external energy field, and they join in with it. For example, if you walk into a boring meeting where everyone is bored, do you become bored as well? If someone is miserable, do you become miserable around them too? Do you pick up on anxiety in others and feel anxious? Do you find it easier to be happy with other people who are also happy?

Perhaps you are an energy shifter. Do you shift the energy unconsciously? Do you liven up boring meetings and change the energy? Perhaps you invoke some humour to liven things up? Or perhaps you raise your energy and inspire people in some way to get motivated in the activities ahead? Calling time out on a meeting to ease the tension is another example of shifting energy at work.

You will already be doing this competently in some situations. Be conscious about what you want to do with the energy around you. Leadership requires you to make powerful choices in every given moment. Don't sit in a boring meeting being bored. Change it!

Your personal energy has an impact on the energetic field. As a leader, you need to be able to shift the energy to something else in service of the greater good. You can play with this. Consider what the energy is of the energetic field, and then think about what you want and create it. Try making your voice louder or softer. Expand or collapse the space you inhabit. Keep noticing the impact. Notice what your default impact is. Notice where you collapse your energy e.g. in confrontation, conflict, or when you are not sure of yourself. If your energy is collapsed, expand it to increase your presence.

Horses mirror the energy around them. When clients show up in fear, the horses are more lively and energetic. If clients create a space of calm, the horses will soften and relax in their presence. Clients soon learn the impact of their default energy and become skilled in being able to change it.

As a leader, your role is to notice what is happening in the energetic field and decide what action needs to be taken. You notice the body language of each person. Who is engaged? Who is shut down? Who is not being listened to? Who wants to run because it feels uncomfortable? What needs to happen now? What is the powerful leadership action you can make based on all the information you have? Does someone need to be invited to share their opinion and be given the space to do so? How can you create a safe space for people? How can you lead by example and inspire everyone to shift from fight and flight to collaborate effectively through the differences?

Assertive energy

Until he retired from Leadership with Horses work, Opus was a master at teaching clients about their default energy. He would expect you to get it spot on before he would consider engaging.

There is a fine balance between passive, assertive and aggressive, especially when you get to the limit of leadership capability. When you are out of your comfort zone and entering new territory, you will most likely either reflect and go along with things (passive), or use a small amount of pressure (coercive). I'm talking fine-tuning here. I believe there is a knife edge of assertiveness we are all trying to find, and when we do, it's effortless, pure leadership in full flow.

Opus showed me and many clients how to master my energy to be able to be fully assertive. Whereas with Kalle, I needed to be soft, with Opus I needed to match his masculine dominant energy. I continue to fine-tune this today. If I match his strong dominant energy with too strong an energy, we enter a power struggle where each one of us fights for control and the right to lead.

That's hierarchical leadership rather than shared leadership; the latter comes from a meritocracy style of leadership. I've seen many clients trying to get one of the horses to move his feet by pulling them. The more they try to force them, the more the horse digs in its heels.

Of course, people do the same at work. They resort to coercive behaviour when they risk losing control and not achieving the result they want. Since people are more polite than horses, they are more likely to come with you begrudgingly. That means they are coming with you because they fear the consequences of not, rather than because they respect you as a leader.

Notice the difference because keeping your team engaged is essential in times of substantial change. Many people have no idea they use coercion until they work with the horses. What you think is your default style is often different from the reality. That's why it is essential to be conscious as a leader and learn your impact in every given moment.

In order to fully respect you, your energy needs to be

fully expanded to the edge of your energetic field. The following scenarios are indicators of your energy being collapsed:

- People don't pay attention to you or listen to you
- You get overlooked in meetings
- You feel uncomfortable speaking out
- You don't feel respected
- You feel anxious
- You feel tired
- You can't be bothered

If you extend your energy too far, you may notice some of the following scenarios:

- People don't do what you ask them to do
- People feel intimidated and don't speak up
- People stay away from you
- Your team may appear to be weak
- You do most of the talking in meetings
- You get resistance from people

Being conscious as a leader is essential in business, especially when you lead through change. If you want to inspire people to do great things, mastering your energy to bring them with you is critical. People often misinterpret power as being external power – the kind yielded by those in a more senior position. Your leadership power comes from within you. Influential leaders strike the balance between power and compassion. They find the strength of energy to be as powerful as they need to be according to who they are with, whilst creating a softness of compassion that engages and brings people with them. Holding the polarities of power and compassion is incredibly compelling.

Case Study

Many clients have powerful experiences related to the use of their energy. They learn what their default energy is and whether it is too soft or too hard, and they learn how to modify it to different people and situations. This is profound learning for many people and has a significant impact on their leadership in ways they often cannot articulate.

James had strong energy and was intimidating on first meeting him. He had brought his team because he thought they needed to be stronger in their leadership. He thought they backed down too much with clients and needed to stand their ground more. He was working with Opus in the arena without a head collar or lead rope and was trying to get the horse to come to him. Opus rushed off, bucking and rearing. James was surprised, but his team were not.

Previous conversations with James informed me he cared about his team, so I asked him to drop his energy and calm Opus down. James dropped his energy, showed his gentler side, and gradually Opus dropped his energy too and came towards James. Opus walked with James, but it was clear he did not entirely trust him. Opus was poised, ready to run off again.

One member of James's team provided feedback: "That's the impact you have on everyone the first time you meet them." Everyone physically took a step back. James had no idea. He thought his team knew how much he cared, but they didn't. They saw his energy as strong and intimidating. The way he spoke to them made them feel there was no room for their opinion, so they held back and didn't raise opposing arguments in discussions. They didn't think they had the space to, and they had no idea how much compassion James had for people.

The next time I met James, his energy was softer. He was more engaging, more interested in other people than he was before, and he explained his team were discussing things more openly and honestly now.

Putting it into practice

What is the impact of your energy currently?

Where is your energy soft?

Where is your energy high?

Where do you feel powerful and compelling?

Where are you feeling disempowered and are not getting the result you want?

Expand your energy to its full bubble. What has changed about the situation now?

How might you use your energy more in future?

Chapter 14

Alignment

*Kalle is turned loose into the arena. With her mane flying and
tail up high, she charges up and down, snorting.
I enter the arena. She pauses, connects and joins me.
At once soft, gentle and sweet, we walk side by side then come
to a stop. Kalle looks me deep in the eye.
I feel her connect with my soul.
She nods. My heart lurches. I am chosen.*

Meeting Kalle, November 2011

There was never a question mark over leaving my
corporate career. My whole body said it was time to move

on. When I left in July 2010, it felt right. I set up my leadership business, signed a six-month leadership programme with a corporate team and never looked back. Running my own business hasn't been the easy path. It's the most challenging job I've ever had. Nothing could come close to the challenges I overcame on a daily basis. I have no doubt this is what I'm meant to be doing.

After all the dramas I had with Kalle, everything indicated I should give up, but it seemed wrong to give up on something so right in other ways. I persevered against all odds.

Our next test came when she was moved to a new field. It had rained extensively, and there was a pool of water filling the width of the gateway. It was fifteen centimetres deep and two metres long and muddy either side. There was no other way in or out of the field. I had been struggling to get Kalle through the gate, and I had a client workshop the following day. I knew I needed to find a way. I didn't want to ask people at the yard for help because they kept telling me to slap her, and I didn't want to. I also knew if I could get Kalle out of the field, she always did outstanding work with clients. I had a two-metre long pool of water to navigate, and I needed to gain her trust.

Holding an electric gate in one hand while trying to persuade Kalle to get her feet wet was almost impossible. Every time the electric fence touched the ground, it clicked in the wet grass, making it seem all the more frightening to Kalle. I lacked confidence in my ability, so

I asked my husband for help. I knew he couldn't help me with Kalle, but I thought he could hold the gate open while I concentrated on my horse. I thought if I could lead her through the gate once, we could do it again.

Kalle resisted. She wanted to come with me, but she was afraid of the pool of water, and I lacked the confidence for her to lean into as a leader. A horse needs utmost trust in her leader to walk through muddy water when she can't see the bottom. I hadn't shown a lot of leadership for Kalle to trust me.

Eventually, she came with me and rushed through the gate, to get it over and done with quickly. In the process, I slipped in the middle of the pool of water. I hung onto Kalle's lead rope to get my balance and almost brought her down on top of me. She panicked and leapt out of the way, head-butting me by mistake in the process. I ended up face down in the mud, and Kalle ran off. I stood up and said to Paul: "Is there building work going on? I can hear someone hammering." He replied there wasn't. I felt as though there was a washing machine in my left ear. I later discovered I had mild concussion.

I had to ask the yard owner for help and with the aid of a bucket of food, she coaxed Kalle back across into the field. I knew I couldn't carry on like this. With one drama after another, I was in danger of being seriously hurt. I'd had my three accidents around horses, and I didn't want to have another one.

I asked my friend Wendy for help. As a coach and trained horse instructor, Wendy had proven to be an invaluable friend every time I had a drama with Kalle. I called her over, and we talked at length. Wendy said: "You could send Kalle back. She's the wrong horse for you. It's like having the wrong man in your life. There are plenty more out there. Send her back and find a horse you can handle." I'd spent six months with one drama after another with Kalle, having one conversation with Wendy after another around my kitchen table where I was nearly in tears and didn't know what to do. I think Wendy was getting fed up of listening – and with good reason. I'd only known Wendy less than a year, and she had proven to be so patient with me and such a source of strength.

All the information indicated: "Kalle's the wrong horse. Send her back and find another one. It makes logical sense. Better still, give it all up and go back to work again. There's no shame in having tried and failed. There are other ways to make a living than this. Go and be employed. It's easier and better paid." It made perfect sense intellectually to send Kalle back.

My heart said: "She's beautiful and amazing, and you love her. You are doing the work you are meant to be doing. You can't give up now. You are doing great work with clients, and Kalle is incredible at what she does. She's very intuitive and knows exactly how to help clients learn. You need to learn how to handle her."

I wasn't aligned. My head said one thing, my heart said another. Which one was I supposed to listen to? In my previous corporate career, I had worked in IT and learned to follow logic and reason. I'd never managed to get technical teams to do anything based on emotion or gut feeling. This time I knew I needed to be fully aligned. It wasn't one or the other. I lay awake for nights on end wondering what to do. Being misaligned can have that effect.

I went to see Kalle the following afternoon. I stood in the field with her and massaged her neck. As I stood there, I felt everything come to a place of stillness. I stopped trying to work it all out and enjoyed being in her presence. As I stood massaging her neck, she let out a sigh.

Immediately, I knew I would keep Kalle. As I relaxed and became wholly present, I became open to feeling my intuition, which was saying: "Keep going. Get the right kind of help and find an environment that works for Kalle and you, without people telling you to slap her." Intellectually I knew I could do this, but I had to do it a different way. I knew I had to move Kalle from the current yard, and I needed some help. My heart and soul loved the work Kalle and I were doing. When we ran workshops, I enjoyed every moment. It was not an option to stop now. Everything in my being encouraged me to dig deeper for courage than ever before to keep going.

The following day, I asked Kalle's owner Julie to take her back while I decided what to do. It felt like an enormous risk. I was terrified Julie would remove her beloved horse from me, tell me I was a novice and wasn't capable of handling Kalle. After all, everyone else on the yard had told me that story for the last six months, and I was starting to believe it myself. I didn't know what else to do though, and I knew Kalle could not stay on that yard. It was no good for either of us. I trusted that everything would work out for the best.

Julie arrived immediately with the horse box and took Kalle back to her yard. I followed in the car, and we put Kalle in a stable so she could adjust to being moved. I stood by Kalle's stable with Julie, feeling deflated and insecure. I'm not sure what Julie saw in me, but I remember her saying: "Don't let them bully you. You want to carry on with this work, don't you?" I replied: "Yes, I think so," but I wasn't sure I could or how.

Julie continued: "You can run your workshops here while you work out what you want to do. Don't let other people erode your confidence when you and Kalle are doing such great work together." My confidence was at an all-time low, and I doubted whether I could continue. Julie was the chink of light I needed at that moment. Her belief in me helped me believe in myself and Kalle when I needed it most.

Kalle came to the door of her stable and rested her head on my shoulder. I was moved to tears. She had never done that before in the six months I had cared for her. In her previous stable, she was always stressed and pacing. I knew she was thanking me for moving her back to safety, and I knew we were meant to be working together. With the right support, we could make this work, and I could continue to do my best work with

Kalle. I was aligned. We were aligned. When alignment happens this deeply, there are no longer questions, only clarity. We might not know how to make it happen, but we knew what we had to do.

I'm enormously grateful to Julie for throwing me a lifeline. I ran a few workshops in the next five weeks while Kalle was at her yard. She told me to ask her grooms for support when I needed it. They helped me with Kalle, and my confidence grew. Five weeks later, I took on my second horse Opus, moved Kalle to a new yard with him, and we never looked back.

Sources of information

In business, there is a tendency to make decisions based on the information provided by the brain and the mind. There are other sources of wisdom to guide you. Let's explore some of these.

1. Intellect - The information processing part of the brain is the neocortex. It processes logic and data and performs reasoning. You are likely to be highly skilled in operating from your head. You gather the facts and figures and make decisions. You make a plan and execute it. You follow a process, analyse data and do something with it. Facts and figures, planning, logic and information are all well used in business and a key part of any decision-making process.

In the western world, great emphasis is placed on logic and reason, with school exams focussing on intellect first and foremost. Some subjects test creativity e.g. music and art, but there is little emphasis on emotional intelligence and intuition.

2. *Emotions* - The limbic system part of your brain processes your emotions. I shall refer to this as the heart. Historically people have shut down their emotions in business and made expressing them wrong. We are all emotional beings. The more you understand your emotional responses and those of others, the more adept you can be in building relationships and inspiring people. You need to use your emotions in harmony with facts and figures as a source of information. Emotions provide an opportunity to see whether something is working and help you build relationships with people.

Research has shown you make most of your decisions emotionally and then use facts and data to back up those decisions. If you decide you don't like someone upon meeting them, you notice the things you don't like rather than recognising their strengths. In this way, data can be manipulated to serve your emotional response. It's therefore essential to keep your emotions in balance to enable you to make decisions in alignment.

3. *Gut instinct* - The reptilian part of the brain governs your instincts that create the fight, flight or freeze response. Kill the threat or run away. Freeze at your peril. Your instinct creates an active response that manages your safety or wellbeing, based on your feelings about a situation or person. If you feel a situation is dangerous, your instinct may be to run. If you were faced with an aggressive dog, your instinct would inform you to

run away or fight it off. Some people might freeze in fear too.

When your instincts kick in, action occurs quite quickly. There is little time for rationalising when your safety is in question. However, you need to know when to follow your instinct in a crisis and when to align it with the other information.

4. *Intuition* - Intuition is your instinctive knowing without rational processing. It is sometimes referred to as the gut feeling although it differs from your instinct.

Intuition is a sensing and feeling about a situation or person and often precedes the gut instinct. You sense something, but you may not have the logic or tangible information to prove it. For example, if you walk into a dangerous part of town, you feel it and sense it. You know something isn't right. At that point, it is merely providing you information that you can choose to listen to or ignore before your gut instinct kicks in to drive an action.

Intuition also gives you the opportunity to address what is not being said before it becomes a major issue, e.g. you may intuitively recognise when someone is not happy or not aligned. If you pay attention to it, you can talk about the issue openly and resolve it before it escalates. Often you have to make decisions without all the information. The more adept you become at trusting your intuition, the easier it becomes to make decisions without having all the tangible facts and data.

Which source of information do you over-rely on?

Which one do you ignore?

What is alignment?

Business in the 21st century is more than processing logic and reason. Complex business problems require inspiring leadership rather than a robot churning out the same thoughts. You need to build relationships in business and use your limbic system skilfully to operate your emotions.

The other skills included in this book are not created from facts and figures, logic and reason. You develop them primarily by following your intuition and paying attention to your emotions. When you expand your range beyond tangible data into the unknown, innovation and business transformation can occur.

Successful entrepreneurs like Richard Branson make intuitive decisions all the time because it's rare to have all the information. If you are going to be innovative and creative as business needs you to be, you will think new thoughts and do new things. That means you need to rely on something more than the facts and figures. You need facts and figures too but not in isolation, and when they are missing, you need to take a leap of faith. The more you hone your ability to listen to your emotions, intuition and gut instinct, the easier it will be to be courageous in your leadership.

Alignment is a deep knowing that gives you a surety. You feel grounded and at peace. There is a sense of "this feels right". Everything is joined up; your whole being knows it's the right decision, and there is no option to do it another way.

Scientific research shows that when you are around horses, you align your head, heart, gut instinct and intuition. When you align all four, you are at your most compelling as a leader because you are authentic, congruent and open. You make your best decisions from this place.

Every time you have challenges in life or business and your head, heart, gut and intuition say different things, you are not aligned. While you're not aligned, you're never going to make a powerful decision. It's essential to be aligned when you make those big decisions. Being aligned requires practice and awareness. If you shut down one of the four elements of alignment and are not aware of its wisdom, you are likely to make decisions that don't serve the greater whole.

All four components are critical sources of information. None of them is more important than the other. They all provide their unique form of information and need to be combined to enable you to make the best decisions.

Where are you currently not aligned?

Which source of information is missing?

Intellectual overload

You probably use your brain to process vast amounts of data and information every day. You become highly skilled in intellectual reasoning and may over-rely on using words to get you out of a crucial situation. You negotiate, collaborate and discuss things though with others. You engage your intellectual brain continuously to do your work.

Few people in business shut down their intellect. It's a founding principle of everything you do and is critical to your success. Knowledge and information are developed through experience and help you expand your capabilities.

When I first led Kalle, I had no experience of working with horses. I had to rely on inspiring her to follow my lead, by engaging with her on an emotional level. Without the experience and knowledge, it was almost insurmountable. As I've gained in experience and knowledge, I am now able to lead her with much less effort as I combine my information with an emotional connection. Both are needed in alignment.

There is often an over-reliance on the intellect, and some people may even use it in isolation. As relationships and people are a significant part of business, ignoring other forms of information will lead you to be ineffective as a leader.

The head often overrules the heart and gut, especially when the path is not clear. The head gets in the way when you don't know how to do something. Your head says you can't do it because your head works based on facts, figures and logic. If you only operate from your head, you are likely to stay in your comfort zone because you won't do anything you don't know how to do. The head wants to know how. Often you won't know how;

often the how has to be worked out later.

Often in leadership, you don't have all the information available and need to draw on other indicators from your emotions, gut instincts and intuition.

If you inspire people rather than manipulate them, you are likely to build a long-term relationship based on trust. You can exploit data, facts and figures. You inspire people from the heart and gut. If you combine the head, heart and gut with your intuition, you have solid reasoning on which to influence others more easily. You need to consider more than just rational and analytical reasoning in your decision-making process.

Once you know why you need to do something, you can connect emotionally as well as with your gut instinct and intuition. When all four align, it's not an option to do something else. You have to do it. I had to do this work with Kalle. When I was completely aligned, I knew I wanted to continue and expand the work I was doing to work with teams, and to do that, I needed another horse. The obvious question from the head was: "Where will you get another horse from? Can you manage another horse?" I didn't know the how, but it was not an option to give up.

When you align the why with your heart and gut, you can work the how out later. The how can almost always be worked out if the desire is great enough. Let's imagine that you know you are meant to sail around the world single-handedly with only one leg. Everything indicates you shouldn't because nobody has ever done it before.

Most people would decide not to do it. Many people never innovate; they never do anything new because they don't know how to do it. When you don't know how, you need to find your courage and find a way to be aligned.

Against all odds, at the time when I was having all the dramas with Kalle, within two weeks of making the decision to carry on, I'd taken on another horse. Everybody said: "That's courageous", or they said: "That's bonkers, and you should stop this madness now!" There was never a question in my mind not to take Opus on once I was fully aligned. That doesn't mean it always feels easy when you are fully aligned. Often, it is incredibly challenging.

Sometimes, clients do an exercise with the horses where they ask themselves a question that is critical to how they move forwards. Some people don't want to ask the question because they don't want to know the answer. It may sound strange, but some people are scared to get clarity on the answer because then they've got a hard decision to make and bold actions to take. Sometimes, they prefer to sit on the fence and prevaricate in "Can I, can't I? Should I, shouldn't I?" When you are aligned, you get absolute clarity, and then there is no longer an option to sit on the fence. You have to take action.

You need to be courageous and have compassion for yourself because when you do something that you've never done before, you may get things wrong. You need to respect your decision, manage your boundaries and trust you are capable of working things out. You'll find a way. That's what alignment is.

The head can get in the way of alignment, often more than the heart and gut can because the head will try and overrule the heart and gut. The head will confuse you until you don't know what the emotions are, and you feel completely weird! We've forgotten how to use our emotions, stuffed them down and made them wrong. It's time to be more cognisant of the value that they bring to business.

Where is your head taking over the decision-making?

What impact do you have when you shut down your emotions?

Emotional takeover

Your emotions have enormous wisdom and information, but it's important to keep them in balance with the intellect.

If you've ever felt scared or unsure about taking on a new job, doing a presentation or doing something new, you're probably not aligned. If your head and gut instinct say it's right, but you're scared, you're not aligned. Whenever there is fear, there is a chance you are not aligned. When you are aligned, the fear reduces because you know you're doing the right thing. You're no longer afraid of whether you might fail or how you might do it; you only know you have to do it. There is a solidity that comes with it.

Fear is an excellent pointer to indicate you may not be aligned. Of course, there are times when fear is a sign of alignment. For example, if you walk into a dangerous part of town, your head may know it is dangerous from previous experience; your heart may feel fear, and your gut may tell you to run. It's worth paying attention to that kind of aligned fear!

Fear gets in the way of you doing your best work and building powerful relationships. The more you stuff your fear down and pretend it is not there, the more it takes over and leads you to overwhelm. Procrastination and prevarication are the results of fear taking over. Instead, find a way to listen to its wisdom. People usually lose their temper when they no longer know how to deal with their emotions. It's an unresourceful use of emotion. It has an impact but not necessarily a powerful one. It leads to mistrust and a breakdown in relationships. It's essential to pay attention to your emotions and look for the information that they provide to help you navigate the situation you are in.

When emotion is present, be curious. Use the information in your head and gut and tap into your intuition. If you're scared about a new job, what is the fear? How does your fear inform you? Are there aspects of the job that are new where you lack the skills? Your head has the information to look at your track record to see if you have the experience. Your analytical brain may identify the parts of the job where you need help, or you may decide you need a mentor to guide you through unknown territory. Tap into your intuition. Does it feel the right thing to do? Are you getting a big Yes? Or is there some doubt? Doubt is another indication of not being aligned.

When I was not sure if I could carry on working with Kalle, I was being pushed around by fear. I was scared that I couldn't handle her and scared that I would have to give up. The fear was overwhelming and prevented me from being able to reflect rationally. I was driven by fear rather than making a powerful leadership choice. I knew I needed to reduce the fear so I could reflect and tap into an alignment of logic and reasoning, gut instinct and intuition, as well as the heart connection I had with Kalle.

Once I stopped over-analysing and allowed myself the space to reflect, I knew I could manage her as long as I was supported. Instead of stuffing the fear down and ignoring it, I was curious about it. How could it inform me? Intellectually, I knew I could not do this work alone, and I could not do it with people telling me to slap Kalle. I needed to seek help from the right people – like Julie and Wendy, who had supported me so far.

My intuition led me to believe I could do it and was meant to be doing this work. To reduce the fear, I looked for more practical and emotional support. The fear lessened its hold on me as I paid attention to it and took steps to create a safe way of working. Fear is real. Don't ignore it because it can provide enormous wisdom in guiding you forwards when you are in uncertain situations. If you ignore it, it escalates and takes over and makes decision-making much more difficult.

When I moved to a new yard and took on Opus, I had

new challenges such as how do I muck out a stable and care for a horse? I asked Opus's owner to show me. I asked people on the new yard for help when I needed it. The more the right kind of support became apparent, the more my fear dissipated. I found alignment in every moment to guide my next step.

On the first yard I was on with Kalle, I was a victim of circumstance. I allowed my fear of being judged to get in the way. I didn't speak up for what I wanted for me or Kalle. I allowed myself to be pushed around. I wasn't leading. On the new yard, I still had fears, but now I was leading powerfully again. I paid attention to the fear instead of stuffing it down, and I used the information it provided to help me get the help I needed. As a result, I was no longer a victim of my circumstances but a leader making conscious choices.

Similarly with anger, be curious about it. How does it inform you? What do you want to happen? Anger is a form of unskilled behaviour. When you no longer know what to do to achieve something, you lash out or get frustrated internally. Neither is useful. Instead, use curiosity. Explore what the emotion is trying to tell you. Who needs to do what and why and how? How can you articulate that in a way that doesn't have your emotion taking over?

How do you articulate what you want in a way that is inspiring and influential rather than coercive?

Courageous conversations are needed in these

situations. You may need to ask for help, or maybe you need more compassion for those who are doing their best. Whatever it is, let your emotions provide information rather than sabotaging your success.

Instinctive reactions

The gut instinct is so innate that in today's business environments, it can be triggered by situations that are less life-threatening than your caveman ancestors experienced. It's critical to be able to manage the emotions that get created from those instincts and align them with other information that is available to you. Otherwise you may find yourself being reactive without knowing why, and it can cause you to be unpredictable to others.

Sometimes, your gut instinct is wrong. It is often driven by the fight, flight, freeze response, which isn't as appropriate in the 21st century. If the new job you are considering or the presentation you are about to do is a big stretch, your gut instinct might be to run away. You can't collaborate if you run, so you need to train yourself to be more aligned and be curious about what the wisdom of the gut is. Check in with your head to see if you have all the skills to do the job or the presentation. If not, that's useful information to help you explore how you might be supported to make it a success. If you completely ignore your gut instinct, you could set yourself up to fail. Pay attention to it as much as you do to the information in your head.

Instinct is often aligned with emotions. If your emotion is fear, the instinct is often to fight or run away. That's your innate response. When I was scared and not sure if I could look after Kalle, my inner turmoil told me it wasn't working. It was right. It wasn't working, and I was physically and emotionally unsafe to a point of overwhelm. I was operating in the danger zone, and the gut instinct in the danger zone is nearly always to run, to give up. I knew my instinct in fear needed to be aligned, to stay, collaborate, work it through and learn in the process.

When you are in conflict with somebody, your instinct is often to run away, to avoid the conversation, but that doesn't make logical sense. If you listen to the logic in your head and avoid the conversation long-term, you intellectually *know* that the relationship will break down. So why do people do that?

Courageous conversations invoke fear. There is a possibility of failure, of not getting the result you want. Your desire to manage your physical and emotional safety is so innate that it can cause you to ignore other sources of information that are now needed in today's business. That's an example of not using the head and allowing the emotions and gut instinct to take over. By ignoring the facts and figures that say if you don't have a conversation with this person, the relationship will break down and the situation will get worse, your fight, flight, freeze response is running the show!

Eventually something will happen, and it escalates and

blows up out of control. It's far better to have the conversation even when it's uncomfortable. When your head says you need to have the conversation, and your heart says yes, but I'm scared, you need to go back to being aligned with the head, heart, gut and intuition together. Be curious about the fear. Are you afraid that the person involved will yell at you? Or are you attached to a particular outcome?

What is the fear and is it real?

What is the outcome you want to create, and how can you create that from a fully aligned place?

Whenever I felt like giving up with Kalle, it was fear talking in isolation. The focus was on the problem. I was looking backwards instead of forwards. My attention was on not knowing how to do something, i.e. look after Kalle, and fearing it couldn't be done. Every time I explored what I was moving towards, I knew I wanted to create powerful learning experiences for corporate leaders. I wanted them to make a difference in their business and not feel the pain of the challenges that I felt with Kalle.

Intellectually, I knew that Kalle and I were doing great work already, and it was helping leaders be more skilled in their leadership. I was leading by example – being vulnerable, afraid, courageous – and this was inspiring to those who worked with me. Knowing that helped get the fear in check and enabled me to align all four sources of information.

293

The fear of doing something is often far greater than the experience itself. Having a courageous conversation takes only a few moments, yet the prevarication that can precede it can take weeks or months of painful, exhausting energy. These are the moments when you need to be courageous. You need to trust that no matter what happens, the right answer will emerge.

If your gut instinct is telling you to run away from the conflict, pause and explore what the other sources of information tell you. People are innately decent at heart. If someone appears to be sabotaging your success, have compassion for them. They are hurting, scared, wanting something but unable to express it. Having an open dialogue can be an incredible way of transforming a relationship through conflict.

One of my closest friends and colleagues is someone that I initially started off in conflict with. We seemed to disagree on everything, and the obvious thing was to avoid each other and not build a relationship. Instead, we agreed to sit down and talk about our differences. In doing so, we discovered that we were aligned on 90% of things or more. We had never realised it because we had put all our attention on the things that we both disagreed on. By understanding our differences and exploring them with curiosity and compassion, we were able to see how we could work together. I'm proud that we delivered an outstanding project for a client team.

What are your instincts telling you?

Ignoring intuition

Whilst the head, heart and gut often take control and shut down the other sources of information, most people have learned to ignore their intuition. Logically, intuition often doesn't make sense, and you may have learned to shut it down. However, it has innate wisdom and depth that is rarely wrong and is therefore always worth exploring.

Intuition often appears to be misaligned with the other sources of information at first glance, and it's almost impossible to influence by pure intuition. If all four sources of information are not aligned, you're unlikely to make decisions that work out well. Your intuition may tell you that the new job doesn't feel right. It may stack up on paper, you may have all the experience, and you may like the person you're going to work for. If for some reason it doesn't feel right, pay attention to it because it probably isn't.

Have you ever thought about taking an umbrella with you in case it rains and then decided to leave it behind? When you got wet, did you wish you'd paid more attention? That's your head overruling your intuition. Of course, that's a simple example that mostly has minimal impact (unless you are going to a job interview and get soaked on the way!).

I once intuitively had some doubts about a job, but my rational brain told me to go for it. There were many logical reasons why I should. It turned out to be the worst job of my entire career. The minor concerns I'd intuitively feared were far bigger than I ever could have imagined and prevented me from doing great work. In hindsight, I was not aligned and I wished I'd not taken the job.

In my corporate career, I often knew what to do intuitively. My intuition would kick in, but it wasn't enough on its own. I couldn't get a team of technical people to pay attention to something that "just feels right". I needed facts and data to back it up as well. You can't work in IT and in business purely from intuition, but you can't afford to ignore it either.

In my early IT career, I managed a critical client issue that resulted in the service being down for several days. As I was not technical, I was managing the client and liaising with the technical teams. My intuition told me the problem was with some particular disks, but I didn't want to impose my non-technical thoughts on the technical teams. However, after a couple of days I suggested they look at the disks. The technicians assured me they did not need to because there was no way the problem was related to the disks.

Each day I mentioned it again. I had no idea why I kept mentioning it, but to me it seemed the obvious choice, whereas technically it appeared not to be relevant. Five days later, with the service still down, I insisted that they explore the disks. The technical teams were irritated with me for interfering, but as they were running out of ideas, they agreed.

My intuition turned out to be right, and the problem was solved quickly. There was no logic or reason and no technical indication that the problem was with the disks. If we had all been willing to explore the information provided by my intuition rather than shutting it down, the problem could have been fixed in one day instead of five. I take as much responsibility for that as the technical teams as I was uncertain and lacked the confidence in my intuition too.

The more you learn to pay attention to your intuition, the more confidence you will get in its wisdom and the greater your chances of success. I'm not suggesting you do this at the expense of rational processing but rather integrate all forms of information available to you and get completely aligned around those major decisions.

Your intuition will guide you when working with people too. Intuition is the ability to hear what is not being said and to read between the lines. Sometimes it is based on experience, and sometimes there is no logical reason for an intuitive thought or feeling.

You may be surprised that accountants often intuitively feel there is something wrong with the figures. It points them to explore the data at a deeper level. Everyone, no matter what job they do, can use intuition to guide them, and when it is aligned with the head, heart and gut as well, you set yourself up for making decisions that are powerful and solid.

Clarity and commitment

When you are aligned, you get clarity. When you get clarity, there is certainty. You know exactly what you need to do. When I was fully aligned around keeping Kalle and taking on another horse, there was absolute clarity about what I needed to do. I knew I would keep Kalle, I knew I needed to find the right yard, I knew I needed to take on a second horse and work with teams as well as individuals. With the clarity came a confidence that I was doing the right thing. I committed to making it work. I didn't know where I would find a yard or a second horse, and I didn't know if I could make it work with Kalle. I didn't know the ifs, the buts and the hows, but I had clarity, which led to commitment which led to me taking decisive action with confidence.

Alignment —> Clarity —> Commitment —> Action

Why do so many people hold back on making a decision? Or stop themselves taking action?

Making the decision is often the hardest part for people, and it's not being aligned that causes the prevarication and procrastination. As soon as you are aligned, you get clarity – which creates commitment and then the action is no longer in question. The decision to act is effortless.

Alignment. Clarity. Commitment. Action.

Sometimes people are scared to be aligned because you may worry that when you are fully aligned, you get the clarity you've been afraid of having. With the clarity, you have to look the situation in the eye, and you have to make a decision that leads to taking action, and there is an associated impact of that. That's frightening when it's a big decision.

When I left my corporate career, I was fully aligned. Everything in my whole being said it was time to set up my business. I had no idea if I could make it work. I had no idea how to run a business or what I needed an accountant to do. What do I want on a business card? How do I have a sales conversation? Some of the decisions I had to make felt excruciating and ridiculous in equal measure. I lay awake at night agonising about the small stuff that didn't matter. It was a complete waste of energy.

Lying awake at night doesn't solve those problems. It's the time when you are most likely to go into your head, have analysis paralysis and go round and round the same problem. You don't get clarity, and none of it makes sense. You get noise that gets in the way because you are operating solely from an overload of information from your head.

If you can find a way to be aligned in the middle of the night, you don't need to agonise over what to do. Find a form of relaxation that helps you get aligned, and then ask your head, heart, gut and intuition. I have a meditation track on my iPhone that I listen to that takes me through a breathing exercise. Within a few minutes of listening to it, I get aligned. I get clarity, commitment and a clear plan of decisive action. Sleep is easy again.

Clarity and commitment don't always lead to easy actions though. Keeping Kalle and carrying on was an easy decision to make once I was aligned, had clarity and commitment, but the actions stretched my leadership to a whole new level.

How do you develop alignment?

If your thoughts, feelings, gut instincts and intuition are aligned, your behaviour will be congruent. Have you ever met someone and although they appear to be friendly, you think there is something not quite right about them? That's a lack of congruent energy. They are not aligned in thought, feeling and action, and it results in exhibiting an unbalanced energy.

Most of the time, you won't need to be aware of which source of information is the most dominant one. However, when making big decisions, or whenever there is uncertainty, being aligned is critical. How can you tell? Ask your head, heart and gut.

1. Consider what the key decision is that you need to make. Turn it into a Yes/No or X/Y decision e.g. Should I take the new job? Yes or no. Should I take job 1 or job 2?

2. Put your hand on your head and ask your head the question. Go with the first answer you get; don't over-think it. The answer might be yes, no, not sure, don't know or yes with some constraints. Trust your instant response.

3. Put your hand on your heart and ask your heart the

question. Go with the instant response again.

4. Put your hand on your gut and ask your gut instinct and intuition the question. Go with the first response.

You will know if your head, heart and gut are all aligned because you will have absolute clarity. If you are not sure, ask them all again in turn.

If you are still misaligned, one of your sources of information is taking over. It is likely to be your intellect or emotions that are dominating the decision-making process. Find a way to relax before you make the decision. Depending on how good you are at doing this will determine how easy it is. It's like building a muscle: the more you practise it, the easier it becomes to do it quickly.

One of the reasons that people enjoy sport so much is that it is one of the times that you are fully aligned. A squash or tennis player will use their intellect to strategise about various shots, will often be emotionally driven to create a sense of elation that comes with winning and will respond to certain strokes based on gut instinct and intuition.

The intellect focuses on the game in hand. It is fast-paced, so there is no time to worry about work issues. The feeling of connection to the body generates a sense of emotional wellbeing and happiness, whilst developing self-confidence based on gut instinct and intuitive action. It's a fabulous example of full alignment that continues beyond the game into the conversation you might have in the changing room or the bar afterwards. These are moments of relationship and connection based on congruent behaviour and alignment. It's not uncommon for the discussion afterwards to turn to work and for you to find you have your answer. It's because you've found alignment. No wonder many sports buddies look forward to their weekly match.

Other options are to go for a short walk, stand outside and take a couple of deep breaths, rotate your shoulders to release any tension. If you meditate or do yoga or any other form of exercise that relaxes you, try asking the question afterwards. Singing, dancing, or any other form of activity that allows you to stop the incessant chatter in your head are all useful to help you be more grounded and embody the whole of your leadership wisdom.

Scientific research shows that when you are around horses, you are more able to access the wisdom of your head, heart, gut instinct and intuition and therefore be fully aligned. Research also shows that when you've had a powerful experience around horses, you only need to recall that experience to be fully aligned again.

One of the major benefits for clients who work with the horses is the ability to get aligned quickly. Many of them use a photo of a horse or screensaver to help them re-connect to the experience. Find your way of creating an embodied experience, so you too can be aligned instead of agonising about decisions that you don't know the answer to. Otherwise, you'll continue to lie awake at night worrying about whether you should do X, Y or Z.

Case Study - Overcoming analysis paralysis

Many clients are used to analysing problems and working their way out with logic. Although their business requires them to be creative in problem solving, they have not honed other skills and don't know how to do it, so they rely on facts and figures. That obviously doesn't work with horses, so a lot of the day is spent being more creative, using emotions and intuition in harmony with the information at hand.

Angela tried to lead Opus. She stood with a furrowed brow, trying to work out how to get Opus to move his feet. Opus stood waiting for her to get going. Angela had no idea what to do. She was seeing Opus as a problem rather than as a team member to collaborate with. Eventually she realised she was over-analysing it. She needed to lead with confidence and stop over-thinking it. Once she stopped prevaricating and over-thinking, Opus went with her although it was stop start all the way round.

Angela explained she can spend hours or days prevaricating about how to do something. She likes to have the facts and figures before she gets going. She said she often spends time in her head trying to work things out. It had caused her to be static many times before and stopped her from achieving things.

Working with Opus, she learned to take a step forwards and trust her intuition, to feel her way into what the next step is and to create from that, instead of over-relying on finding "the right way". She also learned that every time she retreats into her head, the relationship with others is momentarily broken. She now knows that re-engaging with others and working things through together is much more likely to create a result than disengaging and over-analysing a problem in isolation.

Putting it into practice

Which of the four sources of information do you rely on the most? Intellect, emotions, gut instinct or intuition?

Which one do you shut down?

Where are you lacking clarity and commitment currently?

What does your intellect have to say about moving forward?

What is your emotional response and how does that inform you?

What is your gut instinct?

What does your intuition tell you about this challenge and other similar ones?

How do you find a place of stillness to get aligned?

Find a way to get aligned and identify your decisive action.

Chapter 15

Letting go

Scared and panicking
A dangerous beast
Release your chains
There is nothing to fear
Sweet, gentle healing soul
Let go of the mask
You are safe with me
With Tiffin, August 2014

The first workshop with Kalle went like a dream. I was reasonably relaxed and trusted the clients would get powerful learning. I was willing to explore the work and see how I could improve on it. I let go of needing it to be perfect. It was, after all, my first workshop.

The final exercise of the day was to take Kalle over an obstacle course the clients had built in the arena. I went to get Kalle out of the stable, and she was on her toes, bouncing around, clearly spooked. I could hardly handle her. I couldn't possibly hand her over in this state to people who had no horse experience. It was a disaster waiting to happen! I led Kalle to the arena, listened to my intuition, trusted my instincts and decided Kalle needed to let off some steam before she did anything. I asked the clients to leave the arena, and I turned Kalle loose in it.

As soon as I let her loose in the arena, she went crazy. She charged up and down, her mane flying and her tail held high like an Arabian horse. She showed no signs of stopping. I felt my heart rate shoot up with hers. I had no idea what to do. This was my first workshop, my first clients with a horse I had had for only three weeks, and I was seriously out of my depth! Five minutes later, the local hunt passed by within fifty metres of where we were. No wonder she was spooked. She had heard them coming long before we did. With thirty horses and the same number of dogs, there was a lot of energy and Kalle understandably wanted to join the equine herd. Instead, she charged up and down the arena, snorting. Thankfully she stayed in it and didn't jump the fence.

I found myself matching her anxious energy, wanting my clients to get a good experience and wanting Kalle to relax. The more we focused on her and tried to get her to relax, the more wound up she was. I tried entering the arena, but she was so out of control I soon left it again! I shared with the clients how scared I was. I told them my heart rate was high, and I was scared, not knowing what to do. It gave the clients permission to share what they were also feeling. They explained they were also mirroring fear. I suggested we tried deep breathing to steady our heart rates. In all of this, Kalle continued to charge up and down uncontrollably.

We talked about what you do when someone in the team is distracted, and the project gets derailed. As soon as our attention was taken away from Kalle, she calmed down and our heart rates dropped too. We forgot to be anxious because we were in dialogue and exploration. It was a great lesson of sometimes needing to let the energy take its course and stop trying to control and fix it. There was nothing to fix! By focussing on Kalle, we were turning her into a problem rather than a horse who could help us with our leadership!

Forty-five minutes later, Kalle had still not calmed down, and I was still unable to get her out of the arena. I had to send the clients home, and they never did finish their obstacle course. I offered for them to return and finish another day, but they never did. They got the learning they needed.

Afterwards I realised whatever happened in a workshop, I could handle it. My role was to play with whatever showed up and create learning from it. That I could do! Kalle and I were a great team as long as I stuck to my end of the bargain and let her be the raw horse she is! That required me to let go of a specific outcome and play with whatever came up

This work never ceases to amaze me. After three years of workshops, I now know I have not seen it all and never will. Each one of us is unique, each one of us has powerful and compelling strengths, and each one of us gets stuck somewhere and needs to find new ways to navigate those places.

Letting go and unskilled behaviour

If you asked me if this work was easier than my corporate career, I would willingly admit the horses are the most demanding team I've ever led. They expect nothing but the highest level of leadership from me. They question my leadership and my actions every day, and sometimes I am found wanting. I spend a lot of time not knowing what to do, and I've learned to let go of getting it right. I'm largely operating from a place of unskilled behaviour, out of my comfort zone, and that's what leadership requires of all of us. I model leading through uncertainty with the horses and letting go of getting it right because we can't know what that looks like!

One of the things I've learned around the horses is to be gentle with myself when I get things wrong. I desperately want to be a great leader, to lead with courage and compassion, and sometimes I find myself wanting. I've learned to be ok with what I can do, both with horses and people. I've learned to let go of getting it right when I'm doing things I've never done before.

Letting go is counterintuitive at best. At its worst, it is terrifying! It requires courage and trust by the bucket load. The more you allow yourself to let go of a specific outcome, the more breathing space you give for something more powerful to emerge. Letting go of control gives you the ability to be flexible, to adapt to whatever emerges and to lead powerfully. Leadership is far more compelling than control!

You don't always have the skills you need in a particular moment. That came as a surprise to me. I'm learning to notice, to accept it, embrace it, try again and learn from the experience. That's much easier to say than it is to do, but the horses are such a forgiving team. They won't hold your mistakes against you. They come back in the next second, willing to question your leadership and follow you when you do stack up!

You can't be in control if you have reached the level of your skill set. Those are the moments more than ever to let go. Trust that you are resourceful and can navigate solutions to meet the needs of the situation, just as I did with Kalle and the clients.

What is letting go?

Stress occurs when you have a tight grip on everything and feel the need to be in control. Western education systems encourage a right and wrong approach and focus on achieving a specific outcome. That's why leaders find the concept of letting go of control to be so alien.

You can't be in control of everything, but you can choose to lead and influence in every moment. Letting go requires you to disengage emotionally from a situation and release your grip on it. It means letting go of what you know, of a specific outcome in the future and of needing to be right. It's a place of surrender to what is meant to be. Of course, it's important to have goals and objectives, plans and desires, but you can't control them. The best you can do is work towards them, taking actions to move you towards rather than away from the desired outcome.

It's exhausting trying to be under control. It's a myth. You are never, ever going to be under control. You are never going to know everything, especially if you're leading and going to new places. Of course it's useful to weigh up the facts and figures and spend time in planning and preparation, but you also need to create space to collaborate and be creative in every moment.

Letting go of control allows you to sense the emerging reality using your intuition and to act in harmony with it. It creates an empowering space for others to co-create with you and reduces tension.

When change occurs, you need to let go of the old and let go of trying to be in control of everything. Instead, allow space for new patterns to emerge naturally, and see what wants to happen rather than forcing your own thoughts and opinions. When you let go, you create a space of trust in yourself, in others and in the process, and you create mutual respect in relationships.

If business is to embrace new ways of working and allow new emerging realities, you must release your grip on the old and the familiar and allow space for natural change to occur.

Let go of habits and behaviours that no longer serve you and create space for new habits and behaviours to emerge. Find new attitudes to create your happiness. Accept yourself for who you are and have compassion for yourself when you fail to live up to your high expectations.

When the hunt came by during my first workshop, my clients and I were initially attached to wanting Kalle to calm down and allow us to finish the day. When we moved to a place of non-attachment and let go of how to finish the day, the emerging conversation was powerful learning for the clients. In letting go, there was space to see what might emerge. I was unattached to the outcome. I played with the situation in front of me and created from it. It was powerful learning for us all, and it showed me how to be flexible and creative no matter what.

Attachment, detachment and non-attachment

Attachment creates huge amounts of stress and wastes so much energy. It has a sense of right and wrong, good and bad. It is full of judgment around how things should be rather than spacious and allowing possibilities to emerge. When you are attached to an outcome, you create stress for yourself and others, and you cease to create space for solutions to arise. Attachment prevents you from fully listening to other people. You no longer work as a team. You can't collaborate, you can't influence, you're not leading. It's important to have goals and intentions, but you never know where you're going to end up. The future is uncertain. That's why you need to be able to lead through uncertainty.

When I was trying to calm Kalle down initially, it's because I was attached to the clients finishing the day with the planned exercise. I soon realised it was not possible and let go of the outcome. If I had stayed attached to my clients working with Kalle, I would not have been able to have a conversation with them and create the learning environment. I would have stressed about doing things a particular way, and they would have felt the end of the day was a failure. Instead, they went away on a high, knowing they got useful learning.

Detachment implies a sense of not caring and giving up. That's a bit like throwing your toys out of your pram. "I'm not playing because I can't get my own way!" There's no hope and no point trying. I'm not suggesting you do this. It's important to care about your goals, your team and your clients. If you are detached, you'll disengage and so will your team and clients.

If I had been detached with Kalle and the hunt, I would have given up and said: "Well that's it then. We can't finish." I would have sent the clients home. There are times when it makes sense to detach yourself, to accept you need to disengage. That would not have been powerful in that situation with my clients.

Non-attachment requires you to let go of trying to be in control and do your best to achieve your goals and objectives. If you do your best, there is no more you can do. Have you ever turned up to work with a great big long list of things to do and then reached the end of the day and achieved none of it? Did you beat yourself up (*attachment*), or did you let it go and accept you did your best and dealt with the essential things (*non-attachment*)?

When I let go of needing to get Kalle to work with the clients, I was able to work with whatever was happening in the moment. I never expected to have a conversation about derailed projects and distracted team members, and I never knew it would be so useful to my clients to have such a conversation. If you allow things to flow, it's effortless, and you create an opportunity for endless *possibilities*.

Relationships vs. outcomes

When I lead my horses, I rarely use a head collar with Kalle or Opus. I trust we can work together based on the relationship we have. I need to let go of getting to the field in a straight line. In my desire to be in relationship with them, we create trust and respect. In giving them an opinion, I know we'll head towards the gate, but it doesn't matter how we get there. We don't have to go in a straight line.

There are some days when I am in a hurry, so I might use a head collar then because accomplishing the task quickly is critical. If I did this all the time, I'd never build the relationship I have which allows the horses to cooperate with me more effectively. These are the choices you have to make as a leader.

How do you do something effectively to get the job done and build a strong long-term relationship in the process?

If I only ever focused on getting the horses to the field as quickly as possible, I would not have the relationship I now have with them. Allowing them to have an opinion takes longer, but it means we work together much better as a team. I have to let go of doing it my way.

Very little of what you do is linear. You may see the straight line from A to B, but in reality you usually go in a roundabout way because you are working with people with different opinions and largely with the unknown. That's what leadership is. I'm able to do that with both Kalle and Opus because of the relationship built on trust and respect. It's taken us two years to create that.

As a result of our relationship, I can ask Kalle to do all sorts of things. Last year I asked her to stand still while a vet put four needles in her back leg and then lifted her leg and cut away half of the sole of her foot until it bled. She did it because she trusted me. That's what we create with trust. Isn't that incredible? Two years ago I never would have believed this was possible. Letting her have an opinion has helped her be more cooperative too because when I insist she does something, she normally understands there is a good reason.

That's what you can create with your teams too. Hopefully, you're not going to ask your team to stand while you cut the soles of their feet away! But you can create things in teams you can't even dream of if you let go of a specific outcome and open up to the possibilities.

Tiffin is a newer member of my team. I have not yet built up the trust and respect with him to be able to lead him without a head collar from the stables to the field. On the one occasion I did, he was silly and rushed up and down the yard. I trust him to a point, but he has not yet learned what is acceptable behaviour and what is not. Instead, I am finding other ways of building the relationship with him to enable me still to manage our safety. As our relationship develops, it will be interesting to see how much of a free rein I can give to him.

Everyone in your team is going to be different. Some people want you to stay close because it gives them confidence. Others will want free rein to do whatever is needed to get the job done. In my corporate career, the jobs I chose to do required me to develop something new and create the job into whatever I wanted it to be. I needed free rein. I achieved little working for the one manager who tried to control me. You need to decide how much of a lead rein you give to each of your team, as well as your clients too. Some people want all the detail; some want a summary. You need to make choices as a leader.

If you pay attention to people and notice whether they are engaged and inspired, you will know how to work with them to get the best out of them. That requires you to be flexible as a leader and not do things all one way.

Allowing possibilities to emerge

Possibilities are created when you let go of what people think. When you allow yourself to explore possibilities, there is space for creativity, expansion and innovation. Business certainly needs more of these things right now.

I came to a point in my corporate career when I just didn't want to be there anymore. I'd done some interesting and challenging roles and had some incredible experiences. I was rewarded (mostly) for my performance and received pay rises and promotions. I was highly respected in the organisation as someone who could be relied on to do an excellent job. Something was missing, and I needed time out to work things out, so I took a year's sabbatical.

It was a year of letting go. I let go of who I thought I was as a person, in relationships, in a team, organisation, system. I'd previously defined myself by the job I did. My self-esteem was based on it rather than a solid foundation of who I really am. I measured myself by what I did rather than who I am at my core. I see this as a common problem with clients too. As a result, they hide behind the masks of who they think they should be, in case they don't stack up and aren't respected.

In the process of letting go of my masks and the roles I did, I learned who I am as a leader as well as who I am in relationship. I learned how to use the environment as a source of information and include it. I learned how to find something to say and do in those moments when I don't know what to say and do.

I became aware of my impact at a deep level, noticing the impact I have on people, whether it was an intended impact or something that happened by mistake. I developed courage and compassion to do things I'd never done before and continued to find my leadership power. Once you let go of who you think you are, you create the space for all of you to emerge, and that can be incredibly exciting. I never knew I was eccentric before, but I learned it as soon as I let go of being something else that I wasn't.

After a year's sabbatical, I wanted to leave the IT corporation I worked for, but I couldn't see how I could make it work financially. Letting go of a big salary was a big challenge! I lay awake at night worrying about how I could leave and make it work financially. I was exhausted and anxious, and I realised that this was the result of hanging on to a specific outcome. Exhaustion and anxiety! They are not the keys to fulfilling life and work.

I decided I'd let go of a specific outcome, set the intention that I was going to leave at some point in the future and see what emerged. I had an idea to set up my own leadership business. I let go of needing to know how and when and created the space for possibilities to emerge. As soon as I'd decided that I was going to allow the outcome to emerge, I felt a huge weight off my shoulders. Lying awake worrying at night hadn't been a good use of my energy. It exhausted me, left me tired during the day and unable to think clearly.

Now I was enjoying my last few months of sabbatical again. As soon as I'd allowed myself to let go of a specific outcome, everyone around me started asking me what I was going to do. Friends accused me of being in denial and not taking charge of my life. Family were concerned that I didn't know and didn't seem to want to talk about it.

It was counterintuitive, but in giving myself the space to see what wanted to unfold, I was able to focus on what I did want. I knew I couldn't afford to leave, so money needed to come from somewhere. I realised that if I could get a redundancy package, it would give us financial leeway while I got my business going. I was fortunate that a voluntary redundancy package was announced, and I returned to work for nine weeks to work out the consultation period that had to be done legally.

Something had emerged, and I was free to set up my business.

In leaving my corporate career, there was a lot more letting go to do. I had no idea if my leadership business would work or whether I'd get clients. It was a massive lesson in letting go. I let go of the career I once had, the rewards, recognition and high salary. I let go of being defined by my job and career. Suddenly I was no longer part of a big organisation doing great work in the world. I was a lone entrepreneur having a small impact. I let go of needing to be part of something big. I let go of everything I knew about me as a leader and the roles I played. I let go of the relationships I'd built with colleagues and the reputation I had as a leader. I was out in a crowded marketplace and unknown.

I leant into trusting that I could make it work. When I held onto success, I felt the fear that comes with not knowing, the fear of failure, the fear of not being paid each month. At times, it was almost paralysing. I gradually learned to lessen my hold on outcomes, to let go of what I wanted and accept what came my way. That didn't mean I gave up. On the contrary, I worked harder than I've ever worked before, but at the same time, I was open to possibilities and whatever opportunities came across my path. I noticed them more because I was open and available to creating possibilities.

Letting go is a challenge for most people. It's the hardest one of the skills for me to embrace. You spend your entire life trying to be in control of everything – your work, family and social life. It's a myth to believe that you can ever be in control. The best you can ever do at any moment is to lead!

People will tell you to be in charge of your destiny. I do believe that you can be clear about where you are heading, and the actions you take each day either move you towards or away from it. But let go of the how, let go of the finer details, let go of a specific outcome. When you do, possibilities transpire.

Where are you holding on tightly to a specific outcome?

Letting go and fear

Fear creates attachment. I sometimes worry about where my next business is coming from. Will my business be profitable? Can I pay the bills this month? Will my clients get powerful learning? Do they enjoy the Leadership with Horses workshops? These are fears that show attachment to a specific outcome. The best I can do is do the work I love in the best way I can and trust that clients will get the outcomes they need. All the evidence in the last three years indicates that they do. I've learned over time to let go of my anxieties around my business and focus instead on creating what I do want – which is powerful learning for clients, to make a difference, to create a profitable business and have the ability to pay my bills!

Whatever you focus on is what you create, so it makes sense to focus on what you do want and then let go of how it happens. That way, you create space for creative solutions and endless possibilities that you might not otherwise see. You put your energy into creating what you want rather than into worrying about what ifs.

Letting go is about stepping out of your comfort zone. It requires courage to do this, to trust that you are resourceful, to have compassion for when things don't turn out right. Use your energy and intuition to guide you and lead.

If you hang onto control, you do so out of fear. Fear that things will not turn out the way you want them to.

How do you know that your outcome is the right one anyway? How do you know that there isn't something else behind your current challenge wanting to emerge?

When I run workshops with clients, I have to let go of whether they will get powerful learning or not. My role is to lead throughout the day and let go of needing a specific outcome. Of course, I want all my clients to love the horses and have a great day, but I can't make it happen. I have to set the intention that they will, do everything I can to make it happen and be unattached to the experience they have.

When I am out of my comfort zone, I tend to be courageous. I'll give new things a go and dig deep. When I first started running workshops, I wanted the same for my clients. I wanted them to be courageous and bold and achieve incredible things. I was afraid that if they didn't, they were not getting the learning they needed. I soon realised that everyone learns in a different way. I had to let go of my fears and trust that everyone gets the learning their way. Some people throw themselves in; others hold themselves back. Either approach is fine, and it's interesting for the client to recognise what their default pattern is, so they can decide whether or not that is a pattern that serves them.

Staying present

Horses live in the present moment. They don't worry about the past. The past is done and cannot be changed. Let go of beating yourself up about the past. What is done is done.

Horses don't worry about the future either. They focus on the here and now. They want to know: "Are you a compelling leader who can keep me safe now in this moment?" The moment you demonstrate you can, they come with you. The moment you show signs of being unsure, they take over the leadership.

Let go of the past and the future. Life happens in the present moment. Feelings, thoughts and actions are happening now. Is your emotional response relevant to your current situation?

Let go of worrying about the future. Decide what action you want to take to create your best outcome, do it and then let it go. You can't keep a stranglehold on everything. That stifles creativity, and you use far too much energy worrying about things.

How do you let go?

Before you can let go, you need to know what holding onto control feels like for you. For most, there will be tension somewhere in your body. Are your shoulders raised? Yes? Then know that you are hanging onto something. Hanging onto stress or fear or wanting to get things right or doing a good job or trying to persuade someone... Or something. Tension in your body is a great source of information as well as the negative emotions you feel like fear, anger, frustration. These can be a starting point to explore where you are hanging onto being in control of someone or something.

It's excruciating trying to be in control. It creates a tightness that prevents flexibility and agility, physically, mentally and emotionally.

Letting go is a lifelong practice. Here are some of the places to practise:

Let go of needing to be right. Every time you feel discomfort, are you hanging on to being right? If so, let go and see what can be created through relationship with others. Dare to fail. Dare to do things differently from your way. What is important about your way? Find the underlying need and make sure it is met some other way in collaboration with others, so their needs are also met. Conflict arises from unmet needs, so make sure the needs of everyone are met, and you'll have a powerful solution that everyone can engage around.

Let go of fear. Easier said than done, I know. This is the biggest inhibitor to you achieving anything. Be curious about your fear. How is it trying to inform you? Is your physical safety threatened or is it emotional? Find people to help you when you feel scared, whether it is to explore a situation with you or give you moral support. Or a mentor who has previous experience. Or a coach who can help you go deeper into the fear and explore what information it has that serves you. Don't squash the fear. It will keep coming back until you learn to deal with it.

Let go of being attached to specific outcomes. Find ways of being creative with others, so the needs of everyone are met. Have respect for those you are in conflict with so you can collaborate together to meet the needs of everyone. When I let go of trying to calm Kalle down, I found a place of collaboration and exploration instead.

Let go of old habits and behaviours that no longer serve you. The easy thing to do is to keep repeating the same behaviour over and over again. If what you are doing is not getting the required result, try something else.

Let go of being in control. Instead, lean into leading, inspiring and influencing. Trust that you are doing your best and so is everyone else. If people are not doing what you want them to do, change the way you lead them. Try using a different leadership position (refer to the 3 Positions of Leadership model in chapter seven).

Let go of the past. It is done. Don't waste your energy on it.

Let go of worrying about the future. What ifs don't serve you. Instead, plan and prepare appropriately and trust that you are skilled enough to create and collaborate from any person or situation, without having all the facts and figures in front of you.

Practise being creative and flexible. Be bold and courageous and see what wants to happen from unknown situations. Feel into the space and feel what is needed without over-analysing.

Case Study

Many clients like to be in control and letting go is a big stretch for them. They quickly learn that you cannot control 600kg or more of horse – that you need to let go of making it do what you want and inspire, influence and lead instead. That's what the majority of the workshops are about. Inspiration and influence.

Cathy was an experienced manager and saw herself as a team player and collaborative. She led Kalle with a fairly loose lead rein and got halfway round the arena when Kalle stopped. Kalle had become distracted. Cathy didn't know what to do. She stood there and gradually moved her hand closer up the lead rein underneath Kalle's head. She didn't pull her, but her knuckles went white. She let her hand go from the lead rein and put one hand on Kalle's neck. Kalle turned her head and off they went again. She used her relationship skills (her strength) to get Kalle moving again.

When she came back, the team fed back that they thought Cathy was trying to control Kalle. She didn't think she was. The team explained that when things weren't going well, Cathy would give them strong direction and they felt they had to do it. They didn't feel that there was space for them to discuss it as a team. Cathy was surprised. She had no idea.

Afterwards, Cathy said that most of the time she was collaborative, and she had realised her relationship skills were a strength, but she had noticed in meetings that if things were not moving fast enough, she would take control and make it clear that the team had to follow. She hadn't realised she was doing this before. Now when she feels her body tightening, she remembers the situation with Kalle, leans back in her chair, breathes and thinks: "Drop the lead rein and bring the team with me". The team reported that they are working more in harmony together and have more space to discuss problems together.

Putting it into practice

What have you let go of in the past?

What enabled you to let go?

Where are you holding onto trying to be in control?

What stops you letting go?

What are the fears that get in the way?

What are the rules that you make up?

What new rule can you make up that helps you release
the hold?

What will you do to let go of control in your current
situation?

PART FOUR

Lessons from the Horses

*In which I describe
some of the client experiences
and explore how the horses teach*

Chapter 16

Client experiences

In the last three years of providing Leadership with Horses workshops, I sometimes think I've seen everything and yet I know I haven't. I've had the privilege to learn alongside each and every client because we can all learn from each other every day when we pay attention.

There is no end to the learning that can be created when working with horses. Horses give willingly and unconditionally of their time, love and wisdom. They are generous animals. They connect on a profound level that moves the heart and soul. People leave changed forever, often not knowing how or why. What they do know is that everything changes when they've been touched by a horse.

The learning experiences that people have with horses are embodied leadership experiences. They feel the difference in their bodies as much if not more than intellectually. Often people know they have learned something, but they can't always articulate it. That's fine, because much of what we do is embodied.

Few people can describe how to find their balance on a bike, but most people can do it. Few people can explain exactly how they walk, but most people can walk. These are examples of embodied activities that we do regularly throughout life. Leadership is often the same. Yes, you can learn how to do it, but once you've had the experience and found *your* way, it is repeatable in all future situations that you find yourself in. If you can be courageous and articulate in one situation, you can do it in another.

In addition to the case studies throughout this book, here are some of the benefits that clients have gained along the way. All of these examples have been experienced by several clients at different times. Names have been changed to protect those clients who have had these or similar experiences.

Creativity and play

Often in workshops, we encourage clients to be creative and playful. Leadership is a serious business at times, and humans have to be reminded to make it easy and fun too.

Some clients find it uncomfortable to play. They are so used to taking leadership seriously that they've learned to squash playfulness down and judge it as silly. Play is how we learn as adults as much as children, so it is an essential part of leadership.

Many clients report that they have remembered to liven things up for their team and to make work a bit more fun. This is desperately needed in business and welcomed by teams. There is a serious side to creativity too. Clients who are willing to be creative are more likely to find solutions to problems because they are willing to attempt things they've never done before. The fear of looking silly gets in the way of creativity and innovation. Innovation requires a willingness to explore without attachment or perfection.

Power and compassion

Kalle models power and compassion brilliantly. She will only walk with a client who builds a relationship with her and shows her compassion. When she connects with a client, it is sweet and tender, yet she loses none of her own power and expects her leader to be powerful too. She shows how you can hold the paradox of power and compassion in perfect balance.

Horses respond well to assertive leadership and show the fine balance of being passive, assertive and aggressive. The horse requires the leader to be powerful and compelling, as it shows they are capable of keeping the horse safe. The horse also requires the leader to be kind, caring and compassionate too and to respect the horse's needs and opinions. Be too nice (passive) or too forceful (aggressive) and the horse will make it clear they don't respect you. They show up the subtle nuances of each, so you learn to find the knife-edge of assertive behaviour.

Some clients lean towards being compassionate in a desire to be nice, in the belief that this will make them well liked. The horses show this up as fake compassion. If your compassion comes from a place of weakness or insecurity and a desire to be liked, the horses will see it as such and plant their feet. The horses will deem this approach to be too passive, and they take charge. If they believe your compassion is honest and real and in service of being in relationship with them, they will recognise it as assertive leadership and go with you willingly.

Other clients pull the horse when it refuses to move. If they've tried everything they know how to do and are at the edge of their skill set, some people resort to force. This coercive approach lacks compassion, and the horse will plant its feet. If you've ever tried to drag 600kg of horse, you'll know how impossible this is. The horses always re-engage when the client shows a fine balance of power and compassion and a desire to build a relationship and do it together. People in the workplace also require connection and relationship, but they often go along with a leader because they feel they must. Would you rather lead, inspire and influence, or drag people along with a sense of duty and resistance?

Once clients have found their own balance of power

and compassion, they are able to recreate it repeatedly in the workplace. Better relationships are built, teams become more cohesive, employees are more willing to share their emotional experience, and they collaborate more easily with compassion.

Importance of relationships

Clients who have a tendency to focus on the task and the process often learn from the horses about the importance of relationship. The horses are forgiving but refuse to move until a relationship is created. Every time the relationship is broken by the person, the horse will stop and wait for them to reconnect. This shows clients how to find their own way of connecting and building relationship, as well as demonstrating their default patterns where they typically break connection.

Clients who are good at relationship building can sometimes forget to use that strength in a crisis. Working with horses shows them how good they are in building relationships and reminds them to use that skill more.

It's not unusual for task-focused clients to fall in love with the horse and want to take it home. They learn the power of connection and are able to recreate the same connection with people in the workplace in future.

Self-belief and confidence

For those clients with horse experience, they arrive feeling more confident and more in their comfort zone. They are often excited about working with the horses. Yet the expectation on them is higher. The rest of the group expects them to find it easy. They put pressure on themselves to make it look perfect.

After all, clients with horse experience may have led a horse before, but they've never before had the spotlight on their leadership skills during the process. They are even more vulnerable as the expectation is higher. It takes courage to overcome their fear of failure. It takes courage to find new ways to lead when it doesn't turn out as expected. When clients work with the horses, most of them exceed their own expectations and achieve things they never thought they could.

Chris was a senior executive. He was confident in his leadership and his abilities. He was dealing with some major challenges at work, and he worked on them with the horses. What transpired was that he lacked confidence and self-belief. He was surprised because he thought he was confident in his own abilities, and most of the time he was. Where there was minor resistance from the team and organisation, he had a small amount of self-doubt in his capabilities. Every time he did that, the horses planted their feet.

By the end of the day, Chris was moved by the experience. He said he felt more self-confident and had more self-belief than he'd ever had before, something which he had never expected to gain. He felt uncomfortable articulating that because he believed someone of his level was expected to be confident and have self-belief, and he had always thought he did. Often the more senior people are, the more they fake their confidence and self-belief – and they have no idea they are doing it. What they learn with the horses is real, authentic confidence and self-belief. It has a stronger foundation for future decision-making because it removes doubt.

Chris made some major decisions in his business afterwards and said he was able to make them knowing they were the right thing to do. He was able to deal with any opposition more calmly and confidently, and as a result he was more assertive and less coercive. He felt he had made the decisions because they were right for the company. As a result, he made some tough decisions with more compassion because he was confident in what he was doing.

Focus and determination, perseverance and patience

It's not easy to ask a horse to go with you when you've never done it before and don't know how to do it. For some clients, there is a stop, start, staccato approach as they persevere.

Jenny had a stop, start result to leading Tiffin. Each time he stopped, she tried to re-engage with him and rebuild the relationship. She never lost sight of the exercise she was doing and continued to bring him with her, albeit slowly. She showed enormous patience in trying different things each time he stopped. She never gave up, persevering right to the end. When she came back to the group with Tiffin, everyone let out a massive sigh, including Tiffin!

Jenny had never experienced patience before. She had always considered herself to be impatient. She had also not realised that her focus, determination and perseverance were great strengths that kept her and her team going in difficult circumstances. She learned that having these as strengths enabled her to trust that no matter what, she could achieve the end result she desired. She said that gave her permission to be more patient in future. No doubt her team would benefit from that.

Congruence

Sometimes when clients work with the horses, they try to hide their fear. What happens is they exhibit a mixed message. The horse senses the fear underneath and gets confused by the other message of pretending to be fine and confident. Horses refuse to engage in this mixed message behaviour and will often plant their feet. Incongruence prevents horses from feeling safe around you. People are more polite and more willing to engage with the masks. People will engage mask to mask. When you do so, you are playing a role, no longer being who you really are and unable to form true lasting relationships.

Andy was terrified but didn't want to show it, so he went up to Opus with a fake confidence and said: "Come on. We're going." Opus didn't believe him and refused to move. I suggested to Andy that he tell Opus how he feels and ask for his cooperation. Andy said to Opus: "Be gentle with me as I'm a bit scared and don't know what I'm doing." With that, they headed off together, and as long as Andy continued to be honest about his feelings, Opus supported him and cooperated fully.

Andy said everyone always expected him to know what he was doing, and he didn't feel he could admit it when he wasn't sure. He learned that being fake is misunderstood by humans as much as it is by horses. He later reported that he was more honest about his feelings and found people responded well to it. He was surprised how willing people were to offer help and support whenever he wasn't sure of something. He no longer saw it as a weakness but as an opportunity to draw on the strengths of the team and build a better relationship with them. After all, people are usually only too keen to offer support.

Paying attention to the environment

Verity was leading Kalle in perfect harmony. Their relationship was sweet as they walked together completely in sync. Kalle was going with her willingly because she felt the depth of the relationship. There was a sudden noise in the environment, and Kalle stopped. Verity was completely taken by surprise. She didn't understand why Kalle had stopped and didn't know how to get her moving again.

The sweet relationship had stalled, and Verity didn't know why. She was so focused on Kalle and the relationship between them that she had lost sight of what was happening around her. She said she couldn't hear anything and wasn't aware of us watching her either. She had tuned everything out, which meant she wasn't prepared for a distraction.

Verity learned that when she is focused on one person and the task in hand she can sometimes forget about the bigger picture. She explained that she would sometimes get derailed because she didn't spot distractions early enough. She learned that she needed to pay attention to what is happening in the environment as well as the thing she is currently working on. It gave her a greater sense of expanding her vision of where she is going and how to get there, and to watch out for distractions along the way. She went away with more confidence in her ability to prevent future problems by spotting them earlier and dealing with them before they become unmanageable.

Direction - Clarity, purpose, intent

When clients set clear intentions and are purposeful and focused, the horses respect them, engage with them and come with them willingly. Often clients focus on the horse as a problem. In so doing, they lack the clarity and direction of where they are going. They may spend a long period of time trying to work out how to move the horse. The horse knows how to move, so the focus needs to be on the direction you are heading in rather than the horse being a problem. The horse is not clear what the client wants, so they wait. As soon as the person is clear where they are going, commits to making it happen, is purposeful and intentional about it and communicates with clarity, the horse comes willingly.

One group didn't trust that the horses would follow them over an obstacle course in a team exercise, so they spent 45 minutes working out how to do it. In the meantime, the horses fell asleep whilst they waited for direction. Although I offered to help the team a number of times, each time they turned it down and said they could work it out. Eventually they ran out of time, and I said: "If you want to create movement, stop talking about it and do it." One of them moved, the horses woke up, and they walked effortlessly as a team over the obstacle course.

This team and many others demonstrated the trap you can fall into of analysis paralysis, where you talk endlessly about the problem rather than focusing on where you want to go. As soon as they committed to where they were going, the horses came with them. They learned that instead of focusing on the problem, they needed to focus on where they were heading and take steps to make it happen. People want to be led with clarity, purpose and direction as much as horses do.

Leading through uncertainty

When clients work with the horses, they model what it is to lead through uncertainty. They have no idea if the horse will go with them or not. For some that is daunting. Most people find more courage than they ever thought

343

possible and as a result become more comfortable with their vulnerability. Once they are able to lead powerfully through fear, that fear no longer has a hold on them. In addition, they become more resourceful in managing themselves through uncertainty. They learn to say and do things they've never said or done before.

Sarah was uncomfortable leading a horse. She wanted to know how to do it before I handed her the lead rope. She had never done anything without being told exactly how to do it. She had recently become a team leader and was finding it difficult to lead in situations where there was no process.

When she first led Tiffin, she got frustrated when he stopped because she didn't know why. She wanted me to tell her how to get him to move again. I explained that she needed to find her own way of leading. Throughout the day, she gradually became more confident in trying new ways, and her frustration lessened.

Afterwards, she said she was less frustrated with her team when things didn't go the way she wanted them to, and she was learning to try new things without being told exactly how to do them first.

Mastering emotions

Many clients report being able to recognise emotions in other people better as well as using their own emotions to inform their leadership decisions.

When watching the horses loose in the arena, Rob, a senior leader, felt uncomfortable naming his emotion. He had never realised he even had emotions before. He said he was scared and found it difficult to admit it, especially in front of others. He admitted that he often felt scared when leading in new situations, but he thought he was the only person who ever did and thought admitting it would be a weakness, especially for someone of his experience and seniority.

We invited him to share his emotional response regularly throughout the day. He learned that being open about how he felt about different situations helped other people to work with him more openly and more closely.

On returning to the workplace, Rob had some difficult organisational changes to make. He openly shared his feelings with his organisation and invited them to do the same. It was a bold move and created an environment of trust, openness and a desire to create positivity moving forwards. It was well received by his organisation and showed an understanding that the employees were human beings who have feelings. It had a powerful impact in re-engaging people after a difficult year of substantial change.

Cohesive teamwork

Teams quickly learn what their default roles are within the team, and their normal default patterns of team behaviour show up around the horses. They learn how well they communicate and where they get stuck as a team. They learn about the leadership model and how to work with that as a team. They also learn to focus on what everyone else is doing as well as themselves and sense into what is needed in every moment.

Teams often discover that when they are solely focused on their own role, they can lose sight of what everyone else is doing and lack the responsiveness needed to help the team work cohesively together. They also learn how energetic their team is. If they rush things, they lose the horse in the process. If they go too slow or over-analyse each step, the horse gets bored and wanders off.

Once you have worked in a cohesive team and felt the effortless flow of it, it is magic and easy to recreate in the office.

Final Thoughts

Jane came back to the group with Kalle and stood still, tears falling down her face. As we stood in silence, Kalle dropped her head and nuzzled Jane, and her tears fell even more. She said she had never felt supported by another being before. She had always tried to be self-sufficient. Kalle lifted her head and nuzzled Jane's face. In that moment, Kalle was soft, gentle and nurturing. She looked at Jane as if she were a foal. My heart was full of love for Kalle, for Jane and for this work, as I felt tears fall down my face too.

Could this be the snorting beast that I had worked with only three years ago? I looked at Wendy, who was co-leading with me. She had been with Kalle and me as we navigated the last three years. Wendy had comforted me in my struggles in the beginning and always believed in us both. It felt right that she was now standing with us in this moment. What a transformation, in both me and Kalle! How far we have come.

In the first workshops with Kalle, I would lead her from the stable, her head held high, snorting as she mirrored the fear in me, as well as my clients. Now she has grown into the work and shows such maturity, compassion and wisdom. What a powerful leader she is, and so soft and gentle with it. Is that a mirror for me too, I wonder? Have we both transformed from snorting, powerful, scared beasts into wise, mature, intuitive beings with so much to give to clients and this work?

347

Fear is over-rated. We put far too much energy and attention into fear. It gets in the way of you doing your best work. Imagine putting all that energy into courageous action and compassion instead. The seven skills in Part Three of this book are the antidote to fear, the antidote to being stuck, frustrated, static and not knowing the way out.

What a journey it has been, and I know it is just the beginning. I have dug deep and walked alongside my equine soul mate, trying to be the leader she wants me to be, yet compromising none of my vulnerability and authenticity along the way. I have failed repeatedly, picked myself up and carried on with dogged determination. Some might call it resilience and perseverance. Where we go from here, who knows. I have hopes and dreams and goals. I do know that when I commit fully, I achieve them. Better watch this space!

I'm lucky to have had the experience of working in some high-performing teams. However, it wasn't until I worked with horses that I fully understood why some teams worked effortlessly and some didn't. I do believe that if you can lead a horse, you can lead anyone.

I'm grateful that I had the three accidents that led to me being afraid of horses. In subsequently overcoming my fear, I found the work I was born to do and have finely tuned my own leadership skills on a daily basis through working with horses and caring for them. The residual physical pain from my first two accidents is a constant reminder that leadership is a continuum, and there is always more learning to be had and more effective leadership to step into.

Leadership is not the easy option. I have huge respect for anyone who works in business. Leadership starts with self and the majority of the skills in this book are about raising your self-awareness, so you can be more effective as a leader. These skills can help you in your interactions with others too, so your relationships can be more harmonious and teamwork can be more cohesive.

You are a leader by nature. Deep down, your innate wisdom knows what to do in any given moment. Dare to get it wrong, learn from your mistakes and keep trying. Know that you are doing your best in any given moment. You can't do more than that. The leadership skills in this book are natural leadership skills. Relinquish conforming and learned behaviours that no longer serve you. Be congruent, act with integrity and just be yourself.

1. *Be courageous* – Take one bold action every day. Have a go and take a risk.

2. *Be compassionate* – Be kind to yourself when you make mistakes. Be kind to others too. You never know what mistakes they are battling with.

3. *Create mutual respect* – Respect yourself and others and don't make either of you wrong. Create respect from others by being clear on your boundaries.

4. *Create trust* – Trust that whatever happens, you are safe and you are loved. Trust others too. They are doing their best and trying to be safe

349

too.

5. *Use your energy consciously* – Raise your energy to inspire and motivate. Lower your energy to create calm and peace. Don't sit in boring meetings. Shake it up.

6. *Be aligned* – Align your head, heart, gut and intuition to make your decisions. All four have important information for you, but when they are aligned, you are on the right track.

7. *Let go* – Attachment stifles creativity. Being in control is a myth. Let go and lead from your heart and soul in service of the greater good.

The horses teach us how to be more effective in leadership. They have taught me how to be courageous, to dig deep and overcome enormous challenges. Equally, I've learned where I hit overwhelm and need to seek help. When I find myself getting too comfortable, I know the horses will shake me up. Nothing stays the same for long.

I try to meet everyone with compassion, even when we don't agree. I continue to have compassion for myself when I get things wrong. That has been one of the biggest gifts in my learning. Beating yourself up can be such a terrible waste of energy, and it's exhausting and demoralising. I've learned to listen at a deep level to what is needed for everyone. In the process, it means I can make more informed decisions.

I have a deep respect for everyone, including those with whom I am in conflict. Whenever I find myself getting frustrated, I come back to the place of respect for myself and for others. It's from that place that we can truly listen and seek to understand each other. Misunderstanding increases the conflict, so when we hold ourselves in mutual respect, we are able to create unimaginable outcomes!

I trust myself at such a deep level, which means I can trust other people at a deep level too. I don't get scared as easily in new or complex situations because I trust that I am resourceful enough as a leader to know what to say and do in those moments where you don't know what to say and do. As a result, I build better relationships quicker. People sense my open-heartedness, and I meet them human being to human being. It allows those around me to open up too.

My energy is such a powerful tool that serves me constantly. I can masterfully lower and raise it according to the situation. I am a calming influence in a crisis, something that would have surprised my parents some years ago! I am often told I'm inspiring, influential, powerful and enthusiastic. I am of course all those things as many others are too. Working with the horses has helped me to access those energetic levels authentically and transparently, so people see them and are inspired by them.

I trust my intuition. It is the one thing that has enabled me to keep going when this work has felt so challenging.

Many others would have given up, but my intuition was strong enough to remind me that this is the work I am meant to be doing. I can't sell out on myself and my dreams and the difference this makes to people's lives and work. I align my head, heart, gut and intuition when making critical decisions.

Letting go continues to be a work in progress for me. When I find myself attached to a particular outcome, I let myself lean back and ask: "What is needed here?" That allows me to go to a place of what is needed for me, others and the environment. It's a place of the whole and allows me to co-create with others to make a difference.

How bizarre that we look to horses to become more human! How right it feels too. They have evolved over 60 million years, adapting to their environment, learning to live in harmony with humans who must seem as confusing to them as horses are to us at times. Throughout it all, they never judge us. They accept us for who we are, working with us, being clear about their own needs along the way. When we listen at deeper and deeper levels, we can live and work truly in harmony with them. And with each other.

My wish for the world is that every human being meets every other sentient being with love, compassion, respect and trust. By mastering ourselves, we raise the energetic vibration in our homes and workplaces, in society and on the planet. I know this can become a reality, and together we can end the conflict, fear and stress that no longer serve us.

Be courageous and powerful. Be compassionate and loving, both to yourself and others. Trust one another and respect everyone, including yourself. Align your head with your heart, gut and intuition, and pay attention to the whole. Use your energy consciously to influence positively and let go of being in control. It's a myth. Know that you are making a difference in this world. Choose powerfully and consciously how you do that.

You are a leader by nature.

Use your innate wisdom and lead consciously in life and work. It is time to be vibrant, compelling and courageous. The world needs you.

With love,
Jude

Gratitude

I've been surrounded by dear friends, family and colleagues who have believed in me, challenged me, sparked ideas, supported me when the going got tough and never allowed me to play small. I'm grateful to my clients for helping me process my thoughts and learn at a deeper level with every interaction.

Many people helped me before the book started, especially Lucy Lloyd-Barker for stopping me mid-sentence one day and saying: "I think you have a book in you!" To Jim McLean for inspiring me as a corporate leader. To Okokon Udo for challenging and supporting me in equal measures and suggesting that life can be easy and fun. To Art Shirk for encouraging me to live my dream of bringing corporate leaders into nature even though I had no idea how to do it. To Ronnie Clifford for telling me to get over myself. I did and continue to do so. To Melanie Dewberry-Jones for holding me at the highest level and never allowing me to play small. To Jim Lawless for inspiring me to be focused and disciplined to write this book, amongst other things.

I am blessed to be part of a forward-thinking equine community. Enormous thanks to David Harris for getting me started and modelling leadership, Sharon Harris for powerfully holding the space, Gerhard Krebs for the work of HorseDream and the community that supports me. To Julie Keatinge for trusting me with your beautiful horse Holme Park Krystal (Kalle) and encouraging me when I was close to giving up. To the HorseDream and EAHAE community for shared learning and support. To Dana Reynolds for your astute insights and for helping me to shape my jumbled thoughts into this book.

I have enormous gratitude for all the equine partners who have crossed my path and willingly shared their leadership wisdom. Thanks to Floozy and JohnJo for helping me overcome my fear of horses, the racehorses at the Racehorse Trust, Jodie and Mr Bojangles at Warwickshire College, the retired police and military horses at the Horse Trust, especially Aurora and Sam Slick. Special thanks go to Hermi and Rchi for being my working partners. Your power, strength and humour are an inspiration.

My own horses have given unconditional love, forgiven my mistakes, helped me raise my game and been gentle with me as I learn (sometimes). To Kalle, my equine soul mate, for your majesty and grace, power and strength, gentleness, sweetness, nurturing and inspirational leadership. Thank you for your massive range, for learning to trust me and for head-butting me back to the present. To Opus for showing a novice the way and especially for giving me the privilege of being by your side as you end your days. To Tiffin for trusting me enough to have a meltdown, express yourself fully and come out the other side.

I'm hugely grateful to Ed Phillips and John Cleary who provided stunning photographs of the horses, some of which are included in this book.

Thank you to my dear friends who walked beside me every step, picked me up when I was down, held me in my fears, ignored the drama and above all trusted that everything would work out. Thank you especially to Wendy Prior for your practical and emotional support in owning horses, running a business and living life to the full. To my dear friend and business partner Emma Taylor for raising me bonkers, for your horse wisdom and for so much more than words can say.

To my dear sister Sue, thank you for knowing me deeply and championing me in the light and dark. To Paul for your unconditional love and support and for believing in me.

About the author

Jude Jennison is an international speaker, author and Horse Assisted Educator with 16 years of senior leadership experience, leading UK, European and global teams in a global IT organisation.

Jude leads by example in everything she does. Her extensive business and leadership background provides her clients with a solid foundation for learning, where everything they learn is mapped back to real life situations and practical applications. She combines bold, visionary thinking with transparency, vulnerability and humility to create profound learning experiences that lead to sustainable behavioural change.

Jude regards herself as a global citizen and an agent for change. She challenges her own status quo in service of her clients. She has a passion for creating peace and believes that it starts with each of us finding our own inner peace, so we can live and work in harmony with others.

A pioneer of Leadership with Horses, Jude is highly regarded in her profession and speaks regularly about this work and her personal experiences, including at the

Global Horse Assisted Education conferences.

Married to Paul, who never wanted pets, Jude now owns three horses, two dogs and a cat, and they all live together in harmony in Warwickshire.

Contact Jude

Contact Jude about speaking engagements, to discuss your leadership strategy, to explore Leadership with Horses or to chat at:

Email: jude@judejennison.com

Twitter: @JudeJennison

Facebook: www.facebook.com/leadersbynature

Website

www.judejennison.com

www.leadershipbeyondmeasure.com